John Thomson

The land and the people of China

A short account of the geography, history, religion, social life, art, industries, and

government of China and its people

John Thomson

The land and the people of China
A short account of the geography, history, religion, social life, art, industries, and government of China and its people

ISBN/EAN: 9783337131623

Printed in Europe, USA, Canada, Australia, Japan

Cover: Foto ©Andreas Hilbeck / pixelio.de

More available books at **www.hansebooks.com**

OPIUM SMOKING.

Frontispiece. *Page* 150.

THE LAND
AND
THE PEOPLE OF CHINA.

A Short Account

OF THE GEOGRAPHY, HISTORY, RELIGION, SOCIAL LIFE,
ARTS, INDUSTRIES, AND GOVERNMENT OF CHINA
AND ITS PEOPLE.

WITH MAP AND ILLUSTRATIONS.

By J. THOMSON, F.R.G.S.,

*Author of "Illustrations of China and its People," "The Straits of Malacca,
Indo-China, and China," &c.*

PUBLISHED UNDER THE DIRECTION OF
THE COMMITTEE OF GENERAL LITERATURE AND EDUCATION,
APPOINTED BY THE SOCIETY FOR PROMOTING
CHRISTIAN KNOWLEDGE.

LONDON:
SOCIETY FOR PROMOTING CHRISTIAN KNOWLEDGE;
SOLD AT THE DEPOSITORIES:
77, GREAT QUEEN STREET, LINCOLN'S INN FIELDS;
4, ROYAL EXCHANGE; 48, PICCADILLY;
AND BY ALL BOOKSELLERS.

NEW YORK: POTT, YOUNG & CO.

1876.

CONTENTS.

CHAPTER I.

Geographical position and physical features of the Chinese empire 1

CHAPTER II.
THE PROVINCES OF CHINA.

The Eighteen Provinces of China Proper—Peichihli, Shanse, Shense, Kansu, Shantung, Kiangsu, Honan, Nganwhui, Hupeh, Szechuan, Chekiang, Kiangsi, Hunan, Kweichow, Fukien, Kwangtung, Kwangsi, Yunnan. Islands—Formosa, Hainan 13

CHAPTER III.
SUMMARY OF CHINESE HISTORY.

Early chronology—The accession of Fu-hi, 2852 B.C.—The Black-haired race—The first dynasty—The Emperor Yu—The worship of God—Yu's labours—Invention of the compass—Birth of Confucius—Chi-Hwang-ti, builder of the Great Wall—The Classics destroyed—Buddhism introduced from the West—"The Three States"—Literary examinations—The influence of a Queen—Tartar sovereigns—Kublikhan—Marco Polo—The present dynasty 53

CHAPTER IV.
POPULATION.

Population of the empire—The first settlers—Populations of England and China compared—Chinese census—Some recent causes of depopulation—Emigration—Chinese labour abroad—Clannishness—Assimilating power of the Chinese race—A plea for the Chinese in foreign lands 78

CHAPTER V.
CHINESE CITIES AND VILLAGES.

A Chinese city viewed from a distance—Fire walls—Suburbs—Foochow-fu—The great bridge—Streets—Shops—Signboards—Walls—Boats—Villages—Huts—Village life—Village warfare—Hired braves—Robbers—Government interference—Settled communities 95

CHAPTER VI.

SOCIAL CONDITION OF THE PEOPLE.

Different races of China—The savage Yao—Puntis—Hakka, Hoklo, and Tanka of Kwangtung—Social ranks—Mental and physical characteristics of the Chinese—The condition of women—Births—Marriages—Burials—Beggars—Dress of the people—Gambling—Theatrical performances—Music—Opium—Food—Etiquette—Guilds and trades' unions—Coinage and commerce... 117

CHAPTER VII.

ARCHITECTURE, ART, AND INDUSTRY.

Origin of Chinese architecture—Dwellings of rich and poor—Architectural geomancy—Interior of a gentleman's house—Graves—The art of painting—Enamelling—Porcelain—Carpentry—Wood-carving—Ivory-carving—Paper—Working in metals—Barbers.. 159

CHAPTER VIII.

RELIGION.

State religion—Human sacrifices—Confucianism—Taouism—Buddhism—Mahometanism—Christianity—Feng-Shui, or Chinese geomancy.. 189

CHAPTER IX.

AGRICULTURE.

Rice cultivation—Terracing hills—Irrigation—Agricultural implements—Tea culture and manufacture—Black teas—Green teas—Tea season—Sugar—The mulberry—The silkworm—Silk—The loom—Silk embroidery 216

CHAPTER X.

THE GOVERNMENT OF CHINA AND CHINESE POLICY.

Form of government—Central government—Provincial governments—The Peking boards—Political divisions of the empire—Official responsibility for the crimes of subordinates—Chinese aristocracy—Punishments of crime—Official corruption—Weakness of the central government—The Yunnan mission—Signs of progress... 240

CHAPTER XI.

The Chinese language and literature 263

THE LAND AND THE PEOPLE OF CHINA.

CHAPTER I.

GEOGRAPHICAL POSITION AND PHYSICAL FEATURES OF THE CHINESE EMPIRE.

THE geographical position which China occupies in Eastern Asia, and the physical features of the country itself are so remarkable, as in some measure to account both for the antiquity of the empire, and for the long-continued isolation of its people.

Shut in all round by the vast mountain chains of Manchuria, Mongolia, and Thibet, the dependencies of the modern empire, and watered by a river system unsurpassed in the world, the low-lying plains of China proper were prepared for tillage, in times long previous to the advent of their present inhabitants, by a gradual process of denudation in the highlands, and the resulting deposit of alluvia carried seawards with the streams. The land was thus made ready for its busy occupants, and the soil rendered suitable by its depth and richness for maintaining a large population. In the records of the earliest Chinese dynasties frequent allusion is made to waste lands reclaimed by deepening the water-courses, or by cutting channels for the swollen floods.

In this way many of the most fertile plains were drained and redeemed to supply the wants of an increasingly numerous race. But the vastness of its habitable territory, and the native richness of its soil were not the only features which favoured the growth, stability, and independence of this great empire. Within the mountain chains which isolate China and its dependencies almost every variety of climate is to be found, from the cold of an arctic winter in the northern latitudes to the heat of a tropical summer in the extreme south. The natural products in consequence are of such diversity as to render the people practically independent of the outer world.

Thus the Chinese have been able from the most ancient times to maintain a spirit of proud independence. With a language and literature exclusively their own, and with a land so capable of supplying their every want, they disdained intercourse with the outer barbarians in the islands along the seaboard, or with the nomadic tribes scattered over the desert wastes and sterile mountain regions to the north and west. Eminently suited to become permanent settlers, the Chinese are nevertheless supposed to have been originally a wandering pastoral race. However that may be, they must at any rate have taken possession of the fertile plains and valleys which they now occupy at a period somewhat anterior to the commencement of their authentic history, that is, more than

4,000 years ago. Favoured by fortuitous circumstances, by national industry, and by the character of the country they dwell in, the Chinese population has gradually increased, retaining its individuality all the while, as it extended its dominion and its investigation to what appear to be its natural geographical limits in Eastern Asia. The boundaries of the Chinese empire are well defined by a series of vast mountain ranges, whose alpine heights are in many regions mantled with perpetual snows. In North-Eastern Manchuria the great Altai rise from the Sea of Okhotsk, and with their spurs and ramifications sweeping round in a great barrier divide Manchuria and Northern, or outer Mongolia from the Russian empire. These stupendous mountains follow a course of over 2,000 miles. The average elevation of the chain above sea-level may be estimated approximately at 7,000 feet, but many of the isolated peaks tower far beyond the snow-line. The mountain boundary is continued by a range which stretches in a south-westerly direction and separates Tomsk from Kobdo. It has been said by a recent explorer of this region that no natural boundary line could be more complete than that which severs Russia from China.* Not only does it divide the river systems and the northern pine forests from the barren rocky deserts of Mongolia, but it constitutes the wall which parts the territory of the Mongols from that of the Kalmucks. Other well-defined mountain chains, standing at various angles to the Altai range, border the frontier of Zangaria, and finally unite

* Ney Elias, Journal of the Royal Geographical Society, Vol. xliii. p. 138.

with the Himalayas; while these last, sweeping round the southern limits of Thibet, extend their ramifications down through the rocky regions of Yunnan, so as effectually to shut off the Chinese empire from the races of Indo-China. Thus the circuit of the empire is nearly completed by a natural great wall, stupendous in its altitude, but for all that unable any longer in the days of steam transport by land and sea to prevent China from entering into intimate relationship with the more highly civilised nations of the world.

Besides these outer mountain chains, there are also a number of inner ranges of greater or less magnitude and extent, some of which will be noticed in the general description of the provinces. To these inner mountains China is indebted for the sources of a multitude of minor streams, which, after watering and fertilising her plains and valleys, fall into the channels of the greater rivers, or into the lakes which help to feed the volume of their waters. The Yangtsze and Hwang-ho are the two largest rivers of China. The latter, although the less important of the two, has an extremely ancient historical fame, and has thus won for itself something akin to sacred veneration among the people who inhabit the classic land through which it flows. Several centuries before the time of Confucius the Hwang-ho formed the main water-way through what was then the nucleus of the greater Chinese empire, the scene of the labours of Yu, the founder of the Hea dynasty, and the assuager of floods. This was at a time probably 2,000 years B.C., when but little was yet recorded of the great Yangtsze, or of the barbarous tribes dwelling along its banks. The Hwang-ho is a river, which in historic interest, in the uncertainty of its primary source, and in its function as the fertiliser of the great plains of Northern China, where millions of human beings depend upon its turbid waters for sustenance, may be fitly compared to the sacred Nile.

The Hwang-ho taking its rise in a marshy region of lakes which lie between the Yan-ling and Nan-shan mountains in Thibet, runs thence in a northerly direction through Kansu, passes the great wall in its course through Southern Mongolia, and after a tortuous journey of some 600 miles re-enters China proper between Shense and Shanse. The river here divides these two provinces in nearly a direct line from south to north. At the southern extremity of Shanse it takes a sharp bend eastward through Ho-nan, and passes within two miles of the provincial capital Kai-fung-foo. Between the years 1851 and 1853 the river changed its course at Sung-mên-kow, a point not many miles below the last-named city. Its northern embankment, which was partly artificial, gave way, and the waters sweeping in an impetuous torrent over the fertile lowlands of Shantung caused incalculable destruction to life and property. The Hwang-ho thenceforth abandoned its old channel, the once prosperous region through which it flowed becoming thus transformed into a barren waste. The old bed lay through Kiangsu, the river finally disemboguing in 34° N. Lat. It now flows through Shantung in a north-easterly direction, and empties itself into the Gulf of Peichihli, about 240 miles distant from its former mouth. The Hwang-ho is said to have changed its course no less than nine times within 2,500 years. It is impossible to picture the destruction wrought by such a calamity as the breaking down of the bank of a river which has gathered strength from affluents along a course of 3,000 miles, and whose bed stands above the level of the surrounding country. The most recent catastrophe, with all its fearful consequences, had been predicted by the Abbe Huc years before it happened, and yet the government, in spite of the sad lessons of the past, took no measures to strengthen the weak embankments, so as to save the province from inundation. The result of the rapid deposit of alluvium from such a stream is seen in many of the flooded districts, where the waters as they subsided have left entire villages more than half buried in mud. It is at present difficult to determine to what extent the river is navigable. It is certainly available as a highway of intercommunication for the small craft used by the natives, but it is unserviceable for steam traffic, at any rate in its present condition.

The Yangtsze-kiang takes its rise in the mountains of Thibet, in the same region as the Hwang-ho, but one or two degrees further to the south. Such, however, is the number of tributary streams that feed its head waters, as to make it doubtful which of them is to be regarded as the true source of the river. The Yangtsze, after emerging from the mountain gorges of Thibet, follows a winding course of 1,300 miles to its point of confluence with the Yalung river in Yunnan; thenceforward its general direction is north-easterly, through the provinces of Szechuan and Hupeh, where it receives various affluents, and becomes navigable for large vessels up to the great Tsin-tan rapid at the mouth of the Metan gorge in about 31° N. lat., near the western frontier of Hupeh. The rocky defiles through which the river here makes its way are narrow, so narrow indeed in some parts that boats passing up or down are careful to keep their own side of the stream, in order to avoid collision. The gorges appear as if the mighty rocks had been split and slightly parted by some violent shock. The river is thus confined to its channel by great parallel walls of stone rising in sheer precipices more than 1,000 feet high.

To the Chinese the Yangtsze is navigable for at least 1,000 miles above Tsin-tan, but their boats are comparatively small ones, inexpensive to build, and specially adapted for their perilous work. Even such craft as these can only be piloted through the rapids by the united efforts of from 50 to 200 men, trackers from the villages on the banks, who earn their subsistence partly by towing boats, partly by pillaging* the many wrecks that are thrown upon the shore. In ancient times this part of the river was unnavigable, its bed being completely blocked up with rocks. Afterwards the local inhabitants were set to the task of clearing the channel, which they partially succeeded in

---

* "*Pillaging wrecks.*" It is only fair to explain, that by a long-established and well-recognised Chinese usage, derelict property becomes immediately the property of the first finder. These wreckers are not robbers. Even if a junk with its cargo were to drift from its moorings while all its crew were ashore, and were to be carried in the sight of its owner to the opposite bank of a river, the Chinese law would seem to authorise its appropriation by the first man who could seize it.

doing. They have, however, been careful, with true Chinese instincts, to leave some of the most dangerous obstructions, so as to obtain a living out of the haulage and wrecks. Steam traffic in this region would be attended with constant danger, on account of the velocity of the currents, the jagged rocks in mid-stream, and the frequent recurrence of rapids over a distance of at least 100 miles. Should the Yangtsze ever become part of the route from India to China, it might be found that small powerful steamers could be so constructed as to overcome the difficulties of navigation at this point, or overland carriage might here be resorted to, so as to clear the gorges and rapids; but without looking so far ahead, a great boon could be conferred, both on the Chinese and on ourselves, if the Upper Yangtsze were to be thrown open to foreign commerce, for it flows through some of the largest and richest provinces in the empire.

The Chinese carrying trade on the Upper Yangtsze is worthy of special notice, for the traders who engage in such a traffic must be men endowed with the most indomitable courage and coolness, possessing a determination which recognises no obstacle short of death itself. To shoot the Metan rapid in a boat badly put together, laden with all one's worldly possessions, and swept along by a nine-knot current towards sharp rocks in midstream ahead, is an exploit fit to test the strongest nerves, and yet it is of hourly occurrence in these waters. Boats may, and do get frequently wrecked, but the owners, should they survive, calmly begin life anew.

Between the gorges and Hankow, the highest

part on the Yangtsze open to foreign trade, the river alternately narrows and widens; at some parts its long reaches spread out to four or five miles broad, at others to not half a mile across. In Hunan it unites with the outlet of the Tungting lake, one of its chief affluents, and at Hankow it receives the river Han. Thence it flows, a noble stream, in a south-easterly direction to the Poyang lake, another great affluent in the province of Kiangsi, and strikes upwards from this lake to the north-east, through Ngan-whuy, till at last, in about lat. 32° N., it mingles its waters with the sea.

The rivers of secondary importance in China are the Peiho, the Min, and the Chu-kiang, or pearl river.

The Peiho is the principal river of Peichihli, and forms the communication between the imperial capital Peking and the sea coast.

The Min is the great artery of the Fukien province, down which the Bohea teas are brought to the foreign market at Foochow.

But the Chu-kiang, or Canton river, is probably the most interesting of these streams. It has three tributaries—from the north, the east, and the west—which together drain an area of 200,000 square miles.

The lakes of China—that is of China proper—are neither numerous nor important, but the Tungting in Hunan, and the Poyang in Kiangsi, are worthy of notice, for besides draining plains of great fertility and extent, they unite, as has already been pointed out, with the mighty Yangtsze-kiang, and also supply a number of navigable waterways, by means of which a network of communication is established over a vast and populous region.

In the Chinese dependencies the inland salt lakes lying to the north of the desert of Gobi may be referred to as geographically interesting, and Thibet, where the great rivers take their rise, also contains several lakes possessing special and peculiar characteristics.

This brief description of the chief watercourses of the Chinese empire would be incomplete, if the Grand Canal, the most important public work in China, were passed over without remark, more especially as it is desirable to point out the bearing which the features of the country have upon the industry and social condition of its inhabitants. If the antiquity and utility of the Grand Canal be both taken into account, we may set it down as an unique specimen of human wisdom and enterprise. Access into the canal from the Peiho is obtained by the river Yanho. Thence the course of the canal lies through Shantung and Kiangsu to the Yangtsze. It also crosses the Hwang-ho, and not only renders important aid in draining off surplus water from the latter stream, but forms the connecting link in a system of water communication which extends from the metropolis to the majority of the eighteen provinces of the empire. But during the present dynasty this great work has been allowed to fall into decay, and in some places—for example, in Shantung—it has been altogether abandoned of late years, having so silted up with deposits as to be reduced to the dimensions of a mere ditch. In other districts the canal by denudation has sunk below the level of the surrounding country, whereas once the latter stood below the level of the canal, and was irrigated by its fertilising waters. For a considerable distance northwards, beyond the bed of the Hwang-ho, or Yellow River, the canal is now dry during ten months in the year, and communication with the north is consequently cut off. The wreck of so considerable a portion of the Grand Canal may be attributed partly to the recent change in the course of the Hwang-ho, partly to the negligence of a weak government.

The Grand Canal, as the most important of the artificial channels in China, and as a great artery for the purposes of irrigation, supplies us with the grandest example of the canal system which forms a network throughout every province of the land; indeed, nothing is more remarkable to the traveller than the ingenious manner with which the people avail themselves of the bountiful water supply, both for the purposes of irrigation and of transport. On the other hand, it is difficult to find a more depressing spectacle than the wide-spread misery which everywhere follows on the withdrawal of the water supply from the main channels, a disaster of frequent occurrence, brought about by neglect of those classical maxims which urge the Chinese rulers to deepen their channels, repair their embankments, and establish water-courses for the benefit of the people. Unfortunately for China, there seems at the present moment to be no engineer comparable to the famous Yu, who deepened the channels, drained the flats, and thus prepared the soil everywhere for the husbandman's toil. There are indeed native officials who compile reports, notably one who now holds high office, and who has produced a treatise on the Hydrography of

Peichihli, but there are few practical engineers. The work just referred to consists of about forty volumes, and let us devoutly hope that it may lead to the drainage of that oft inundated province, and thus rescue the people from the misery which their perpetual floods entail, securing the government at the same time from the menaces of a desperate and starving population.

Some idea may be gathered from the foregoing pages of the value of the mountain and river systems to a large industrious population such as that of China. There we see the rivers drawing their supply of water from the slopes of the outer and inner mountain chains, and the people depending for their sustenance on the distribution of those waters throughout the numerous channels, natural and artificial, which constitute the real wealth of the empire.*

---

* It appears from the most recent intelligence that the authorities have set themselves earnestly to work to repair the broken banks of the Yellow River; 100,000 men are said to be employed on the undertaking.

CHAPTER II.

THE PROVINCES OF CHINA.

The Eighteen Provinces of China Proper—Peichihli, Shanse, Shense, Kansu, Shantung, Kiangsu, Honan, Nganwhui, Hupeh, Szechuan, Chekiang, Kiangsi, Hunan, Kweichow, Fukien, Kwangtung, Kwangsi, Yunnan. Islands—Formosa, Hainan.

WITHOUT attempting to be minutely accurate, I may divide the surface of China proper into two halves, one made up of the mountainous and hilly regions, and the other consisting of plains and fertile valleys. The former division is sparsely peopled, but rich in yet undeveloped mineral wealth, while the latter is highly tilled, and supports by far the largest and densest agricultural population in the world (with the doubtful exception of the valley of the Ganges). The region known as the great plain extends from the great wall to the Yangtsze, and from the sea to the eastern boundary of Szechuan. South of the Yangtsze the plains are more broken than in the north, by mountain ranges, high lands, and richly wooded hills. Many of these hills have been carefully terraced and brought under cultivation; and this is especially the case in the tea-producing districts, where the tea plant is found growing at a great altitude.

China proper is divided into eighteen provinces, and these taken in their order from north to south, and east to west, may be catalogued thus: Peichihli, Shanse, Shense, Kansu, Shantung, Kiangsu, Honan, Nganwhui, Hupeh, Szechuan, Chekiang,

Kiangsi, Hunan, Kweichow, Fukien, Kwangtung, Kwangsi, and Yunnan. The island of Formosa is included in the province of Fukien, while the island of Hainan forms a department in the Kwangtung province. Each province is again subdivided for separate purposes of civil and military jurisdiction, the subdivisions thus constituted being known as fu, chow, and hien, or departments, districts, and hundreds.

To every province a capital of its own is assigned, and there the provincial government is carried on. These provincial capitals are cities of the first class, while the departments and districts are respectively administered from cities of the second and third rank. The whole of the land is so portioned out that each city has under its control an area corresponding to its class or rank. The Emperor exercises despotic sway over the whole territory, and the imperial power, which in the provinces is directly represented by a certain number of governors-general, who hold the highest civil and military rank, descends through a host of mandarins of inferior grades, until it is at length brought to bear on the mass of the people.

The province of Peichihli occupies the northern extremity of the great plain, and has an estimated area of about sixty thousand square miles, nearly double the size of Scotland, and contains a population fully ten times as great as the latter country. The soil of this province, although light and sandy, is nevertheless well adapted to the growth of cereals and a great variety of other products common to the north of China. The lower plains towards the sea have been subject of late years to frequent and disastrous inundations, so that many thousands of the people thus deprived of food and shelter have either perished altogether, or been driven to the towns and villages on the higher land. Many fell by the way, and many more, when they had reached a place of safety, succumbed to the cold winds that sweep in winter time over Peichihli. To Li-Hung Chang, the present governor-general of the province, belongs the credit of having made, either from motives of humanity or good policy, a genuine and great effort on the occurrence of the last inundations to alleviate the misery in the flooded-out districts, but he found it necessary, at the same time, to hold the military in readiness to suppress the threatened rising of the starving people.

Peking, the metropolis of China, stands further inland, and on a higher level than the submerged plains. It may be approached from the sea by the Peiho river and **the Grand Canal**; but the city of Teintsin on the Peiho is the navigable limit for vessels of large tonnage, while even for smaller craft the nearest and most readily available point by water to the capital is Tungchow, about four days' boat journey higher up stream. From Tungchow to Peking there is the old Mongol stone road, which has now fallen into such utter disrepair as to be in some places almost impassable. It is nevertheless constantly used, and a good horseman, following this once magnificent route, may reach the capital in an afternoon's ride.

The seasons are well marked in Peichihli; and the climate, although subject to excessive changes of temperature, is bracing and salubrious during half the year. London is fully ten degrees further north than the Chinese metropolis, yet the cold in winter is so intense at Peking that the Peiho is annually frozen over, and remains blocked to trade for several months. This low temperature is due to the prevalence of cold winds which sweep over the frozen steppes of Mongolia. During southerly winds, when the sky is clear, the atmosphere recalls that of an English summer, but with this important difference, that the heat of the mid-day sun in Peichihli is far more intense. Yuen-ming-yuen, the imperial pleasure grounds where the famous Summer Palace formerly stood, is about eight miles north of the capital. This spot, with its lotus lake spanned by great white marble bridges, its deer parks, its wooded hills crowned with temples, palaces, and pagodas, must at one time have been a charming retreat; but it still remains a heap of ruins, as the allied forces left it after the sack of 1860.

The great wall runs along the northern outskirts of Peichihli province, dividing it from Inner Mongolia, which may be reached by the roads that lead through the Nankow and Kupikow passes. In ancient times these roads were kept in good order, but they are now in such a condition as to render them suitable only for the trains of camels, donkeys, and mules that carry produce and merchandise between Mongolia and China. The average difference in altitude between the level of the plain of Peichihli and of the Inner Mongolian plateaux is from 4,000 to 5,000 feet. The nomadic Mongols of these plateaux are chiefly shepherds and herdsmen, whose movements are determined by the nature of the pasturage obtainable for

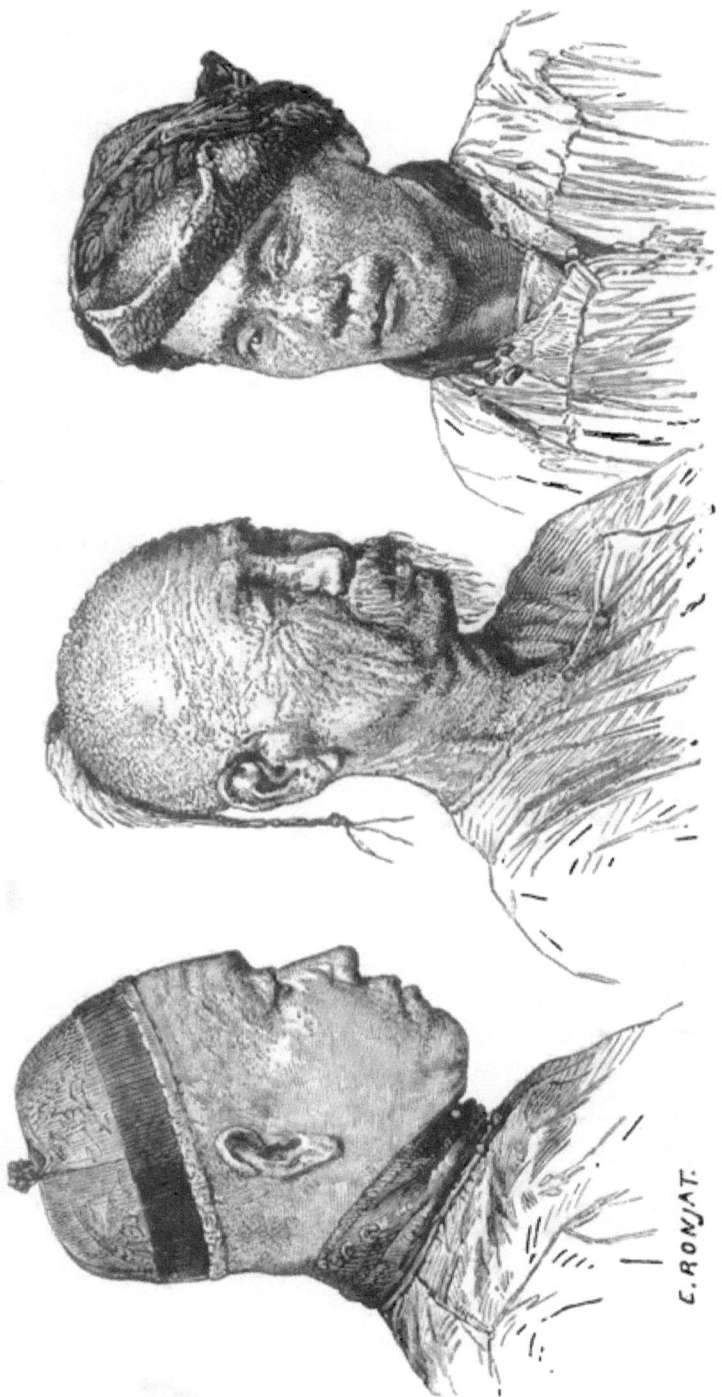

MONGOL. CHINESE.

Page 17.

their flocks. The occupation of the Mongols, the great elevation of their plains above those of China, together with the plentiful supply of animal food to which they are accustomed, account for the differences in physical characteristics which distinguish the nomad highlander from the lowland Chinese. The former has generally a large bony frame, high cheek bones, strongly developed jaw, square chin, well-marked facial muscles, large prominent teeth, and full lips. The natives of Peichihli and the north of China, who enjoy an abundant supply of the animal food imported from Mongolia, partake of the same characteristics, but in a degree modified by the nature of their varied, though more settled occupations, and by the difference in the climate to which they are exposed. Traces are not wanting of the intimate connection between the two races, or rather of the process of amalgamation and absorption by which the Chinese have, so to speak, conquered their conquerors, and impressed their own physical characteristics and their own civilisation upon alien tribes and nations.

Shanse is one of the smallest provinces in the empire, it is nevertheless said to possess four cities of the first class, besides its capital Tai-yuen-fu, and a large number of second and third class towns. About half the size of Italy, it contains a population considerably greater in proportion to its area. The capital, although it has lost much of its ancient splendour as the first residence of Chinese emperors, is still numerously inhabited, and enjoys besides a special reputation for its manufacture of felt. Shanse is bounded on the east by Peichihli, and on the north by a section of the great wall. Its surface abounds in hills interspersed with fertile plains and valleys which support a hardy industrious population. Shense, the adjoining province, is separated from Shanse by the Yellow River, which hereabouts, fed by a number of affluents, carries off the drainage of both provinces, and forms the main channel of communication from north to south. Shense is thinly peopled, probably owing to the mountainous nature of the country and to the poor quality of its soil, which, however, grows wheat, millet, cotton, tobacco, and various other products; nevertheless the two provinces of Shanse and Shense are extremely important if we take their mineral resources into account, and it is indeed to these resources that China must look for her future material development. Shanse alone is said to contain 30,000 square miles of coal fields, for the most part still untouched, as the mining appliances of the natives are of an exceedingly primitive kind. Mining operations are only carried on to a very limited extent, and yet the abundance of coal and the cheapness of labour enable the miner to sell the mineral at the pit's mouth at the rate of seven pence a ton. That is the price paid for the finest quality of anthracite coal in some parts of Shanse, but bituminous coal is sold for less. In the province of Shense lead is found in such quantities as already to form an important article of commerce, and indeed the mountains of this region possess stores of undeveloped mineral wealth which, ere long, will play an important part in the destinies of the empire.

Shense is, however, not unknown to fame. Singan-fu, its capital, was for many centuries the ancient metropolis of China, while in recent times its city of Hwa-chin is said to have been the birthplace of that Mahometan rebellion which has since spread its ravages over Central Asia. Fired with the zeal of the Faithful, these Mahometans, though greatly inferior in numbers, gained easy victories over their less warlike foes. To Pagans they gave no quarter, slaughtering cities full of men, women, and children, but sparing the native converts to Christianity who were all Roman Catholics. At last came the day of retribution—the Mahometans were in their turn subdued; and now fifty thousand sons of Islam are said to be confined within the walls of Singan-fu. These men, if report speaks true, dare none of them stir beyond the city gates, their Pagan fellow-citizens being only kept from falling on them like ravening wolves on carrion, by the restraining power of the authorities.

Still further westward, and also cut off from Mongolia by the great wall, is Kansu, occupying the north-west corner of China proper. The area of this province is something less than that of Shense, but its jurisdiction extends over the desert of Gobi to the borders of Zungaria. Its surface characteristics may be said to resemble those of the two provinces just described, while its population is nearly four times as great as that of Shense. The inhabitants are partly Mongolian, but there is also a large agricultural community settled to the west of the Hwang-ho, or Yellow River, which flows in a north-easterly direction through the province.

Kansu is intersected by a number of mountain ranges, whose peaks attain to an elevation of 10,000 feet above sea-level. These irregular chains are rich in minerals—gold, silver, and copper being among the metals found there.

The region derives additional importance from one of the trade routes between Central Asia and China running through the valley of the Yellow River, on which the capital Lanchow-fu stands.

The principal depôt of this trade was Singan-fu, in Shense, from which town there is a perfect network of communication, by rivers and roads, to the southern and central provinces of China.

The facility with which railway communication could be established, "leading through the province of Kansu, the oasis of Hami, and the region of Ili," from Lanchow-fu to the Russian frontier, has been a frequent and favourite theme among writers on commercial intercourse with China.

Shantung, the province south of Peichihli, is distinguished by the great promontory which forms the southern shores of the Gulf of Peichihli. The hill ranges, plains, and valleys of this fertile region are held in profound reverence by Chinese scholars as the most classic land in the world. Confucius and Mencius, China's greatest sages, were born and buried in Shantung. But objects are to be found in Shantung of even more ancient historical interest than the tombs of these sages: the central mountains cluster around the everlasting peak of "Taishan," held sacred by the Chinese for 4,000 years. Notwithstanding all its ancient glory, Shantung is, in some respects, most unfortunate. The Hwang-ho, or Yellow River, when it abandoned its old bed, swept in a destroying flood over some of the richest plains of the province before it finally settled into its new channel. It has thus transformed a once smiling land into vast shallow lagoons and pestilential marshes, and has taken from tens of thousands of the wretched inhabitants their only means of sustenance; unless indeed it be true, as has been reported, that 100,000 men are now employed in repairing the banks of the river. Let the Chinese bestow honours on their ancient sages if they will, but by all means let them see to their water-courses and avert such calamities as the submerging of half a province. If rapacious mandarins would but follow the virtuous maxims of the sages, they might earn far more money for themselves than the most extortionate squeezes can now bring in, by repairing dangerous embankments and saving the poor tax-payers. But no! each man's term of office is but short, and his brief labours might be suddenly arrested, so he must profit by his opportunities; and should the common people, his rate-payers, perish by thousands, the succeeding official must find his constituents where he can. The chief duty of the lower orders in China would appear to be to till and sow and reap, and even to perish, if need be, for the benefit of those who rule over them.

Shantung possesses a number of good harbours, both in the north and south sides of the peninsula. The best known is Chefoo, the only port in the province open to foreign trade, but Wei-hai-wei and Chong-tan are also commodious, and well adapted to steam traffic. The climate is salubrious; the seasons are well marked, and while the summer heat, which would otherwise be excessive, is tempered by land and sea breezes, the north-west winds of winter are softened in their severity by their passage over the low lands of Peichihli.

The soil of Shantung is rich, and its productions varied; cotton, millet, mulberry, rice, tobacco, and arrowroot are successfully cultivated and form articles of export. The mulberry and wild oak are widely distributed over the silk-growing districts, where different sorts of raw and manufactured silks are produced. The Shantung silks are famed for their special qualities. One kind is said to be almost impervious to stains, and the woven fabric of another sort defies the attacks of the moth. The Pongee silk combines the advantages of softness and durability, and would certainly become an important article of export but for the illegal transit dues and other imposts exacted by the authorities, who, although they affect to despise trade, are not above taking the lion's share of its gains.

The chief minerals in Shantung are coal and iron. The coal mines are worked with fair success, but the shafts are all of them shallow, as the natives abandon them for new borings whenever the water becomes troublesome to mining operations. For this reason the finest seams of coal are left wholly untouched, and the soil is honeycombed with shallow workings.

There are writers who urge with the most perfect good faith the desirability of introducing steam machinery to the manufacturing districts of China, and they are not without merchants and others to support them in their schemes for the regeneration of China.

Chinese traders and manufacturers are thoroughly practical and far-seeing; it cannot therefore be doubted that they themselves will ultimately follow the example of their compatriots at the coast ports—who now use steamers and telegraphs—and erect steam power factories.

Manchester merchants ought to pause and think how such a change will affect their interests in a province like Shantung, where labour is cheap, where cotton is largely grown, and where coal and iron are ready to the hand of the engineer.

Kiangsu, the next maritime province south of Shantung, presents a long irregular line of coast, broken by a multitude of sand-banks, by the old entrance to the Yellow River, and by the broad outlet of the Yangtsze-kiang. It is at once the smallest and the most populous province in the empire, and possesses a rich and well-watered soil. Besides the Yangtsze and Grand Canal it contains also a number of inferior rivers, lakes, and watercourses. Nanking, the capital of Kiangsu, stands on the south bank of the Yangtsze, and is one of the largest cities in China, enclosing within its walls an area nearly equal to that of Peking. In ancient times, when the empire was divided, Nanking was the southern capital. It afterwards, for a time, became the metropolis of the greater empire, when Hung-woo—the first sovereign of the Ming dynasty—ascended the throne. It was Yung-lo, the third emperor, who removed the court to Peking. In modern times Nanking and its famous porcelain tower were destroyed by the Taiping rebels under the so-called Tien-Wang, or "Heavenly King," who there rearing a sumptuous palace amid the general desolation which he had spread around, conferred upon his chosen city the title of "Heavenly Capital." But the rebellion was at last stamped out, and Nanking is again rising from its ruins.

The walled city of Chin-kiang, about 150 miles from the mouth of the Yangtsze, at the junction of the Grand Canal with that river, was at one time one of the chief trade marts in the maritime provinces; but it received a terrible blow at the hands of the rebels when they held their sway over the whole course of the Yangtsze, and it has never fully recovered from the destruction with which it was then overwhelmed.

In 1861 this port was thrown open to foreigners, and since that time an imposing foreign settlement has sprung up upon its shores, so imposing as almost to remind one of an English sea-port, were not the illusion soon dispelled by the presence of native craft moored to the mud-banks of the stream.

Honan, the province to the west of Kiangsu, is noted for its fertility, which is so remarkable as to have obtained for it the Chinese name of " Middle Flower." In the eastern part of the province a change in the course of the Hwang-ho has cast a blight over some regions formerly among the most productive, which lie along the old dry bed of the stream. The Hwang-ho still flows from west to east across the north, and emerges from Honan at a point some miles below the capital, Kai-fung-fu. This city has fallen in commercial importance, although yet one of the distributing centres of trade in this part of the interior. It is also the head-quarters of the Jews in China. There are only about 200 individuals left as a remnant of the Hebrew colonists in this land, and they have so conformed to the national customs and usages as to have forgotten their ancient traditions. It is even said that the last of the race who understood the Hebrew tongue died about seventy years ago.

Nganwhui province lies between Kiangsu and Honan. It has two large cities, Ngan-king, the capital, and Whui-chow, but it also contains a multitude of minor towns and villages dotted over its fertile plains. It is watered in the north by the river Whui, and in the south by the Yangtsze and Lake Tsao. The soils drained by the lake and by the great river are the most productive, and indeed are capable of raising almost every sort of grain. Cotton, silk, and hemp also figure among the exports from Nganwhui. The inland scenery of this province is agreeably diversified by low-terraced and cultivated hill ranges, many of them crowned with the graceful plumes of the bamboo, which grows in great profusion in southern China. Nganwhui is considerably smaller than England and Wales, and supports a population of more than 34,000,000. China is constantly spoken of as the most densely-peopled country in the world, and every acre of its surface is said to be under cultivation. These statements are based upon facts derived from the census, and from the agricultural industry apparent in populous provinces, such as Kiangsu and Nganwhui; whereas the population of the entire province of Yunnan, spread over an area exceeding that of Great Britain, is probably only about 2,000,000 in excess of the present population of London.

The superficial extent of any Chinese province cannot therefore afford the slightest clue to the number of its inhabitants. In the same way the area of soil available for the purposes of agriculture cannot be taken as supplying incontestable evidence of the presence of great agricultural communities. Allowance must be made for Chinese ignorance of the physical geography of their own country, for their neglect to construct proper roads, for imperfect drainage, for the silting up of old water-courses, and for the havoc wrought by inundations, and by the Taiping, the Neinfi, and other rebels, from which the country has not yet recovered. All these causes have served to limit the acreage of arable land. These remarks, though they would not warrant us in concluding that the present population of China is actually less than what it has been supposed to be by the best authorities, still may teach us that the theories upon which various writers, in the absence of trustworthy statistics, have hitherto based their calculations, must be accepted with caution.

Hupeh, the most central province in China, has an estimated area of 70,450 square miles, and a population of 37,370,098. Even if he knew nothing of the geography of the region, the reader, supposing he at all understood the genius of the Chinese people, would make up his mind that so populous a province must needs boast a soil well adapted for the industry of the husbandman, and that it also must be well watered by a close network of those rivers and streams which form the highways of trade in that part of eastern Asia, and in doing so he would find that his conclusions were borne out by facts.

The great Yangtsze flows from west to east through the entire length of the province, and is joined by its mighty tributary the Han-kiang opposite the capital city, **Woochang**. Besides these navigable water-courses, and connected with them, there are a number of lakes and minor streams, forming a commodious system of water communication over a vast and fertile country.

Woochang-fu stands on the south **bank of the Yangtsze**, nearly opposite to the city **of Han-yang**, with its densely populated suburb, Hankow. **These two** large cities, separated from each other by the breadth of the river, formed at one time the central nucleus of commerce, from which communication was established all over the empire.

The ancient name of the river Han **was the** Mien, and at that **time** it **flowed close** beneath the walls of Han-yang-fu. But the course of the Han and its point of confluence with the Yangtsze have been subject to frequent changes, which have now so transferred the trade of the city to its suburb, Hankow, as to render Han-yang-fu little more than a place of official residence.

The suburb has been noted for its trade since the time of the Mings, but it was entirely destroyed by the Taiping rebels, and is only slowly recovering its former status.

The restoration of trade there has however been facilitated **by** the presence of a large foreign community established in a splendid settlement on the banks of the river. Still, for all its splendour this foreign settlement is not without its disadvantages, and the least of them is perhaps its proximity to a great Chinese city. The well made roads and streets which run between the English-looking villas of this little suburb are not unfrequently submerged towards the end of the summer season, and at such times the dwellings can only be approached by boats. After the novelty of aquatic visits and boating parties has worn off, when the hall stairs have been transformed into jetties, and the lower apartments and offices into swimming baths, the residents, perched for safety among their mouldy furniture on the upper floors, look down drearily enough upon the brown flood that threatens to sap the foundations of their buildings.

It cannot be agreeable to have the poultry roosting in one bedroom and the children sleeping in the next, while a third is set apart for the accommodation of the milch cow and the native domestics.

Notwithstanding this, when the land is not flooded by the annual rise of the Yangtsze and Han rivers, Hankow is a most agreeable place to live in; food is varied and abundant, while every European luxury is supplied by a service of splendid steamers which run between Shanghai and the foreign settlement. The two Chinese cities stand further up stream, and are raised well beyond the reach even of the severest floods. The heights of Wusang, crowned with a bold modern pagoda, and the green slopes of the Han-yang hills lend a characteristic charm to the scene when viewed from the river; but the disappointment experienced on a closer inspection resembles that which unfortunately we too often feel as we look into the details of the picturesque in the far East. The quaint houses that were softened and beautified by the mysterious effect of atmosphere dwindle down into paltry shanties, propped up over the muddy banks by a multitude of lame-looking piles and posts, and disfigured by the slimy deposit of the river. The green slopes of the hill are dotted with wretched, ruinous tenements, patches of kitchen garden, and manure heaps, and their pigs are wallowing in, or fighting over, reeking garbage; while, as for the children, they are as numerous as the vegetables in the garden plots, and as dirty as if they had been manured for growth there.

Tens of thousands of boats are moored close to the shores, each one with its family of small traders, who aid the general uproar and discord by raising their voices in praise of their wares. Such are the impressions that are apt to fill the eye and the ear of the beholder as he gazes upon a river-side population and its immediate surroundings.

Szechuan, to the west of Hupeh, is the largest province in China, having an area of about 166,000 square miles, and a population estimated at about twenty-one and a half millions. The province abounds in mountains and hill ranges, interspersed with extensive highly-tilled plains and valleys.

Coal and iron are found in many parts of the country, copper and sulphur also are known to exist there, although not so widely distributed or in such great abundance as the two first-named minerals. Here again the Yangtsze is the great artery of commerce, following a tortuous course from the south-western to the north-eastern extremity of the province. Coal mines may be seen all along the face of the rocks that wall in this river from the town of Patung in Hupeh, to Chengking in Szechuan. The mineral, in some places, is of excellent quality, but the mode of working it, if simple and inexpensive, is extremely defective.

The Yangtsze is fed by many important affluents, as it travels across Szechuan. Notably by the Wen, which is navigable as far as the provincial capital, Ching-too, about 150 miles above the confluence of the two rivers. From the varied and important nature of its products, and from the facilities afforded by the navigable streams by which it is watered, Szechuan must take a high rank among the provinces of the Chinese empire. Its soil yields more rice and wheat than is required for the support of its inhabitants. Cotton, hemp, silk, tobacco, Tung oil, white wax, and salt, are among its other principal exports, and however much we may regret the fact, opium is largely cultivated on some of the best lands, both in Szechuan, Kweichow, and Yunnan, and has added greatly to the wealth of all these three provinces. In Szechuan, above 6,000 piculs ($133\frac{1}{3}$ lbs.$=1$ picul) of opium are now stated to be annually produced. The quality, however, is inferior to Indian opium, and the native drug is consequently sold at a cheaper rate. The Chinese assert that the poppy has been cultivated in Szechuan, Shanse, Yunnan, and Kweichow for about a century, but that the seed was originally imported from India and Thibet. The drug was at first used only as a medicine, but by-and-by opium smoking became so general that the demand could not be satisfied, owing to the high price of foreign opium at Canton, and then the idea occurred to the Chinese to raise their own supplies.

Chekiang is a small maritime province lying to the south-east of Nganwhui and Kiangsu. Its surface is rather larger than that of Portugal, and its population about ten times as great. The mountains in Chekiang are famed for their grand and picturesque scenery, while its highly-tilled plains produce the mulberry, cotton, rice, and a great variety of cereals. Hang-chow-fu, the capital, stands on a plain, at the inner angle of a great bay, and on the banks of the Grand Canal which terminates at this point. The place has the reputation of being one of the most refined and luxurious cities of China. When speaking of this eastern Paradise, a Chinaman will say, "Hangchow and Soochow on earth, and heaven above."

Ningpo, the only port in this province open to foreign trade, is a fortified town built on the Yuyaon branch of the river Yung. The small foreign settlement on the opposite bank of the stream facing this town is conveniently placed for commercial purposes, and otherwise well adapted to meet the wants of its European community. This spot is intimately connected with the early history of Chinese intercourse with foreign nations.

The Portuguese traders sought refuge in Ningpo in 1522, after they had been expelled by the Chinese from Kwangtung; but some twenty years later the majority of these Portuguese settlers were massacred by the natives, who were incensed by their outrageous conduct. Towards the end of the seventeenth century the East India Company reopened commercial relations with China, by establishing a depôt on Chusan Island, opposite the mouth of the Yung; but it was not until 1842, when Ningpo became a treaty port, that foreigners were again permitted to reside and carry on their trade at the place. The city fell into the hands of the Taipings in December, 1861, was held by those rebels for about twelve months, and finally recaptured for the Imperialists by the British and French naval forces stationed on the Yung. The foreign trade at this port has proved disappointing to the local merchants. The high expectations which its position seemed to warrant have never been realised. The fact seems to be that many of the valuable products of the country find their way to the greater market at Shanghai, while the absence of a system of good navigable channels has tended to check the distribution of foreign wares over the interior. There are, it is true, a number of inland canals, but the undulating surface of the country and the frequent occurrence of locks render these far less serviceable than the level waterways found in the adjacent provinces, and more particularly in the north of China.

The settlement is, however, in high favour among foreigners as a place of residence, owing to the proximity of the islands of the Chusan group, and the lovely scenery met with about a day's journey inland from Ningpo, where one may breathe the bracing air of richly-wooded highlands. The Tiendong Hills, thirty miles or more to the south-west, are also much frequented by Europeans.

These hills, where dark pine woods shade quaint monastic retreats, where crystal rivulets and foaming waterfalls abound, make a very brilliant show in spring-time, when the azaleas are in bloom, for these plants grow in wild profusion all over the district, and mingle with the ferns and flowers common to more temperate latitudes.

The tea plant also flourishes in this region, but it is only cultivated to meet the wants of the inhabitants. The bamboo, too, grows in great perfection, and spreads a pleasant shade over the houses with its graceful plumes.

The province of Kiangsi, which lies to the south-west of Chekiang, has an approximate area of about 70,000 square miles, greater than Scotland and Ireland combined, and a population nearly equal to that of the United Kingdom. This district is drained by a number of streams that discharge their waters into the Poyang lake. The Poyang lake is a large sheet of water supplying the connecting link between the Yangtsze river and the numerous waterways which form the high-roads of commerce throughout the province. The Chang river, which flows from south to north, is the chief artery, and by it Nanchang, the capital, may be reached. Nanchang, a place of great commercial importance, is accessible to vessels of moderate tonnage, but the Poyang lake is closed to steam traffic. The nearest point at which steamers touch is Kiukiang, on the Yangtsze, not far from the outlet of the lake. Foreign goods are distributed from Kiukiang, over the districts of Ningchow in the south-west, Hokow in the south-east, and Wuyuen to the east of the lake. The chief exports from Kiukiang are tea, paper, and porcelain ware. The latter comes from the famous potteries of Kingte-chin, established A.D. 1004, and named after an emperor of the Sung dynasty.

The tea is supplied by the three districts already named, but the principal tea-growing district is Hokow, on the northern slopes of a range of mountains which divides the province from Fukien. About a third of the Hokow teas find their way to the Foochow market, whence they are shipped for Europe. This traffic involves overland carriage from the Hokow tea fields to one of the water channels leading from the Bohea region to the Min river in Fukien, whereas by the proper navigation of the Poyang and its affluents a perfect system of water conveyance could be established between the tea districts and Kiukiang, the treaty port of Kiangsi. The quantity of tea annually shipped from Kiukiang averages about 140,000 piculs ($133\frac{1}{3}$ lbs. = 1 picul).

The manufacture of paper from bamboo, from the bark of a certain tree, and from cotton or hempen fibre, is one of the chief industries of this province, and indeed ranks second only in importance to the cultivation of tea.

The production of porcelain and earthenware affords constant employment to about 15,000 workmen, as well as to a large number of merchants, who are solely occupied in distributing their choice wares over the empire.

Hunan, the central province south of Hupeh, in its physical geography much resembles Kiangsi. One special feature shared by Hunan and Hupeh is the Tungting lake, which, standing at the northern extremity of Hunan, by means of its southern tributaries effects the entire drainage of that province, and finally discharges its waters into the great Yangtsze-kiang. The provincial capital, Chang-sha-fu, is situated on the left bank of the Siang river, not far from the head of the lake. The Siang, in common with the Yuan and Soo, takes its rise in the Nanling range of mountains on the southern boundary of the province. These rivers appear to intersect the country at nearly equal distances from each other, and their commercial importance may be estimated by the number of large towns which we find scattered along their banks, or following the courses of a multitude of minor streams by which the three main channels are fed. The Tungting, though the largest lake in China, and the natural approach to many of the chief emporia of the central provinces, remains closed to foreign trade. Hankow is indeed the highest point on the Yangtsze to which steam traffic has hitherto been carried, and only the main channel of the Yangtsze is open up to this port. The byways of commerce, the natural routes to the great consuming districts of the interior, such as the Poyang lake and the Han river, are kept jealously sealed against external traffic. The Poyang and Tungting lakes are said by the Chinese to be unnavigable when the river is at its lowest; if, however, it is certain that those great sheets of water are bordered by vast shallow lagoons, it is equally certain that they are intersected by navigable channels which are constantly used by Chinese traders.

However, until the lakes have been properly surveyed, it would be unfair to say that the obstacles to steam navigation in these waters exist only in the minds of native officials, although the testimony of one or two travellers who have crossed the Tungting tends to strengthen the belief that it at least presents no serious obstacles to steamers.

Coal of the finest quality is found in great abundance in Hunan. It occurs in the prefectures of Shin-chow-fu and Heng-chow-fu, and in many other places besides. The Hunan coal is both anthracite and bituminous, and finds a ready market in Hankow, at which place, after a water carriage of between three and four hundred miles, it sells for about twenty-eight shillings per ton. At Hankow alone ten or twelve thousand tons of coal are annually supplied for the use of steamers which run on the Yangtsze.

The province of Hunan is broken up by mountain and hill ranges which produce a variety of minerals, notably iron and lead, as well as timber in great abundance. This timber is rafted down the lake to the Yangtsze in huge baulks dotted over with rows of huts, and resembling floating villages. The rafts, when they reach their destination, are broken up for sale, the owners transferring their huts to the banks of the river, where they remain until the cargo is disposed of. These small timber trading settlements look so complete and comfortable as to convey the notion that the woodcutters not only come themselves in charge of the rafts, but bring their villages with them, whereas in reality their huts form a part of their cargo, and are disposed of at the last moment to ready buyers. In this procedure we have a striking example of the social economy of the Chinese—a people who, in so far as their knowledge will permit them, utilise everything that can be turned to account, alike in their commerce, their agriculture, and their domestic life. The soil of Hunan is a rich and productive one, yielding a plentiful supply of grain; while the fisheries on the lake also contribute largely to the support of a population which numbers about twenty millions, and is scattered over an area of 74,320 square miles.

Kweichow, to the west of Hunan and the south of Szechuan, is, for the most part, a mountainous province. The minerals found there are lead, copper, coal, silver, mercury, and iron; but the soil is described as poor, and the inhabitants as semi-barbarous. In the mountain chains to the south there are a number of what are supposed to be aboriginal tribes, called Miautze, who from the most ancient times have not only maintained their independence, but proved a source of constant trouble to their foes, the less warlike Chinese. These savage tribes inhabit the mountains of Kwangtung, Kwangsi, and Hunan. Their language, customs, and usages are totally different from those of their lowland neighbours, and judging from Chinese works in which pictures of the Miautze, carefully drawn and coloured, are sometimes met with, these wild mountaineers bear a striking similarity to the Laos of northern Siam and Cambodia. Both males and females wear their hair long, and gather it up in a tuft on the top of the head, while the colours and patterns used in their garments of silk or cotton also resemble those in vogue among the Laos tribes of Indo-China.

Kwei-yang, the provincial capital, stands on a branch of the Wu, a river which drains the central part of the province and finally falls into the Yangtsze at a point some fifty miles below Chungking in Szechuan.

The area of Kweichow is about 64,500 square miles, and its population 5,288,219.

The province of Fukien, on the sea-board, lies south of Chekiang, and east of Kiangsi, and within its limits comprehends a small but important region where some of the finest Chinese teas are grown and prepared for the foreign market.

Fukien is one of the most mountainous provinces in the empire, possessing only scattered patches of alluvial soil, and these chiefly formed near the beds of its two great rivers, the Min and the Lung-kiang. The Nanling mountains in the north and west constitute the boundary between Kiangsi and Fukien. The road connecting these two provinces crosses these mountains by the "Fung-shui Pass." Here the track becomes steep, narrow, and difficult of ascent, nevertheless great quantities of tea from Hokow—the district already mentioned—are carried annually along this elevated defile in baskets slung on the bamboo poles of coolies hired for the purpose. The scenery on the Fukien side among the spurs of the Nanling mountains and the Wu-he —commonly known as the Bohea hills—cannot be surpassed in its weird grandeur.

For this reason the Wu-he hills have been chosen for the sites of hundreds of Buddhist shrines, and for the homes of countless hermits. The cultivation and preparation of tea is the chief industry of the region which lies between the Nanling range and the hills around Yen-ping-fu. Yen-ping-fu is the central city, and it stands at a point where the Min unites two streams which flow, one from a northern source in the Nanling chain, and the other from the hills in the south. The climate and soil here are probably most favourable to the cultivation of the leaf which produces

FUKIEN WOMEN.

the black teas of commerce. The pure tea of Fukien, however, possesses a delicacy of flavour little likely to be appreciated by the consumer at home, whose palate has of late years become accustomed to the stronger growths of Assam, Japan, or Formosa. But the cultivation of the plant is by no means limited to the north of the province; there are also many other extensive plantations on the Pailing hills, not far from the capital, Foochow. Tea culture, indeed, is carried on all over the province wherever the soil is not suited to the produce of cereals. The river Min is a broad navigable stream up to the foot of the Yenping rapids, about one hundred miles from the sea. Above the rapids all traffic is conducted in boats built specially to meet the difficulties and perils of voyaging. Foochow, the capital of Fukien, stands about thirty-five miles inland, on the plain through which the Min flows. The foreign settlement at Foochow is built in a picturesque locality, among the hills about three miles from the city, and on the south bank of the river. There is an excellent harbour at Pagoda anchorage, below Foochow— a harbour spacious enough to accommodate the merchant fleet of China, and not more than twelve miles removed from the sea.

Amoy is another town on the south coast of this province. Here once were the head-quarters of the famous Koksinga, a Chinese adventurer who, in 1661, expelled the Dutch from Formosa. Amoy and Chinchew, a neighbouring city, were both celebrated emporia as far back as the beginning of the ninth century, at a time when commerce with the West was carried on *viâ* India or Persia.

It was not till the middle of the sixteenth century that Europeans commenced at the port of Amoy to trade directly with the Chinese. In 1544 the Portuguese appeared there in great force and established a settlement, but, owing to their misconduct, the natives rose against them, burned their ships, and drove them from the place. Traces may still be found among the gravestones scattered over the Amoy hills, and the adjacent islands, of European traders and priests who were buried there about three hundred years ago; but it was not until the Treaty of Nanking had been ratified that foreigners were permitted to trade freely at this port of Fukien, and to build themselves a permanent settlement.

Foochow harbour is one of the most accessible in China, and well adapted for the accommodation of large vessels; indeed the depth of water in the inner harbour allows ships to anchor safely close in-shore in front of the merchants' offices and warehouses.

The Fukien coast, from north to south, is broken sometimes by masses of rock towering in bold cliffs and headlands, sometimes by huge granite boulders crowning the low hills that slope down gently to the edge of the sea. The general shore outline is a rugged and irregular one, bordered by numerous islands, among which Amoy and Quemoy are the most important, if not the largest in size. As to the other islands, many of them consist simply of gigantic lumps of granite that look as if they had been riven from the rocks of the mainland and tossed into the sea.

In the neighbourhood of Amoy the soil is

unproductive, and the population is much greater than the district can support. To add to these evils the people have been impoverished by the rebels and crushed under the subsequent pressure of local taxation.

Happily the tide of emigration now carries off tens of thousands of industrious poor to cheapen labour in our own colonies and in America.

The population of the province is now set down at 25,799,000, and occupies an area of 53,400 square miles. Kwangtung, the province which covers the south-eastern extremity of the empire, presents a long irregular coast-line to the China Sea and the Gulf of Tong-king. Owing to its geographical position, this province is the one which foreigners know best; indeed Canton, the provincial capital, and its immediate surroundings, formed the sources from which, up to recent times, we derived most of our information about the Chinese. In and near Canton, too, we fought those battles which gained us our island colony of Hong-kong and many of the advantages which our merchants now enjoy.

The Nanling range of mountains in this region, marks out, under a new name, the limits of the province to the north, and separates it from Kiangsi and Hunan, but everywhere in Kwangtung there are mountains and sierras to diversify the landscape, or isolated peaks and knolls that lend a peculiar charm to the inland scenery. The highlands are well wooded and rich in a variety of bamboos and pines. The best alluvial land is found towards the sea-board, near the mouth of the Chu-kiang, or Pearl River. At San-shui, a point about seventy miles in a direct line from the coast, the Chu-kiang receives the waters of the North and West rivers, while its third great tributary, the East river, joins it at Whampoa, between Canton and the shore. The country below Tsing-yuen district on the North river may be described as a vast alluvial plain, which has been gradually redeemed from the ocean by the denudation of the highlands, and the resulting deposit of soil on the low grounds beneath. This process may be still seen in active operation in many quarters of China. On the western coast of Formosa, for example, as much as three miles of alluvial land have been added in some districts within the last two hundred years. In such regions there is either a river still existing, or the dry bed of some ancient stream may be traced, which has now sought a different outlet.

The Kwangtung plain is to this day broken up by such a multitude of shallow streams and lagoons as to render it difficult to determine which is the true navigable channel.

This delta lies so low that it can never be descried from the seaward, until vessels get close inshore. It is exceedingly fertile; and the careful husbandman has taken up every foot of available soil for the culture of rice, sugar, tobacco, the mulberry, fruits, and vegetables.

The city of Fatshan is celebrated as the scene of a battle during the so-called opium war, when Admiral, then Commander, Keppel, with a handful of British blue-jackets destroyed the Chinese fleet. The men of Fatshan are workers in iron; their city, indeed, is the Sheffield of China, although their native manufactures—in keenness of edge, in temper, and in quality—fall far short of the corresponding

KWANGTUNG BOATWOMEN.

Page 42.

English wares. Population of Kwangtung, about 21,152,000; area, 79,456 square miles.

The province of Kwangsi, which extends westward from Kwangtung, touches Tong-king, with its southern borders, and encloses within its limits a thinly populated mountainous and unproductive region. It is singular to observe that these same characteristics apply in a greater or less degree to all the outlying or frontier provinces of China proper; and that the most productive lands are not reached until rugged, sterile regions have been crossed.

It is at the same time impossible to over-estimate the value of these mountainous provinces in contributing the water supply, upon which the chief industries of China and the lives of so many millions of human beings depend. The same remark holds good also of the inner chains and hill ranges distributed so widely all over the land, which are not only important as affecting the hydrography of the plains, but also as supplying differences in temperature corresponding to differences in altitude, and this independent of latitude, a fact which enables the sedulous tillers of the soil to cultivate an immense variety of useful products. An observant traveller passing through any of the central provinces will at once be struck with the manner in which the poorest and most ignorant Chinese farmers avail themselves of the natural advantages afforded by their soil and climate, and the only solution of the mystery appears to be that they understand enough of the rudiments of natural science to carry on their agriculture with economy and success. In such a province as Kwangsi, the higher mountains are devoted to the growth of useful woods; the lower ranges afford a constant and inexhaustible supply of bamboos, which are largely used by the peasantry for making houses and furniture, while the food staples are grown in the valleys and plains below. Besides these advantages, the wooded heights not only perform important functions in purifying the air and supplying it with life-giving elements, but the mountains themselves contain in their mineral treasures an as yet undeveloped source of natural wealth. What the Chinese call the laws of "Feng-shui," or of good luck, have a great deal to do with the cutting of woods and the opening of land. These Feng-shui doctrines, and the profound veneration entertained for ancestral usages, combine with the landowner's natural love of gain to maintain the healthy custom of rearing pines and bamboos on the mountains and hill-sides of the provinces.

In the south of the province of Kwangsi, many low marshy lands are to be found, reminding one of the region round Lake Albufera on the Spanish coast, and peopled by scattered settlements of rice-planters, who suffer constantly from the relaxing influence of a hot and humid atmosphere. The province is thinly populated, and, excluding the independent tribes of Miautze, who dwell in the mountain ranges, it may contain from seven to eight million Chinese inhabitants.

Yunnan, the province which lies along the frontiers of Thibet and Burmah, at the south-western extremity of China, forms an extensive and elevated table-land broken up by great defiles, plains, and lakes. Its surface is rugged and uneven, and many of its mountains rise above the snow-line, especially in the north. Three great rivers pass through this region, and a fourth takes its rise within its borders. First there is the Yangtsze, making its way through mountain gorges, and curving down into the north of the province before it starts on its northward course through China. Then there is the Lantsan, which rises near the source of the Yangtsze, flows along the west of Yunnan, and finally descends through Cambodia as the great river Mekong.

In Cambodia the Mekong waters one of the most interesting regions in Eastern Asia, for on its banks are to be found the remains of stone cities, palaces, temples, and aqueducts, the relics of an almost unknown civilisation. The rapids of the Mekong between Yunnan and Cambodia render the stream quite unnavigable, while the exquisite architecture of the ancient Cambodian ruins forbids our supposing that their builders derived their arts from China.

The Salween also passes through the west of Yunnan, close by Momein, where Mr. Margary lately fell. Thence it traverses Burmah, and finally discharges into the Gulf of Maetaban, near Maulmein. But the most important among the rivers that have their sources in Yunnan is the Menam, which flows through Siam, and effects the drainage of one of the best rice-producing countries in Asia. In Yunnan there are also three considerable lakes, the Sien, the Chin, and the Urh-hai, near Tali-fu. The Urh-hai is an affluent of the Yangtsze-kiang.

It has been proposed to open up a river route between India and China *viâ* the Brahmapootra and the Yangtsze-kiang, connecting these two streams by means of a road about 250 miles long. The great objection to this scheme is, that the route has never been properly surveyed, and it is quite certain that in the Yangtsze-kiang alone so many obstacles to steam traffic exist, that even a steamer of the most modest proportions might after all be unable to approach within 1,000 miles of the proposed point of junction. There are, however, trade routes through Yunnan already existing, which the Chinese must now throw open to our commerce. These routes will soon be surveyed, and commercial relations can then be established not only with the tribes along the line, but between the merchants of British India and Western China. While we are thus preparing to open up this part of China, our neighbours the French are said to have discovered the shortest and most direct river approach to Yunnan, up the Songca river through Tong-king. Tong-king they have now taken under their own protection, and their recent attempts to navigate the Upper Mekong having proved futile, they are turning their attention to the Songca, which flows from a source in the mountains of Yunnan.

The provincial capital, Yunnan-fu, stands at the northern extremity of Lake Chin, and is the focus of a considerable trade from Burmah, Thibet, and the central provinces. But besides the capital there are about twenty first class cities, which to a greater or less degree share in the import and export trades of the province. The native products are gold, tin, copper, precious stones, silk, musk, gums, and ivory. The inhabitants of the country are hardy and industrious, and are skilled in a variety of handicrafts.

The area of Yunnan is 107,969 square miles, and the population 5,823,000 or thereabouts.

The proximity of Yunnan to Tong-king, and to the Laos states, in the north of Siam and Cambodia, favours the assumption that the Laotians are allied to the primitive Miautze tribes, who inhabit the mountains of Kweichow, Kwangsi, Kwangtung, and other provinces of China. The southern and western districts of Yunnan, according to Dr. Williams, are peopled by semi-independent tribes of Laos, under the rule of their own chiefs. This relationship of the Miautze and Laos tribes is all the more probable, as it can be proved that the territory taken up by the early Chinese settlers did not extend further south than the 33rd parallel of north latitude, and that thence, as they gradually encroached upon the southern lands, they drove the aborigines into the mountains in the south-western provinces of the empire.

ISLANDS.

The largest islands off the Chinese coast are Formosa and Hainan.

Formosa lies between $25°10\frac{1}{2}$ and $21°24\frac{1}{2}$ N. latitude, and is about 85 miles wide across the centre, which is its broadest part. Although separated from the coast of Fukien by a channel no more than 100 miles in breadth the Chinese only discovered its existence about the beginning of the fifteenth century. It was afterwards made known to Europeans by the Spanish, who named it Isla Formosa, or the beautiful island. The Japanese endeavoured to form a colony in the north of

Formosa about the beginning of the seventeenth century, and in 1634 the Dutch established themselves at Tai-wan-fu, the present capital. Interesting traces of this Dutch occupation are still found in the ruined forts at Taiwan-fu, and in traditions and documents carefully preserved by the mountain aborigines. The Dutch were finally expelled from Formosa by Koksinga, a renowned Chinese pirate, who afterwards became a powerful adherent of the imperial government, and received a title of nobility.

Formosa forms one of a great chain of volcanic islands, which may be traced as far north as the northwest coast of America, and southwards through the isles of the Malayan Archipelago into the South Pacific Sea. In Formosa there are numerous evidences of volcanic action in comparatively recent times—lava deposits, chasms and craters, where sulphur is found in such abundance as to render it a valuable article of commerce. Hot springs, too, are met with, and rapid physical changes, such as could only be effected by volcanic agencies, may be still clearly made out. Coal of excellent quality is widely distributed over the north of the island, and is extensively worked at Kelung, where there is a harbour affording anchorage for large vessels. A high mountain chain traverses the island from north to south, in some places attaining an altitude of over 1,200 feet, and descending eastwards in a multitude of rugged spurs, which protrude their rocky cliffs and headlands into the sea. The western half abounds in hill-lands, in fertile valleys, and in vast plains; but these have been taken up for the most part by industrious Chinese settlers, who employ themselves in cultivating tea, sugar, rice, fruit, and vegetables, and also in the preparation of camphor. The mountains are inhabited by independent tribes bearing no resemblance, either in appearance, language, or customs, to the Chinese colonists, with whom they alternately carry on hostilities, or trade by barter. The language, customs, and usages of these mountaineers point to a Malayan origin, although the long-continued isolation of the different tribes in their several hunting grounds has given rise to a puzzling variety of dialects, seemingly of common derivation, but still so unlike as to make the southern aboriginals unintelligible to those of the north. The wild scenery in the central mountain chain, the deep gorges clothed in tropic vegetation, the rugged streams and cataracts, the lofty peaks mantled with primeval forest, present together a combination of the beautiful and the sublime rarely matched in other parts of the world. Some civilised tribes of aborigines are found in the hills which border on the Chinese territory, and are known in the Amoy dialect as Shek-hoan, Shui-hoan, and Pepo-hoan. Many of these tribes have now acquired the Chinese tongue, and the men also adopt the tonsure and the Chinese dress; but the women cling with fond tenacity to their more picturesque native costume, cherishing the traditions of the good old days, when the land was all their own, and when the hated stranger had not yet driven their forefathers from the fertile plains.

The climate of Formosa is much more tropical than that of the opposite mainland, and its products are more valuable and varied. During the northeast monsoon, however, a strong current sets through the channel and renders it extremely dangerous for vessels to approach the coast. On the western side Takow is the only good harbour, but even here the inlet is very rocky and narrow, and the anchorage appears to be gradually silting up through the neglect of the Chinese authorities to dredge the lagoon, which is making inroads on the space available for shipping, or to keep the channel clear by which the port is approached. There used to be, during the time of the Dutch occupation, a harbour at the capital, Taiwan-fu, but the spot where the ships then lay is now three miles inland. Vessels trading to this port at the present day have to moor in the roads outside, and there await till favourable tides and winds enable the boats to cross the long shoals so as to discharge or take in cargo.

In the north, at the mouths of their respective rivers, are the harbours of Tamsui and Kelung, both of them probably more accessible than Takow. During the prevalence of the monsoon, when the violence of the wind and the strength of the current render it almost impossible for sailing vessels to make the western harbours, trading intercourse between the north and south of the island is almost cut off, as the roads through the interior are hardly broad enough to accommodate pedestrians marching in Indian file. Kelung, Tamsui, Taiwan-fu, and Takow, all on the western half of Formosa, are the only ports yet opened to foreign trade. The population of Formosa is estimated at 3,000,000, and its area at 13,100 square miles.

The island of Hainan constitutes a department of the Kwangtung province called Chung-chu. It is about 150 miles long by 100 broad, and though the strait which separates it from the mainland of Kwangtung is a narrow one, it abounds in shoals and sandbanks, which render the navigation difficult and dangerous. The interior of the island is mountainous. In some of the central ranges the peaks are said to rise 17,000 feet above sea-level; but this assertion has still to be verified, as no proper survey of the interior has hitherto been made. It is, however, quite certain that the mountains attain to a very high altitude, and, as in Formosa, what may be termed the Alpine districts of Hainan are peopled by independent aboriginal tribes, who are commonly known as Li. As we traverse the island from the north, the Li-mu-ling is the first chain met with. This range unites with the Yin-ko-ling and Ta-wu-chi, or "Five Peak Mountains."

The entire island is divided into thirteen districts; three rank as chow, and ten as hien, and separate civil magistrates are assigned to each. Ching-chow-fu, the capital, stands on the northern coast, about four miles inland. This town is approached by a river, and at its mouth is Haihow, the port. It was proposed in 1871 to throw Haihow open to foreign trade, but no definite steps have yet been taken to include it in the list of treaty ports.* There are a number of other good harbours in the island used by the Chinese settlers, who from thence carry on a not unimportant trade between the mainland, the Malayan Islands, Siam, and other places. The soil, which in some parts of the interior is a rich one, has been cultivated, and

* Since the above was written Haihow has been formally opened, and a British Consular Agent stationed at the port.

is watered by streams taking their rise in the central mountains. Many of these streams are assumed to be navigable, as in the Chinese maps their courses are dotted with market towns, villages, and customs stations. Copper mines are reported to exist in the Chang-hwa district, but the products both of the interior and the coast are for the most part similar to those found in the Malayan Islands, such as cocoa-nut oil, ground-nut oil, hemp, sugar, areca nuts, pepper, spices, and tropical fruits. The Chinese planters obtain a limited supply of labour from among the semi-savage aborigines, who are, nevertheless, careful to guard their own independence.

The Chinese of Hainan emigrate in great numbers to the Straits Settlements, Siam, and Cochin China, in all which countries they are much prized as labourers on plantations, and as domestic servants.

Hainan was at one time an imperial residence. To this island the uncle of a reigning emperor was banished in 1321, and there he lived in great state until 1330, when he ascended the throne.

From the foregoing geographical and topographical sketch the great dependencies of China have been purposely omitted, as they do not come directly within the scope of a work which professes to deal principally with the Chinese people, their industries and social condition. But the physical characteristics of the empire and all the provinces peopled by the Chinese have been described at some length, with the view of showing how far the natural features of the country have contributed to develop the distinctive national characteristics and industries of the greatest race in Eastern Asia.

CHAPTER III.

SUMMARY OF CHINESE HISTORY.

Early Chronology—The Accession of Fu-hi, 2852 B.C.—The Black-haired race—The first dynasty—The Emperor Yu—The worship of God—Yu's labours—Invention of the compass—Birth of Confucius—Chi-Hwang-ti, builder of the Great Wall—The Classics destroyed—Buddhism introduced from the West—"The Three States"—Literary competitive examinations instituted—The influence of a Queen—Tartar sovereigns—Kubli-khan—Marco Polo—The present dynasty.

CHINESE chronology extends backward to primeval ages, when their gods reigned on earth. After the gods came kings no less mythical, whose lives and government were prolonged for periods of eighteen or twenty thousand years. These latter rulers, besides enjoying a longevity so remarkable, must also have boasted something more than human attributes. If they did not invent Chinese men and Chinese women, they, at any rate, taught them the useful arts of sleeping and eating—arts which in modern times have been brought to such perfection that some sceptics have mistaken them for inborn aptitudes coeval with the creation of the human race.

The world was framed and put in order for the special benefit of Chinamen, at least so their own early chronicles would have us believe. China was in those days the only habitable part of the earth, the centre of the level plain over which the sun, moon, and stars moved in their appointed courses, supplying heat and light, and marking the divisions between night and day, that men might know when to labour and when again to repose. It would appear, too, if we are to be guided by the Chinese historians, that the seasons were either invented or discovered by some wise ministers in order that agriculture might be carried on without confusion, and that tillage, seed-time, and harvest, might succeed one another in due course, and not be mixed up.

The accession of Fu-hi, about 2852 B.C., may be taken as the event which separates the purely mythological from the more trustworthy history of China. It is quite possible that such a personage reigned about that period, although scholars, native and foreign, have shown some reasons for doubting whether he occupied the throne for the traditional space of one hundred and fifteen years. The fictitious element is again prominent in the records of the seven sovereigns who followed the illustrious Fu-hi, and who wore the crown for periods varying from fifty to one hundred and forty years.

There can, however, be no reasonable doubt that the Chinese, or "Black-haired race," as they are designated in the historical classic, appeared about 2200 years B.C., and took possession of the banks of the Hwang-ho. They formed at that time a small colony, but they had brought with them habits of industry, and a rudimentary knowledge of a written language, in which their earliest records were carefully preserved. They seem also to have been acquainted with the culture of the mulberry and the preparation of apparel from woven silk, for we meet with several allusions to this industry in the "Tribute of Yu," as one of their historical classics is termed. The settlers found the land already occupied by alien, and perhaps aboriginal, tribes, but these they either gradually absorbed, or drove back into the mountain districts as their own numbers increased.

The first dynasty recorded in Chinese history is that of the Heaites, who had to struggle against the difficulty of cultivating a flat country where inundations frequently occurred, and also against the raids of those savage aborigines whose descendants, the Li and Miautze, still occupy many of the hill fastnesses of Southern China. It is supposed by some writers that the Heaites as well as the aboriginal tribes migrated from the West, and separated in the region where the two great rivers take their rise—the former following the course of the Hwang-ho, the latter that of the Yangtsze. Be that as it may, the theory is one which gains no light from the ancient Chinese records, and on which philologists and students of history have never been able to agree. There is indeed no trustworthy evidence to indicate that the Chinese had any existence as a nation anterior to the time of Yu, the founder of the Hea dynasty, about 2200 B.C. The historical classic, "Shoo-king," gives us a wonderful account of the virtue, the wisdom, and the mighty deeds of Yu, an emperor famous among other things because he sought out servants of God the Supreme Ruler to be his ministers. Yu established a sort of feudal empire, dividing the land among his chiefs and conferring a title upon each of them. This feudal system, of comparatively modern origin in Europe, arose in China out of the necessities of the times, for the nucleus of the great empire was exposed to danger on all sides from the savage tribes who were steadily being driven back before its advancing power.

The emperor governed the chief state, but drew his revenues from the whole land, and held the feudatory princes liable to military service. Like everything Chinese, this early form of government casts its dim outlines across the ages, so that we may perceive something of its spirit and elements still surviving in the present administrative system. It is true that these outlines have been modified; nevertheless they are apparent in the existing divisions of the empire, each province being governed as a separate state under a viceroy armed, during his term of office, with imperial power, who administers the local revenues, and every year remits a proportion of the sum collected to the treasury at Pekin.

It is reported of Yu that he assuaged a great flood. Some suppose that the story which describes this event is nothing more than the Chinese version of the Noachian deluge; but such a view cannot well be maintained, for the chronology does not agree. Far more probably the record supplies us merely with the earliest reference to one of those breaches in the embankments of the Yellow River which have been a constant source of trouble to the Chinese, or to the first measures taken to construct embankments so as to check the periodical overflow. This opinion seems all the more certain as it is known that the empire during Yu's time lay along the valley of the Ho, extending from the north-west corner of the modern province of Honan to the eastern coast in the shape of a wedge, the thin edge turned inland, and covering the region through which the old and new beds of the Yellow River take their course. This region then was probably drained for the first time, and brought under cultivation by the labours of Yu. So engrossed was the ancient imperial engineer with his task of redeeming the waste lands, that, as we are told, he journeyed to and fro during thirteen years, thrice passing his own door and refusing to enter it. The establishment of the first Chinese dynasty seems to have been pretty nearly coeval with the foundation of the Assyrian and Egyptian monarchies, and there are certain events recorded and characters described in ancient Chinese history which bear a resemblance, almost too close to be accidental, to the incidents and characters of our ancient Scripture history.

Ching-tang, the founder of the second dynasty, is said to have been a wise and mild ruler. On one occasion, during a period of great drought, this monarch repaired to a grove of mulberries, and there, attired as a mourner, fasting and offering up his hair and nails, he prayed to God earnestly for rain. His prayer was answered not long after in welcome showers. Twenty-eight sovereigns followed in the same line, reigning altogether for 644 years. But, alas! there were some among them who proved unworthy successors of the good Ching. The last emperor of the dynasty, a man greatly famous for physical strength and moral depravity, found a fit associate in a lewd concubine. Within his palace grounds he constructed a tank so large that three thousand men could drink at its brim, and then filled it with enough wine to float a barge.

On the surrounding trees hung the most delicate viands, but these no one was allowed to touch until he had quaffed deeply of the wine. Day and night these pleasure grounds were thronged with the gay and profligate, who spent their time in riot and debauchery. These evils ended in the decay of the imperial power, and the chiefs in their several provinces were thus enabled to assume independent sway.

The Chow dynasty, which began about 1122 B.C., introduced the use of imperial posthumous titles, which were inscribed on tablets set up in temples consecrated to the memory of the dead. The compass also is supposed to have been invented during the same period (1122 B.C.) by the Duke of Chow; and it is said that this south-pointing instrument was first applied to the chariots employed in those days to carry tribute-bearers back to distant lands.* Throughout the duration of this dynasty China was still divided into numerous petty principalities, which varied, however, in number and strength, according to the measures put in force to repress the arrogance of the chiefs. In spite of all efforts these chiefs were not brought into complete subjection until the commencement of the Tsin dynasty. Nevertheless the Chow dynasty is one of the most noteworthy in Chinese history, for it was during it that, amid strife and disorder which threatened to break up the empire, Confucius and Mencius were born. Although the wise and timely counsel of Confucius could not arrest the progress of disso-

* The Chinese take bearings from the South Pole instead of from the North Pole as we do. The magnetic needle is, therefore, supposed to point to the south. The course of the chariots was determined by means of the compass.

lution, yet the writings of that sage and of his disciple Mencius have in after ages become imperial text-books, and continue to exercise a power over their fellow-countrymen which has no parallel in history.

The troubles of this period which Mencius has pictured led at last to the overthrow of the feudal system, and to the establishment of a despotic monarchy such as exists in modern times.

The first emperor of the Tsin dynasty is one of the most remarkable of Chinese rulers. After subduing the feudatory princes he next travelled through his dominions, constructing roads, building bridges, and executing many other public works. The Huns he drove back into the wilds of Mongolia, and thenceforward determined to shut them out from the middle kingdom by constructing the Great Wall. Accordingly at an enormous cost of human life and labour, he raised this vast and ineffectual barrier, designed to exclude those very Tartars whose descendants now occupy the throne of China. The name which the monarch adopted, Chi-Hwang-ti, or "The First Emperor," was in keeping with the ignorance and vanity which led him to think that when he had reduced the petty states he was lord over the whole world. The insane attempt he made to destroy all records of the past has won him a foremost place in the annals of infamy. His edict for the burning of all historical documents was followed by a general massacre of the literati. Some things of importance, however, escaped the conflagration, for in after times one or two imperfect copies of the ancient classics were found built into an old wall. From the fact that most of the MSS. were lost irrecoverably, critics have mistrusted the historical value of any of the more ancient Chinese writings.

This emperor, not satisfied with the prospect of a reign limited by the narrow compass of human life, became the dupe of Taouist astrologers, and sought to render himself immortal by drinking their magic potions. He thus hoped to reign from the beginning of his era to the end of time. But fate was too strong for him. When his turn came he passed unwept to his grave. The dynasty he had founded proved one of the shortest on record.

About 212 years B.C., the Han dynasty was formed by a man of obscure origin, who, nevertheless, proved a wise and powerful ruler. The Han period was celebrated for its heroes and scholars, men of high attainments and noble character. The mild rule of the Han emperors and the prosperity of the people during their sway have endeared that dynasty to the nation, and even at the present day he deems himself highly honoured who is addressed as a "Son of Han."

It is curious to notice that the twelfth Han emperor, Pingte, or the "Prince of Peace," was on the throne of China when our Saviour was born. Under Ming-te, A.D. 64, imperial commissioners, it is said, were sent to the West in search of the Great Teacher, and returned bringing disciples of Buddha and the Buddhist sacred works.

China was at this time a warlike nation, having to struggle against the barbarous Huns,* adver-

---

* The earliest name of the Tartars was Hien-yun, which was changed during the dynasty of Chow to Hiong-non, and by Europeans into *Huns*. See De Guignes "Histoire des Huns."

saries who perpetually made harassing incursions into the north-western parts of the empire. But these Tartars, though they played so important a part in overthrowing the civilisations of the West, could not cope with the Chinese. They must, nevertheless, have been both formidable and persistent foes, for we find that peace was more than once patched up with some roving chief by the present of a fair Chinese maiden from the imperial stock, whose marriage with the fierce nomad established an alliance which might last until her beauty declined.

The Han family seems to have degenerated more and more with each change in the succession. But, indeed, steady moral and intellectual decay seems to mark the career of all Chinese dynasties; their founders may have possessed originally all the qualities which enable men to govern wisely and to win the confidence and love of their people, but the end of these dynasties has commonly been heralded and brought about by the sins and incapacity of the last sovereigns.

After a succession of monarchs, whose united reigns extended over 426 years, the last of the Hans gave himself up so completely to indolence and voluptuous ease, that he was finally compelled to abdicate in favour of a son of one of his own ministers, who thus became the first emperor of the After-Han dynasty.

The period of "the Three States" into which the country was divided at the close of the Han dynasty, abounds in startling events and wonderful heroes, for which reason it has supplied the materials for nearly all the Chinese plays and romances. "The native history of the Three States," says Sir T. Davis, "resembles the Iliad, except that it is in prose, especially in what Lord Chesterfield calls 'the porter-like language of the heroes.' These heroes excel all moderns in strength and prowess, and make exchanges after the fashion of Glaucus and Diomed, Hector and Ajax. One shows his liberality in horses, another in weight of silver or iron.

<blockquote>'And steel well tempered, and refulgent gold.'"</blockquote>

The Chief of Wei at last subjugated the States and became first emperor of the After-Tsin dynasty. Hitherto women had exercised cruel influence at Court, but the new sovereign passed a sort of Salic law that females should neither be permitted to reign nor to mix themselves up in the administration of public affairs. This law must have been abrogated soon after it was introduced, for about 371 A.D. the records tell us that the children of concubines, priests, old women, and nurses were carrying on the business of Government.

A number of short dynasties followed the After-Tsin. At one time the country was divided into a northern and a southern empire, at another it became reunited. One monarch interdicts Buddhism, burns its temples, and slays its priests; of another it is stated that he introduced chairs, and that then for the first time the people sat with their legs hanging down. A notice of this sort is not so unimportant as might at first sight be supposed; for by it we discover that the people had already begun to be recognised, and that the emperors, their ministers, and their women, were not all that made up the empire.

There is a striking uniformity of style and matter in most of the earliest histories of semi-barbarous nations — sovereigns, chiefs, and heroes, their deeds, speeches, and wise sayings, statecraft, political plots, and great battles fill the narrative from beginning to end; while topics of infinitely greater importance, all for instance that relates to the men and manners of the times, or to the growth of industries and arts, are briefly noticed in such scant sentences as the one just referred to, where we are told that the people rose from the ground and began to sit upon chairs. It is indeed very possible that the people, the real nation—a subject too mean for the lofty consideration of the ancient annalist—had up to that period squatted on the earth in front of the raised seats of their chiefs, and that the reference to the chairs implies simply that the masses had now become more important in the estimation of their rulers.

The famous dynasty of Tang began with the uneventful reign of Kao-tsu, A.D. 620. Kao-tsu kept the Tartars in check, and crushed all the rivals who pretended to his throne. It is told of one of this emperor's generals that he first disorganised and then defeated the Tartars by the following ingenious stratagem. A company of musicians and dancers were placed on a hill in full view of the foes, and while the attention of those rude warriors was engrossed with the display, a chosen band took them in the rear and put them completely to the rout.

Books were first bound during this period, and were substituted for the scrolls formerly in use. Theatrical performances and literary examinations were also instituted. Heng-tsong honoured the Buddhists, but his successor, a disciple of Laoutze, died the dupe of Taouist sorcerors.

Tai-tsong, the originator of the system of competitive examinations and the founder of schools, also drew up a code of laws, and personally visited the most remote parts of his empire in order to correct abuses and improve the condition of the people. In those days the frontier of China extended to the borders of Persia, as far as the Caspian Sea and the Altai of the Kirghis Steppes; northward it stretched along the mountain chain which shuts in the desert of Gobi, and terminated at the inner Hingan on the east. Logdiana, portions of Khorassan, and the regions around Hindu-Kush, were also tributary states; but the conquest of Corea was not effected till Kau-tsong, a son of Tai-tsong, had succeeded his father on the throne.

The historian, with a praiseworthy impartiality, exposes the pitiful imbecility of Kau-tsong; telling us how he fell completely under the subjection of an able but unscrupulous queen, a woman who after her husband's death engrossed the whole management of affairs, and managed both to extend the limits of the empire and to improve the condition of the people.

Five short dynasties followed the Tang emperors. The first was the Liang dynasty, which commenced in 907 A.D., and the last was that of the Chows, which came to an end in 959 A.D. Each reigning monarch throughout this period had to contend against the descendants of the former dynasties who laid claim to the throne, as well as against foreign foes.

The Lung dynasty ruled from 960 to 1127 A.D. The first emperor in this line was chosen by the general of the army. He was a rude, ignorant soldier, who had formerly served the last of the Chows, and was so besotted that when the messengers arrived to place the imperial yellow robe on his shoulders they found him lying under the influence of wine; nevertheless learning flourished under his fostering care.

The matter-of-fact records of Chinese history are strangely mingled with purely fabulous incidents. Thus the chronicler of this epoch, as if determined to test the limits of human credulity, records that the sun after setting reascended the heavens. Perhaps, however, we should understand this as a clumsy joke intended to enliven a more than usually dull page; and so the annalist, for lack of worthier topics, tells his readers that the orb of day followed simply its ordinary course, and reascended the following morning. The same authority sets forth that celestial books were obtained from Tai-shan, "The Great Hill." The important fact, too, is carefully noted down, that a woman was discovered with a long beard; she must have been an object of envy to every ambitious son of Han, for such an appendage is greatly esteemed among them. Thus in a single brief sentence two important subjects are disposed of. The world turned astern on its axis just one revolution perhaps to signify its approval of some remarkable Chinese event, and there was a lady who wore a beard; she may have been the first agitator for female suffrage.

The Sung emperors enjoyed a high reputation

for their wisdom and virtue. At first learning was encouraged, but in process of time this dynasty too sank into feebleness, until at last the Kin Tartars drove them out of the north and forced them to fix their capital at Kai-fung-fu, on the Hwang-ho, which had anciently been the metropolis of the empire. After thus retiring southward, the Chinese established the dynasty of the Southern Sung, which endured from A.D. 1127 to A.D. 1278. But a mightier power than the Kin Tartars was now gathering like a storm-cloud in the west; the nomadic tribes, retaining all the attributes of their warlike ancestors the Niu-tchi Tartars, and uniting the occupations of shepherds, bandits, and soldiers, confederated under the genius of Genghis Khan, the most formidable of Asiatic conquerors. Led by this irresistible warrior, the nomad hordes swept east and west like a consuming wave till their empire stretched from the Pacific Ocean to the German frontier.

The successors of the great Genghis overthrew the power of the Kin, with the assistance of the Chinese, but were afterwards provoked to a quarrel with their allies and drove them beyond the Yangtze-kiang. The insolence of the Sung emperor, who cast the ambassadors of the Tartar conquerors into prison, caused a second outbreak of hostilities, and this time the war ended in the complete subjugation of China.

The Chinese, though thus for the first time in their history reduced beneath a foreign rule, bore the yoke meekly, and learned to value peace at length under a wise prince—the first monarch of the Yuen or Tartar dynasty—who resolved to encourage learning and to restore the original institutions of China. This prince was Kubli Khan, a most interesting historical character, for it was he who received the Polo family, and among them the illustrious traveller Marco, who has faithfully narrated to us the deeds and magnificence of this great emperor.

The Grand Canal was excavated during Kubli Khan's reign, and is one of the noblest works ever executed by the patient toil of an industrious and peace-loving people.

The Ming or "bright" dynasty arose on the wreck of the Yuens. The Chinese had continued steadily to increase, both in numbers and prosperity, while their conquerors were becoming as steadily subdued by the influence of luxuries little used among nomad tribes; until at last the descendants of the redoubtable Genghis abandoned themselves wholly to voluptuous ease. Meanwhile an obscure personage who had once worn the dress of a bonze* and then borne arms in the field, began to gather followers and to watch an opportunity for revolt. This leader enjoyed a fair fame, which won him countless adherents, and soon after a brief and triumphant conflict he was proclaimed emperor, as the first of the Mings. Hung-wu, for such was his name, began his reign by reuniting the whole of China under one rule, establishing his court at Nanking. Here he encouraged learning, and restored the system of literary examinations; and here he died after a successful rule of thirty years, having appointed his grandson, then but sixteen years old, to succeed him on the throne. This youth, however,

* A priest.

was speedily deposed by his uncle, Yunglo, who transferred his court to Peking.

Among the oldest public buildings in China are the Ming Tombs at Nanking, which contain the ashes of the two first sovereigns of the dynasty. There are certain Buddhist shrines and temples which claim a much higher antiquity than these tombs, but the antiquity attaches to the sites and not to the buildings, for most of these edifices have been at some time or other destroyed, and rebuilt in later times. The stone drums in the Confucian temple at Peking are probably the oldest relics in the empire, and it is believed that they were sculptured and engraved with the primitive characters three thousand years ago.

Yunglo revised and altered the code of laws which to this day remains the basis of Chinese administration.

During the reign of the thirteenth Ming emperor, Kia-tsung, the Portuguese appeared at Macao; and in that of Wanlieh, about 1581, the Jesuits established missions in China.

At length the eunuchs, who had always played an important part in state politics since their introduction into the imperial palace, gradually gained supreme control. Disorders soon followed, and the eastern Tartars, taking advantage of the divisions and internal strife, resolved to redress their own wrongs by invading the north of China. A Manchu chieftain, vowing to celebrate the burial of his father by the slaughter of 200,000 Chinese, took the field with a small but well-organised force, and having routed the army sent to oppose his advance, soon found numerous bands of rebels rallying to his standard. A leader of one of these rebel bands managed to enter Peking, which was delivered up by the treachery of its defenders. The last of the Mings thereupon, seized with despair, attempted to slay his favourite daughter, and then strangled himself with his girdle. The Chinese general who was defending the country against the Manchu invaders determined to sacrifice everything rather than let a treacherous deed, which had ended in the death of his sovereign, go unavenged. Accordingly, after arranging a truce with the Tartars, and securing the assistance of their forces, he proceeded against Peking. He succeeded in his project; but no sooner had the usurper been punished than the Manchus themselves claimed the vacant throne. Thus commenced the reign of the present Tsing or "pure" dynasty, A.D. 1644.

The Tartar conquerors conformed in a great measure to the laws, customs, and usages of the Chinese race; thus the national vanity was flattered, and the people were induced to submit with a better grace to be ruled by barbarians who had shown themselves so enlightened. Apart from this, it was wise in the Manchus to adopt such a policy, for ancient forms of administration in China had been moulded by the experience of ages into the shape best suited to the requirements of a people so peculiar in every way, so thoroughly rooted to their own soil, and whose cheerful co-operation was indispensable to maintain the prosperity of the empire. But there was one condition imposed upon the Chinese by their conquerors, which in many quarters roused the ancient stubborn spirit of the sons of Han and caused much blood to flow. The people were ordered under pain of death to change their national costume, and to display badges of their servitude by conforming to the fashion of the Tartars. No blow more deadly could have been aimed at the pride of a race who had hitherto accounted themselves the one central civilised nation, and their own land the garden of the world. Resistance accordingly broke out afresh, and had the rebel armies but combined their strength the tonsured, tailed Tartar would probably have been driven back to his native wilds. As it was, each Chinese leader sought only to advance his own claims; thus their separate bands were vanquished in detail, and the people at last had to settle down to the practice of shaving their heads and carrying the Tartar queues.

The men of **Fukien** resented the mark of degradation to the last, and there to this day we may find their representatives wearing blue turbans, designed to conceal the tonsure.

Mariners most of them, these non-conforming Fukiens, they are probably descended from the piratical followers of Koksinga, a sea-rover, who in his time was the dread of the Manchus, and who drove the Dutch from Formosa about the middle of the seventeenth century. Fortunately for themselves the Tartars let the Chinese women alone. Had they meddled with the female head-dresses they might never have formed a dynasty at all, for the influence of women has more than once **caused an** overthrow in the "Flowery Land." As it was, a serious insurrection broke out, and stern measures had to be adopted in order to quell the rebels and to cripple the growing power of the Koksinga. Among other orders, the people all along the coasts were commanded to withdraw ten miles inland; yet after all, this rover, who commanded a vast fleet of war vessels, had to be bought over with a title and fair promises.

Some time prior to the accession of Kanghi, about the latter part of the sixteenth century, the Russians overran Siberia and threatened Manchu Tartary; but after a desultory war between Russia and China, which extended over thirty years, a mission was finally sent to the frontier, and a boundary to divide the two nations was settled by mutual agreement.

Kien-lung, who ascended the throne in 1736, reigned for sixty years amid almost uninterrupted peace, but such military expeditions as he undertook he carried out successfully. Thus he vanquished the Eluths, and asserted his sovereign rights over all those tribes which had hitherto been tributary to that powerful nation. He also aided the Thibetans to repulse an invasion from Nepaul, and turned this intervention to such account that not long after he managed to get the control of Thibet entirely into his own hands, leaving to the Grand Lama nothing more than spiritual authority over his subjects. This stroke of policy, however, gave rise to some misunderstanding with the British Government, and the Banjin Lama, who was spoken of as having extended a friendly reception to the English, was summoned to Peking. Reluctantly he went forth to comply with the imperial mandate, taking little pains to conceal his dread of small-pox, or of poison that works more surely still; but the invitation, though clothed in all the suavity of Court etiquette, was far too peremptory to be disobeyed. His worst fears were realised. Welcomed as a divinity, and worshipped by the emperor in person, he soon after fell a victim to small-pox—so at least it was given out, although there was a strong suspicion that poison administered by the emperor's own desire had been the real cause of his death.

Little Bokhara was also added to China during Kien-lung's reign, and now the dominions of that emperor extended over the whole of the table-lands and mountains of Central Asia as far west as the plain watered by the Oxus and Jaxartes.

Attempts were also made to absorb Birma, but both the expeditions dispatched to conquer that country were destroyed on the Irawaddy. China to this day, however, exercises a powerful influence among the scattered tribes, who people the mountain lands which divide Burmah and British India from the Chinese frontier; and as in Kien-lung's time, so now the fixed policy of the Peking Government has been to forbid all overland intercourse between their territory and our own.

About this same epoch a rebellion broke out for the first time among the Mohammedan Tartars. This occurred in Kansu, where the followers of the Prophet had been settled in great numbers for more than a thousand years. Troubles also arose in 1785 with the aborigines of Formosa, who remain still unsubdued.

Kien-lung abdicated at the ripe age of eighty-five in favour of his fifth son, Kia-king, who began his reign in 1820, under the imperial title Tau-kwang.

A rebellion in Turkestan was followed by a rising among the hill tribes of Kwang-tung, and shortly after these troubles, in 1840, the first war with England broke out. However we may regard this war, whether as creditable or disgraceful to the British Government, there can be no two opinions about the inhumanity displayed by our Chinese foes. As a nation they had a right to resist the enforcement of our will, but not by poison, assassination, or any other such cowardly devices; not by concluding treaties with the deliberate intention of perfidiously breaking through them whenever opportunity should serve. If the Chinese were at one time a warlike people, trained to fight for conquest, or for the attainment of righteous ends, they have long forgotten their skill in arms, and have sought to replace it by cunning, treachery, and tricks of statecraft. At various times, and by the mercy of God, plots were discovered that had been laid for the complete destruction of all foreigners in China, such events usually occurring just when the Chinese were gaining time to complete negotiations for peace. In the end the island of Hong Kong was ceded to Great Britain, an indemnity was paid, and a resumption of trade followed on the conclusion of hostilities. Two years later the Treaty of Nanking was ratified, and under its provisions Canton, Amoy, Foochow, Ningpo, and Shanghai were thrown open to foreign commerce. A renewal of the war in 1847 ended in a fresh agreement between the British Government and China.

About the year 1850 the disorder and misrule prevalent in the south of the empire gave rise to the Taiping rebellion, which, starting among the mountains of Kwang-tung, spread thence like a consuming fire all over the southern provinces. Some foreigners have spoken of the Taipings as Christian insurgents; this, however, is an error. Their chief, it is true, had been the pupil of Christian missionaries, and had been to a certain extent influenced by reading the Bible and a few Protestant tracts; but he misinterpreted the message of the Prince of Peace, and himself assumed the titles of the Heavenly King and brother of our Lord. His blasphemous and blood-stained career may be still traced in ruinous cities, depopulated districts, and barren wastes which were once fruitful fields. The Tien Wang (Heavenly King)—for thus the Taiping chief was known to his followers —chose Nanking as his capital, and would probably have overthrown the Tartar dynasty but for the Anglo-Tartar contingent, formed under the leadership of Colonel Gordon, which stamped the rebellion out. In the suppression of this rising it is probable that the imperial forces themselves did quite as much to destroy the people, and to spread the misery which everywhere follows the stoppage of industries, as did their enemies the Taipings.

In 1857 the obstacles to commerce and to intercourse with foreigners in every shape, which Yeh, the notorious Viceroy of Canton, chose to set up, led to a third war, and to the occupation of Canton for nearly four years by French and English troops. The seizure of Canton was followed by an advance on the metropolis, by the sack of the Summer Palace, and finally by the Tientsin Treaty of peace.

Previously to the conclusion of the new treaty the experiment had been already tried of placing the management of the Customs at Shanghai in the hands of foreign commissioners, and this important step had proved so satisfactory to the central government, owing to the increased revenue produced by honest and strict administration, that the native authorities readily sanctioned an extension of the system to all the ports open to foreign commerce.

By the new treaty foreign ambassadors were for the first time permitted to reside at Peking, but the defeated emperor, Hien-fung, seems to have ill-brooked the presence of these strangers at his capital, and accordingly soon after, leaving his brother, Prince Kung, and Wensiang, an able statesman (who still survives), to carry on the government, he retired, utterly broken in body and mind, to Jehol, in Manchuria, where he died in August, 1861. His son, then but nine years old, was named as his successor, and ultimately took the title of Tung-chi. Prince Kung and the Empress Dowager, as the natural guardians of the boy emperor, took supreme charge of affairs during their sovereign's minority, the empress acting as regent, and the prince as a chief minister of state. While still holding office these two great personages managed to discover and crush a plot set on foot to exclude them from power. Two of the conspirators, who proved to be princes of the imperial line, were graciously permitted to strangle themselves, and thus pass to their doom with bodies unmutilated, but the rest were decapitated as common felons.

The Empress Dowager is the real controlling

power, and even Prince Kung himself has been twice dismissed temporarily from office under the influence of her jealous intrigues.

The Tsungli Yamen, or Board of Foreign Affairs, has for some time past been established at Peking, and is presided over by the most distinguished statesmen in the empire. The functions of this Board resemble those of our Foreign Office; that is to say, it carries on all the official business with the foreign ambassadors, which had formerly been transacted through the Chinese Colonial Department, where Great Britain and the other western powers had found themselves placed on the same level with Thibet, Corea, or such-like Chinese dependencies.

The Emperor Tung-chi was married with great pomp and splendour, and died not long after from an attack of small-pox. His young bride dutifully starved herself to death in the palace, and the funeral of both has been celebrated with as much ceremonial as surrounded their nuptials two years ago.

Tung-chi's rule, which extended from August, 1861, to January 12th, 1875, is, perhaps, the most uneventful to be found in Chinese history. The Mohammedan rebellion, which commencing in Shensi in 1861, spread thence to Kansu, till it finally reached the distant regions of Ili and Turkestan, and the war which threatened on the occupation of Formosa by the Japanese, form the principal disturbing incidents in an otherwise tranquil reign.

One of Tung-chi's cousins, a child of four years, is now Emperor of China, where he rules under the title of Kwang-su, or "Continuation of Glory." His selection for this dignity to the exclusion of several other kinsmen of maturer years is attributed to the influences of the old Empress Dowager and her associate, the mother of the late sovereign. The latter is aunt by blood to the boy-king, and the two empresses will, of course, act as regents during his long minority.

Kwang-su has as little knowledge of the dignity of his present position as of the dangers into which the central government has drifted during the past few months, but what these dangers are it will be our business to point out when we review the present aspect of affairs in China in one of the concluding chapters of this work.

CHAPTER IV.

POPULATION.

Population of the empire—The first settlers; their gradual increase—Populations of England and China compared—Chinese census—Some recent causes of depopulation—Emigration—Chinese labour abroad—Clannishness—Assimilating power of the Chinese race—A plea for the Chinese in foreign lands.

The population of China has been variously reckoned by the best authorities at from three hundred to four hundred millions. These calculations are based principally upon the native census returns, for a native census has been taken at different periods; but the vast extent of fertile land in the empire, the skilful husbandry of the people, and their characteristic industry and frugality, have all been taken into account by those who have dealt with this question, and all these circumstances confirm the belief that a very high estimate is by no means an improbable one. The surface formation of the land renders it well fitted for tillage, and for the supply of an abundance of food staples, while the great rivers fertilise the boundless tracts of alluvial plain stretching along their banks, and which annually yield a double or triple crop of grain. The nucleus of the Chinese race settled first along the course of the Yellow River, and there, directed by an illustrious chief, set themselves to the task of controlling and utilising one of the richest water supplies in the world. Four thousand years ago, in obedience to edicts which they held to be almost sacred, they drained the rich soil of the land of their inheritance, sowed, planted, and reaped. Gradually growing in numbers, and developing their arts and industries, they spread from the valley of the Yellow River into regions that up to that time had lain fallow under the sway of an indigenous race. Everywhere they brought the soil into subjection, and compelled it to yield its increase to supply the wants of their rapidly increasing population. These hardy settlers never failed all the while to preserve their intercourse and identity with the parent stock, for by the multiplicity of navigable streams which nature had placed at their disposal a constant intercommunication could at all times be kept up. Thus the nation continued to multiply and to absorb the weaker races, extending their dominion until they reached the barriers of girdling mountains and the wide seaboard of China. The history of their early progress, like that of many other great communities, abounds in records of feudal strife and dissensions, which at various times threatened to break up the race into permanently isolated and independent tribes. But notwithstanding the fierce internal conflicts in which the primitive petty states were embroiled, the necessity for co-operation in carrying out great schemes for the drainage of the land, and the inborn tendency of the race to follow the settled pursuits of husbandry, have preserved for them their language and their national characteristics down to the present day. The wisdom of their primitive laws, the peculiar nature of their customs and usages, and the influence of their classic literature, have also contributed to maintain the identity of the race, and enabled it to gain predominance everywhere over less civilised communities.

The Chinese are undoubtedly a peace-loving people. Wedded to the land of their forefathers by the strongest, most ancient, and most sacred ties, striking their roots so deeply in the soil that no conquering invaders have ever succeeded in dislodging them from it, they appear identified with the land they inhabit as completely as its own indigenous products. Nowhere in the world shall we find a people with such a limited knowledge of arts and science as the Chinese can pretend to, who could continuously extract so much out of the land and yet survive the struggle for existence as each generation increased their numbers uninterruptedly for such a vast period of time. The Chinese for ages have looked to their own land for their food supplies; and with the appliances and knowledge which more than four thousand years of experience have furnished, they force the soil to yield fruits in such variety and abundance as to solve the problem, how on a limited area to support an unlimited population. Apart from statistics, and judging simply from what we actually know of the morality and social economy of the Chinese and of the productiveness of their land, we can hardly doubt that the population of the empire may very possibly, during the present dynasty, have surpassed even the highest number at which it has been set down. But this view will appear all the more reasonable when we consider that the estimated density of inhabitants to each square mile in China —assuming the population to be 400,000,000—after all only slightly exceeds the proportion of inhabitants to each square mile in England.

It may be said that in England we draw a portion of our supplies from abroad, and are therefore able to maintain a larger population; but this apparent advantage is counterbalanced in China by superior fertility of the soil, and by the fact that the mass of the inhabitants are engaged in agricultural pursuits, producing food supplies for themselves and others. Moreover, China possesses few grazing lands, such as are preserved in England for the raising of stock, while in the most fertile regions two crops at least may be raised annually without allowing the ground to lie fallow even after it has been taxed to this extent. Again, in China it has never been the custom to keep vast tracts of land waste for the exclusive pleasure of wealthy proprietors. Peasant farming is the rule, and the land is portioned out so as to contribute its utmost to the support of the people and the maintenance of the revenue.

Everywhere in China, except in the mountainous regions, we find the mass of the labouring population distributed over the soil more uniformly than in England. Our industries tend to the concentration of great communities round the manufacturing and mining centres, and to the neglect of the rural districts. Our towns also are, most of them, more densely peopled than those of China; our local industries, and the arts and sciences developed by our own higher civilisation, combine with our more widely diffused wealth and refinement to strengthen the taste for city life, and thus to increase our city populations.

G

We may thus conclude that in China, where food staples are cultivated more widely and abundantly than in England, and in a more productive soil, and where also, as has been shown, the people depend entirely upon agricultural industry, in which they are thoroughly skilled, there exists the power of fostering the growth of population. But besides all this the average Chinese labourer is certainly more frugal and quite as industrious as the average English hind. His style of life is simpler, his wants always fewer, can be more easily and cheaply supplied, while, if we except opium, he uses no stimulants to paralyse his productive powers.

The vice of opium-smoking has had a fearfully demoralising effect on the Chinese. It has worked most mischief in the cities and villages, but nevertheless its brutalising influences cannot yet surpass those produced by the excessive use of alcoholic liquors which prevails in some of the most populous districts of England.

Several authorities have objected to the Chinese statistics of population as utterly untrustworthy, contending that no proper method is followed in taking the census, and that the numbers set down in official documents are exaggerated. On this important subject Dr. Morrison remarks thus :—

"In the Chinese Government there appear great regularity and system. Every district has its appropriate officer, every street its constable, and every ten houses a tything man. Thus they have every means of ascertaining the population with considerable accuracy. Every family is required to have a board always hanging up in the house, and ready for the inspection of authorised officers, on which the names of all persons—men, women, and children—in the house are inscribed. This board is called the 'Mun-pae,' door-tablet, because where there are women and children within the officer is expected to take the account from the board at the door. Were all the members of a family faithfully inscribed, the amount of population would of course be ascertained with great accuracy. But it is said that names are sometimes omitted through neglect or design; others think that the account of persons given is in general correct."

According to Chinese law any person neglecting thus to register the members of his family is liable to severe penalties. The highest authorities are agreed in according a considerable degree of credence to these native statistics; at any rate we possess no means of controverting them, and those writers who may choose to set them aside on *à priori* grounds as to their general untrustworthiness will find themselves hopelessly adrift, and be fain to base their estimates on mere theory and speculation. It has been argued that the Chinese are so desperately fraudulent and dishonest that they cannot ever be relied on to prepare a census truthfully, and it would be idle to pretend that the charge of general deceitfulness is an unfounded one; we must, nevertheless, bear in mind that a Chinaman only practises dishonesty and deceit when the free exercise of those vices is likely to prove remunerative—a rule of conduct not altogether unknown in more civilised lands. As no possible benefit can accrue to an official who tampers with the census returns in order to swell the population on paper, it may be reasonably contended that in this instance he will adhere to facts. There is nothing for it, then, but to accept the native census as our safest guide in estimating the population of China, and accordingly we here exhibit it in the following table :—

Province.	Census, 1812.	Province.	Census, 1812.
Pei-chih-li	27,990,871	Hu-peh	37,370,098
Shan-tung	28,958,764	Hu-nan	11,652,807
Shan-se	14,044,210	Kan-su	15,193,125
Shen-se	10,207,256	Sze-chuan	21,435,678
Ho-nan	23,037,171	Kwang-tung	19,147,030
Kiang-su	37,843,501	Kwang-si	7,313,895
Kiang-si	30,426,999	Yun-nan	5,561,320
Ngan-whui	34,168,059	Kwei-chow	5,288,219
Fu-kie	14,777,410		
Che-kiang	26,256,784	Total	370,673,197

Some of the chief circumstances which conduce to the rapid and continuous increase of population in China have already been considered; it remains for us to point out what the influences are which in recent times have checked that normal increase. Among these the wide-spread mortality caused by floods, and consequent famine hold a foremost place. But besides these evils the devastating wave of the Taiping rebellion swept over the central provinces of the empire like a blight, and was perhaps the greatest scourge to which the race has been exposed for many centuries. Enormous quantities of the most fertile lands were laid waste by the rebels and were almost depopulated. City after city was made a pile of ruins, and its inhabitants put to the sword. When the rebellion had run its course then came the fearful retaliating scenes of bloodshed and massacre, in which the doom of the

Taipings was sealed. **Thus at** Nanking, the rebel stronghold, the three days and nights following the fall of the city were spent in massacring the inhabitants, and then all who bore the fatal brand of the long-haired rebel were summarily destroyed.

The city moat around the walls flowed with blood, and was heaped with the ghastly relics of the slaughter. Ten years after this dreadful episode Nanking was still in **ruins; acres upon** acres of streets, once busy and teeming with thousands of industrious citizens, stretched out within the walls like miles of grass mounds, hushed, desolate, and overgrown with rank weeds. Here and there, faint as if still subdued by dark memories, the hum of reawakening life might be heard mingled with the fitful sounds of labourers and builders at their task of reconstruction. Outside the walls the **deserted** plains, where little else but reeds and grass were to be seen, testified how completely the region had been depopulated. Fresh labourers at that time had begun to pour in, and were settling like squatters in a new land.

Another instance of the havoc wrought by the Taiping rebellion is afforded by the city of Chungchow, in the Fukien province, and **an** instance by no means exceptional, as the ravages of the war extended far and wide all over the central provinces. It is stated on good authority that when Chungchow fell into the hands of the rebels, from six to seven hundred thousand men were either killed, or perished by disease.

Close on the heels of the Taiping rebellion came the rising in the north-west among the Mohammedan fanatics, who, if they had not been ultimately crushed by the imperialists, would have extirpated all their unbelieving fellow-countrymen in their districts, and so struck a most serious blow at the Tartar predominance. The Mohammedans at last were completely subdued, but not until they had laid waste and partially depopulated large tracts of country by their desultory raids.

Internal disaffection among sundry tribes in Kwangtung and other provinces, although of minor importance, has also had its share in retarding the natural increase of the people. The constant feuds, too, among the clans of Chow-chao-fu, and the enmity raging between the Hak-kas and Puntis in other parts of the province, are examples of the strife which ends in the abandonment of cultivable lands and in the consequent decrease of the food supplies on which the local population depends.

The northern provinces, Shantung, Peichihli, and part of Kiangsu, have suffered from floods to an extent that can never be properly ascertained.

The change in the course of the Yellow River was the first great disaster, but it brought many other calamities in its train. Thus the inundations caused great mortality among the inhabitants, many perishing in the floods and many more by famine and disease. Some of the richest lands were at once transformed into pestilential marshes, while others, drained of their water supply, were rendered barren and unproductive. When, therefore, all these diverse agencies are taken into account, it would appear as if the population of China in recent times ought to have diminished rather than increased. It may indeed be urged that the tide of emigration which now carries labourers from China by tens of thousands to foreign shores is opposed to this conclusion, and that this modern exodus of the race must be caused solely by over-population. But more probably the real causes of this singular change in the habits of what, for so many ages, appears to have been a non-migratory people, are to be found in the disturbed and unsatisfactory condition of their country, in the demand for labour and the high rate of wages obtainable abroad, and also in the increased facilities for emigration.

The Chinese are unquestionably a most prolific race, and this natural tendency of theirs to increase inordinately under favourable circumstances is a characteristic which brings grave political consequences in its train. But the central government has been to a great degree relieved from the difficulty of having to face an overcrowded, half-starving nation, by infanticide practised to a limited extent among the people themselves, and also by repeated rebellions. These rebellions, however, may, in part, be attributed to misgovernment; in part to the neglect of proper precautions for averting floods; in part to local famines, which occur whenever the food supplies which the soil is capable of yielding are suddenly cut off. Religion and fanaticism have also raised the standard of revolt, those seasons being carefully chosen for each such outbreak when the disaffected leaders can enlist adherents in abundance from among the tens of thousands who are fainting under the bitter struggle for existence. Thus it would almost appear as if by some immutable law of Providence the possible increase of population has been steadily kept in check. This law has manifested itself in political convulsions and physical changes by which thousands of human beings, who would otherwise have died miserably of starvation, have been more suddenly, and so more mercifully, cut off.

The influence which Chinese emigration is exercising on other lands is apt to be underrated by those who know but little of the extent to which the coolie traffic has recently been carried. Formerly emigration from the middle kingdom was hedged around with many restrictions. These, however, were never sufficiently stringent to prevent secret emigration, and now the coolie trade is regulated by a new code of laws enabling voluntary emigrants to embark in ships which have first been inspected by the proper Customs authorities. In many of the towns and villages in the maritime provinces of the south professional brokers are to be found. These brokers are the agents of contractors for coolie labour, who are stationed at the ports of arrival in Singapore, Siam, Cochin China, and elsewhere, and their business is to induce the coolies to enter into agreements binding themselves to pay off their passage-money, plus interest, when settled in their foreign homes. The coolie on reaching the scene of his new labours is taken charge of by the contractor, who finds employment for him and deducts the passage-money and commission out of his surplus earnings.

Respectable females rarely emigrate, and the result is, in the Malayan countries, that the Chinese settlers find wives among the native races. Chinese domestic servants are employed by Europeans whenever and wherever they can be procured, their methodical habits, their cleanliness, and their docility rendering them invaluable adjuncts to a household. In this capacity their wages range from three to eight, or even ten dollars a month, out of which they have to provide food and clothing for themselves. Coolies find extensive employment in the Malayan countries among the European and Chinese planters, and are paid from three to five dollars a month. These coolies generally enjoy the additional privilege of squatting on some part of the plantation, and there they soon build themselves comfortable cabins out of material got from the neighbouring jungles, and surround their snug quarters with vegetable gardens. In process of time, if not opium-smokers, they save sufficient out of their monthly pittance to enable them either to return to their own land or to start in trade on their own account and settle down permanently among foreigners. It is interesting to observe how true these poor peasants are to each other, and how fondly they keep up intercourse with their friends in the old country. There is a continual interchange of letters, which are safely conveyed by the hands of clansmen who are either coming from or returning to China. But something more than empty congratulations are contained in these documents. Needy relatives are provided with the means to pay their passage over, or in other cases the entire savings of the emigrant are transferred to his aged parent for the double purpose of contributing to the latter's support, and being invested for the benefit of the son, who will in consequence surely find when he returns home that his interests have been jealously guarded, and that his money has procured him substantial benefits and an influential position among his clansmen. Others there are, and not a few, in whom the love of fatherland gradually dies out as they realise the advantages which surround their improved positions, and the security which a more enlightened government confers even on the meanest of its subjects. Thus in Singapore there are many instances of Chinese coolies who, step by step, have risen from their low estates till they became personages of considerable means and standing. One labourer personally known to the author made the island his home, and died after a residence of thirty years worth about half a million sterling. Yet this is no isolated example of prosperity, for when once out of their own country the Chinese are ambitious and successful.

Everywhere they adhere steadfastly to their national customs, combining together in trades, guilds, and secret societies, and so directing their affairs as to monopolise certain branches of commerce and industry. By acquiring the Malayan dialects, and by intermarriage among the native tribes, they contrive to establish themselves at inland trading settlements all over the Malayan States. Thus they become middle-men or brokers, and through their agency the indigenous products are obtained by Europeans. In the island of Singapore alone the Chinese population already more than doubles that of all the other nationalities put together, and as at least 20,000 additional emigrants arrive there annually from China, the **Chinese element must** be continually increasing. The increment would in fact be enormous were it not that a certain proportion of these Chinamen are regularly drafted off to other quarters, and that every year also a considerable number return to their native land.

To the casual observer Singapore looks more Chinese than Malayan, and really is so as far as the inhabitants are concerned. We might expect that the Chinese born in the island would bear some resemblance to their Malayan mothers, but excepting that their skins are of slightly deeper hue, they seem as purely Chinese in their attributes, appearance, and instincts as their fathers from the "Central Flowery Land." Many of these half-breeds receive European education, but this circumstance does not sometimes interfere with their acquiring a thorough knowledge of the language of the fatherland, and in that tongue some of them conduct their business correspondence. They adhere firmly to their old religious beliefs and superstitions, very few indeed having become Christians, while there is probably not a single instance of a Singapore Chinaman who has embraced the creed of Mahomet.

Something of the predominating and assimilating power inherent in the Chinese race will be gathered from the foregoing facts, and when we consider therefore how widely the race is spreading itself in the Malayan Seas, in Australia, and in America, its ultimate destiny and influence become a question of the deepest social and political importance. In California, Chinese labour was largely and most successfully employed in making the great excavations and in constructing the embankments of the Pacific Railway. This labour arrived at a timely crisis; it was cheap, efficient, and therefore eagerly sought after, but men found out soon that the coolies were to some extent neutralising the demand for the more highly paid labour of European emigrants, or of native Americans, and then the sudden discovery was made that the vices of the Chinese settlers were of the blackest type, and most damaging to the morals of more highly civilised communities.

Their superstitions and religious beliefs all at once became perfectly intolerable to a Christian people, no one caring to remember that these Chinese had been invited to come over, that the glorious advantage of free and enlightened institutions had been assiduously set before them, and that they had never been requested to leave their national characteristics entirely at home. There was some talk of sending them all back, but the Chinese, though a curious, are an extremely useful race, so the proposal to cast them out was never seriously entertained. Politicians hitherto have resisted the popular prejudice, and appear to have secured a measure of tolerance for the Chinese immigrants by pointing out that these coolies, if left to themselves, persist in returning to their own country, though not without a certain amount of wealth which they refuse to leave behind invested in American securities.

Here then we touch the fringe of a most serious political question. The Chinese have evidently taken root in California; they are useful, and for the most part peaceable members of society; there can therefore be no excuse for turning them adrift merely because they manage to hold their own in the labour market ; while if they sell their labour, and receive in exchange the means to return to their own land, it is surely a fair bargain. American or European communities have no more reason to denounce the Chinese practice of returning home with a competency than the Chinese have to cry out against foreign merchants who settle temporarily on the shores of China with precisely the same objects in view.

As to the vices of these Asiatic immigrants, much might be done to mitigate the evil complained of by urging the Chinese Government to promote female emigration from China by every possible means.

In Queensland, where the Chinese are highly respected, their morality does not compare unfavourably with that of other races settled there. But in Queensland Chinese labour still continues in demand, and is greatly appreciated, while some of the European women who have overcome the prejudice of caste, find that even Chinamen may prove gentle, industrious, and devoted husbands.

The influence of Chinese civilisation in moulding the character of inferior races is unquestionable, but it is itself amenable to ameliorating influences, and Christian missionaries, who have already planted the standard of the Cross along the shores and in the interior of the Celestial Empire, believe that ere long they will bring the entire nation to a knowledge of Christ and His redemption.

Surely these highly civilised and truly Christian

communities should rejoice at the opportunity thus afforded of winning over the handful of heathens that bring their cheap labour and their idols to their very doorways.

CHAPTER V.

CHINESE CITIES AND VILLAGES.

A Chinese city viewed from a distance—Fire walls—Suburbs—Foochow-fu—The great bridge—Streets—Shops—Signboards—Walls—Boats—Villages—Huts—Village life—Village warfare—Hired braves—Robbers—Government interference—Settled communities.

THE typical Chinese city, when viewed from a distance, presents a vast area of tiled roofs, rising to a nearly uniform height, and a network of narrow alleys and streets. In most of the densely populated towns the roads are so contracted and the overlapping eaves of the houses so broad as to convey the idea that the place is made up of one unbroken mass of human dwellings; but in cities, such as Peking and Nanking, there are many straight wide roads and open breathing spaces. These two cities, however, are the ancient and modern capitals of China, for which reason they were specially laid out to accommodate the imperial Court and the aristocracy. In towns, where available space is really of greater importance to the people, sunlight and pure air appear to be carefully excluded, hence all the inhabitants who may desire to cheer themselves by a glimpse of the blue sky and a draught of the passing breeze must resort to their house-tops, which are commonly decked with rows of fragrant flowers set out in pots, and surrounded with ornamental rails marking the limits of a small wooden platform. Running along the ridges of the roofs numerous jars may also be seen filled with water to the brim so as to afford a ready resource in case of fire. They have no fire engines, and indeed only those of the most portable kind would be of any service, since otherwise they could never be conveyed to the scene of a conflagration.

We may also notice that the close packed edifices, if the commoner sort of city dwellings may be dignified with the name, are divided at intervals by substantially-built fire walls, designed to check the spread of those devouring flames which too often play sad havoc with the flimsy architecture of the Chinese.

The writer was present at a fire when the value of this wise precaution was singularly illustrated. Roused during the night by the flare and wild tumult he hastened to the spot to volunteer his services, and found that in an incredibly short space of time an entire block in a densely populated suburb had been laid in smouldering ruins. The dividing walls were in many places red hot, but the flames had not extended beyond their boundaries.

The uniform level of the roofs in a Chinese city is only relieved by the imposing proportions of the official residences, pagodas, temples, and guild-houses, or in the southern provinces by the lofty square towers of the pawnbroking establishments. But, strange as it may appear to foreigners, there are in most cities large open spaces of tilled land that might have been used for the better accommodation of the citizens, did they not prefer to crowd their houses and shops together for the purposes of trade and social intercourse, as close as the cells of a bee-hive. Nearly every town is **hedged** around by a high wall, pierced with several triple gateways. These walls are exceedingly massive, and have evidently been constructed for purposes of defence, as they are broad enough on the top to allow troops to pass freely and thus to **concentrate** themselves at any point of attack. It **would,** however, appear, from the almost invariable **existence** of densely peopled suburbs outside **the** ramparts and the wide unoccupied spaces within the town, as if the inhabitants now place little faith in their ancient and impregnable-looking fortifications. But another explanation of this evident tendency to settle outside the city limits may be, that as the Mandarins and their people are not always on the best of terms, the latter endeavour as far as possible to cut themselves off from an intercourse which is certain to bring oppressive taxation and grinding tyranny, with few, if any, counterbalancing advantages. This remark is not levelled against the Mandarins as a class. There are many just men among them, who enjoy well-merited popularity. A civil officer of high rank may sincerely desire so to fulfil the duties of his position as to inspire the people with love and gratitude; he is often, nevertheless, so utterly dependent upon his subordinates, the permanent officials attached to his yamen,* that his plans may be cunningly frustrated without his knowledge, and he may after all leave the city when his term of office expires followed by the curses of the people whom he intended to befriend.

* Official residence.

Foochow affords a picturesque example of the general appearance of a Chinese city; and as it is less known than Peking or Canton a short account of the place may be interesting.

Foochow lies about thirty-six miles inland, and three miles from the banks of the river Min. It stands in the centre of a highly tilled plain of unsurpassed fertility, which is dotted over with villages and homesteads, while mountain ranges close in the distant horizon on every side. The town itself is built around the bases of three hills, whose summits have been appropriated exclusively to temples, official residences, and pagodas. The walls make a circuit of about six miles, and the space they enclose is supposed to be occupied—as at Peking, Canton, and all other great cities—in part by the cantonments of the Tartar garrison, in part by the Chinese citizens. The actual result is a densely populated trading quarter on the west, and gardens, waste lands, and fish ponds in the eastern half.

After the Manchu conquest of China every important city was garrisoned with Tartar bannermen, and a separate allotment was in each instance assigned to the invaders; but in many places, among others in Foochow, these allotments have long ago passed into Chinese hands, the descendants of the ancient warriors having become so impoverished that numbers of them are now miserably dependent upon the charity of the conquered and despised Chinese. Between the south gate of Foochow and the river Min there is a long raised causeway, lined with shops and houses, which connects the city with the river.

Here various industries are carried on by shopkeepers who sell their wares to the merchants going to and from the city. The thoroughfare is always open, and the importance of this particular causeway may be estimated, not so much by the number of people of all classes who frequent it, as by the extent of the great bridge in which it terminates. This bridge, a masterpiece of ancient Chinese engineering, is about a quarter of a mile long from the north bank to Chung Chow island, whence there is a second bridge to the southern shore.

These bridges are said to have been built about eight hundred years ago. They consist of a multitude of solid granite buttresses supporting gigantic masses of hewn stone, each from forty to fifty feet long, over which the granite pavement of the bridge is laid down in transverse slabs. A finely sculptured granite balustrade protects the roadway across on either side. The work is in no way remarkable for artistic beauty or grace, and cannot, therefore, be compared to the light, strong, and elegant bridges of Europe; at the same time the structure boasts a massiveness and simplicity in design that rivet attention, while by its great durability it has fairly won its local name, "The bridge of ten thousand ages."

We should like much to know by what means the builders raised those huge blocks of granite which span the buttresses. Most probably they lifted them into their lofty positions on floating platforms, elevated by the joint action of the tide and the periodical rise of the river.

Many of the Chinese bridges—that, for example, at Chow-chow-fu—are taken up along both their sides with shops and booths, so that only a narrow footway down the centre remains open for passengers. Twenty years ago the Foochow bridge formed no exception to this rule, but all such obstructions have since been removed, and the whole surface is now clear for traffic.

There are some hot springs close to one of the eastern gates of the city, much frequented by the natives for the cure of skin diseases.

The business quarter within the walls is intersected by the usual narrow alleys, and if it offers few attractions to a stranger it has much that will shock his more delicate sensibility. The streets for the most part are extremely filthy. We soon perceive that dogs and pigs are the only scavengers, and that these animals, though dirt and garbage are only too plentiful, seem somehow to thrive but ill upon them. The atmosphere also is oppressed with odours, in their variety and sublimated offensiveness peculiarly Chinese; the unsavoury outcome of extremely defective drainage, which blends its exhalations with the fumes of charcoal, garlic, and oil; whiffs of opium and tobacco being mingled therewith by way of an occasional change. Many of the lower orders in the inner thoroughfares look sadly in want of a washing, and seem as if they had never changed their clothes for a whole season. But, on the other hand, in order to do justice to our subject, we must bear in mind that these narrow lanes, though sometimes closed in with matting on the top, were not purposely constructed to exclude wholesome ventilation. They were built narrow to shut out the hot sun, and thus obtain a sort of underground coolness; and if we may judge from the appearance of the shopkeepers, who spend their entire lives behind their counters, the effect is not so baneful as one would suppose. The tradesmen and merchants are a healthy and contented-looking race, who evidently take a calm pride in their shops and wares, and live on to extreme old age, toiling in the grooves in which their fathers toiled before them during many successive generations.

The architecture of the majority of the streets is peculiarly attractive, though it follows a nearly uniform design; but much of its effect is lost for want of space. The shops have a ground floor and an upper story. This upper story is sheltered by broad ornamental eaves, and has a couple of Venetian windows opening into the street. The roofs inside are low—so low that the native workmen employed at their tasks above look large beyond all proportion, and seem uncomfortably cooped up. The lower floor is entirely occupied by the shop or office, and is quite open in front. The interior is divided into compartments by richly carved partitions of wood. Some of these partitions have merely an engraved surface pattern, some are cut through into graceful imitations of climbing plants. The finest examples of these carved partitions are simply varnished so as to show the colour and grain of the wood, others are japanned or ornamented with paint and gilding. It may be mentioned that the primary colours, red, blue, and yellow, prevail in shop and street decoration.

The shops are separated one from the other by well-built walls of brick, and at the base of these parti-walls, close to the footway, we find small niches containing offerings to the god of the craft. The parti-walls also serve to support vertical sign-boards, each painted in some brilliant hue and adorned with huge ornamantal characters setting forth the nature of the wares to be had within the shop, and the style or designation by which its proprietor is known. "The house of Eternal Felicity," established by Chung five or six centuries ago, will serve as a specimen inscription. These picturesque signboards are largely supplemented by strips of cloth hung across the street beneath the eaves, and carrying letters which are read horizontally from right to left. There are no brass plates or windows in China which may be utilised for advertising purposes, but there are always a number of small boards placed in conspicuous positions inscribed with lists of special commodities for sale. In doctors' shops of the better class we may also see tablets presented by patients in grateful acknowledgment of the physician's skill, and in some interiors where medicine men reside bundles of herbs and grasses hang all around, besides portions of dried animals and such-like curious gear, for it is from materials of this sort that the apothecary compounds his quack nostrums or prepares his plaisters; but in most places of business the fabrics and wares are carefully arranged on shelves or in drawers, so that the dealer can lay his hand at once on the article which a customer requires.

As in our own towns, so in Chinese cities, there are streets of greater pretension and greater cleanliness than those in which retail dealers supply the lower orders with the necessaries of daily life: streets secluded and quiet, wearing an air of larger mercantile importance, and peopled by bankers, silk merchants, and teamen, who carry on their business in calm and dignified retirement, and content themselves with inscribing the simple style or chop* of their firm in modest characters on their closed wooden gates. If a stranger wandered through such thoroughfares at mid-day he would find them almost deserted; but he would not fail to remark the indications of superior wealth about the houses. The grey bricks here look squarer, and are more carefully pointed with white lime; the tiles are glazed; and beneath the eaves there are illuminated scrolls or small figures in bas-relief, while above the doorway a landscape has been cleverly painted on a plaster panel. The gates, however, are shut and barred, as if to intimate that the owner is only at home to visitors who have business on hand. In such establishments the interior is lofty, as there are no second stories; the spacious offices in front are floored with stone or red tiles; and beyond these are a series of courts and warehouses, where many assistants are packing and preparing cargo as only Chinamen can pack and prepare it, for exportation to foreign countries, or for the markets in the interior. Passing on through streets and alleys thus shut in by brick walls, and pierced by doorways here and there, the foreigner traverses the entire length and breadth of such a city as Foochow in the vain hope of discovering some indications of the dwellings of the people, some charming spot where the busy merchant, after a career of enterprise and perseverance, has sought

* Style of firm.

to spend his declining years in peace and retirement. Surely in this "Flowery Land" there must be retreats that will at least compare with the suburban districts of our own towns, where the lot of the aged and successful is cast—smiling gardens fragrant with orange blossom, and lakes breathing the perfume of the lotus. Such places, however, are rarely to be seen in China. How many of them exist, and where, their owners alone can tell us, for the wealthy wall their abode around so that the pleasures enjoyed within may not be intruded on by the vulgar gaze. Climb one of the three hills of Foochow, the Wu-shi-shan, or Black Rock Hill, which rises about three hundred feet above the wall at its south-western angle. As we look down from the summit of this hill, which is partially shaded with groups of banyan trees and clumps of bamboo, towards the east we may discover close beneath our feet several groups of houses, affording each of them a perfect representation of the social exclusiveness of the Chinese. If we approach such dwellings from the plain all we can see are bare walls topped by the branches of trees. Here is the idea of the great wall and of the city wall carried out in miniature in the domestic residence, and thus the Chinaman distinctly intimates that his house is his castle, the fortress where his wives and daughters are kept imprisoned, and in which he himself is very much at home.

It is to his mind the perfection of human abodes, the result of four thousand years' civilisation. If he thinks at all he must reflect that his home is a little world to his women folk. There is a tiny landscape garden with model bridges and model mountains, wherein dwell the blessed genii; living fish in little pools, just as in the ocean and rivers; rocks and chasms like the weird peaks and gorges of Wohea hills; shady nooks beneath bending bamboos, where the ladies may bask in the smiles of their lord, when he is in the mood for their attentions. Here and there miniature pagodas and temples occur, or sometimes a real shrine dedicated to the worship of the ancestors of the family. Food in abundance from unknown sources, rich and costly raiment to put on, paint to bring back the hues of health to the cheek which has shrivelled and faded even in this earthly paradise; above all, a living Chinaman to love and worship, or to hate, as the humour suits them. What more can mere women desire? Hatred is a luxury with which such ladies are by no means unfamiliar, although all their experiences of life have been drawn from the sweet resources contained within the four walls of their homes. This is the sort of establishment that a really successful citizen delights to set up for himself. The more successful he has been, the more thoroughly will he entrench himself within his castle, jealously concealing his wealth and comforts from the greedy eyes of the outer world. In our own land the houses of the prosperous, with their visible comforts, their sloping lawns and their rich flower-beds, afford a genuine pleasure not to their owners merely, but to many a poorer man whose lot it is to dwell in the outskirts of our cities, as well as a powerful encouragement to the industrious to labour on patiently that they too may one day dwell at ease.

Where are the public gardens, the parks, and

promenades of Foochow-fu? We shall seek for them in vain. There are, it is true, parks and gardens within the viceregal palace; "but such resorts are only suited," said an educated Chinaman, "for those whose minds have been refined by study. The toiling poor, even were they given the opportunity of enjoying them, care for none of these things. When they obtain leisure or seek relaxation from the physical strain of labour they have the tea shops, the opium pipe, and the theatre." Nothing can be said against well-conducted city tea shops, where friends may meet and converse over a social cup, and may listen to readings or lectures. But as for the theatre and the opium den, the first indeed might be greatly improved were the ancient heroes who strut the stage in some way compelled to abstain from immoralities, but the opium dens could only be rendered unobjectionable by being abolished altogether.

The scene eastward from Black Rock Hill presents all the customary features of a Chinese provincial capital. Within the walls the space is taken up by the usual low-roofed houses, whose monotony is to some extent relieved by the high tops of temples or official residences, and in this instance also by the rich foliage of the banyan, a plant which grows to great perfection in that part of Fukien. At the south-eastern corner of the city, on Kiu-sien-shan, or the "Hill of the Nine Genii," a white pagoda and several other edifices may be seen, while to the south, outside the ramparts, there is a large suburb containing an extensive military parade ground, and diversified by bright green patches of cultivated ground or placid mirror-like ponds, where pisciculture is carried on. The plain beyond looks like a rich green carpet spread right out to the foot of the mountains, which close in the scene eastwards at no great distance from the town. In the south broad silver bands mark the course of the river, wherein one may descry multitudes of what seem to be little islands and promontories, but which in reality are boats in vast numbers moored along the banks, or anchored in mid-stream. On board these boats dwell thousands of those families who make up the floating population of China.

The surface of the Black Rock Hill is composed of masses of granite. There are also great detached boulders which rest on the top, one of them rounded like a pebble and quite fifty feet high. The sides of this monstrous stone are engraven with classical texts, and similar inscriptions abound over all the other rocks, more especially near the apex of the hill. A great dome-shaped boulder on the summit has been split as if by some sudden heavy blow, and a small granite altar stands above the chasm. To this altar the viceroy repairs during seasons of drought, and at stated periods, to make burnt offerings to the Supreme Lord of Heaven.

From our stand-point on the Black Rock Hill many villages may be seen scattered over the plain, any one of them a fair type of the hamlets in the south of China. The number of these small agricultural communities in China is perfectly astonishing. The writer has repeatedly, during his journeys, looked down from a height upon some fertile plain, and counted as many as fifty or sixty such rural settlements rising like little islands out of a bright green sea, whose waves ripple up to the very cabin door. Bamboo and mud are the principal materials used in constructing a peasant's cottage, although pine and other woods are also sparingly employed. Only the walls of the local temples or the dwellings of the head-men are built of bricks. The thick stems of the bamboo which form into the framework and rafters of an ordinary village hut are either dovetailed one into the other, or else lashed together with bindings of hemp or rattan, for this mode of fastening is found to be less costly and more durable than nails. The walls are next made out of small branches, or thin laths of the same plant nailed together and fixed to the uprights in such a manner as to support securely a surface coating of mud. Pine or the dried stalks of millet are similarly used in some of the northern provinces, for there bamboos are less abundant. Thus the huts of the peasantry of Southern China are almost entirely composed of bamboo and other grasses. When the framework of a hut has been set up with its rafters and sloping roof-beams, it only remains to render the whole wind and water tight by thatching the roof and walls with bamboo leaves or with rice straw. Doors and windows are also made of bamboo, and so, indeed, is the household furniture, as will be shown in another part of this work. That the form of the Chinese peasant's hut or wigwam is extremely ancient may be gathered from the fact that in superior dwellings built of brick and mortar the wooden beams and the rafters which support the roofs are placed exactly as in the simple cottages, and then painted to imitate bamboo stems. The most primitive form of Chinese dwellings was probably the tent of the nomad, made of the skins of wild animals and supported by bamboo poles. As the people settled down to agricultural pursuits the tent was abandoned, although its form was still partially retained, and in the more permanent dwellings which succeeded the tents the indigenous bamboo, so frequently mentioned in the Chinese classics, became definitely established as the mainstay of domestic architecture, a position which it still retains. In some parts of China, in districts where decomposed granite abounds, the houses are built of blocks of concrete, which soon attains to the hardness of stone. In other quarters there are settlements of dwellers in caves; but the great mass of the labouring population live in small village-communities scattered over highly-tilled lands. Many such Chinese hamlets are remarkable for their rustic beauty, and no less so for the simple, peaceful, and contented air of their inhabitants. The houses are often shaded by fine old trees or by waving clumps of bamboo; and the only approach to them lies perhaps along a narrow, grassy ridge, between irrigated rice fields, where blades of vivid green rise above glassy pools of water that mirror all the landscape around. At length we reach a footpath on higher ground, beneath the deep shade of some wide-spreading tree. From the shrine at the roots of this tree the smoke of incense rises in pale blue wreaths of vapour against the dark trunk. Following the path to the village street, the stranger, if he be gentle, inoffensive, and to some extent acquainted with the local dialect, will almost certainly receive an honest, touching welcome, and the thought is then sure to strike him that the ancient civilisation of China must after all possess some merits, seeing that it has thus taught these simple villagers to rest contented with their uneventful lot. It may, however, be said with truth that civilisation in the proper sense of the term has had little or no influence upon villages and village life in China. The village and its inhabitants have been such as we see them at the present day since the time when the Chinese first acquired the art of dwelling together in settled communities, and of subsisting on the produce of the soil. The traveller of to-day may enter a rustic hamlet and find it just what he might have found it had he lived three thousand years ago.

The people go out to the fields in the morning and return after their toil, precisely as in Yu's time; they have the same faith in their images and shrines, offering up the fruits of the earth in their season, and trusting to the paternal guidance of the patriarch or head-man of their own tribe, who is set in authority over them and held responsible to the Mandarins for the good faith of his people. In this way they are contented to live and die after the fashion of their forefathers, so long as floods and famine can be averted, and nature wooed into smiles around their humble abodes. This is no picture of the imagination; the writer has seen many such happy spots in the interior of China, wherever the peasantry are not suffering from neglect and oppression.

Perhaps the people are none the less happy on account of their primitive mode of life. Far removed from the strife and turmoil of cities, they rarely seek to penetrate the mysteries that lie beyond the village horizon; their world reveals itself with every sunrise; its men and women are like themselves, and have precisely the same attributes. Certain individuals amongst them are distinguished for their wisdom, and these are, therefore, consulted as to changes in the weather, treatment of disease, and propitious days for marriage or burial. Here the four walls which elsewhere hedge in the houses of their more pretentious countrymen are unknown; and as for the women folk, the young work in the fields, and are free to deck their raven tresses with the flowers that grow by the wayside, while the old crones may put their grey heads together without interference for the good or evil of their neighbours. But a great power in such rustic settlements is the schoolmaster, who is sure to be looked up to as a man of profound erudition, although he may have failed to pass a single Government examination. Such a man believes sincerely that his poverty was the sole cause of his failure to win the favour of the examiners and a proud position in the State. It is he who could tell the people, if they cared to know, who are the rulers of the land; but as such questions are not supposed to affect their tillage, or to influence the weather, they do not come within the range of village politics in China. The teacher, as he increases in years and in infirmities, transfers his ambition from himself to those among his most promising pupils who are qualified by their birth to compete for the preferment which high literary merit can confer.

It must, however, be admitted that perfect harmony does not always reign among these rural communities even when they are most prosperous. The village elders (a term which comprises all the men who have reached three score years and ten) enjoy certain privileges by right of their age—privileges which may not be disputed by their worst enemies. Thus they are free to invite themselves to any festive gathering or family celebration that may take place in their vicinity, and on such occasions are entitled to the same welcome as the other guests. Their grey hairs perforce must be respected; no one dares to suggest the desirability of their absence. Villagers, too, the matrons as well as the men, have their grievances, and these cannot always be settled without the stirring up of family feuds. In some less settled districts the village feuds break out so continually as to remind us of the ancient raids and forays among the Scottish clans, or of the still more ancient struggles between the primitive petty states of China. Village warfare was carried on in many parts of the Kwang-tung province, when the coolie traffic, or slave trade, as it might be more correctly termed, was in vogue at Macao. One clan found regular and remunerative employment in bearing off captives to the coolie ships; others lifted their enemies' cattle from the neighbouring hostile village, ran off with their women from the fields, or reaped their crops by moonlight. The antagonists, however, seldom closed in pitched battle, though there are instances where this has happened, and then they fought savagely and yelled more savagely still. The average Chinese warrior thoroughly exhausts the pantomime of his craft before venturing upon serious hostilities. With the instinct of the brute he first employs every device in his power to paralyse his foe with panic fear, and when fiendish yells and tragic gestures have attained their end he rushes on to an easy victory. The Chinese do not yet understand how it is that foreign troops can be brought to walk calmly forward to what may prove certain death while they have a clear country behind them, and good sound limbs wherewith to dodge the enemy, so as at a more convenient season to fall upon him unawares.

At the beginning of a village war, when no blood has yet been spilt, prisoners are not so inhumanly treated, and may be redeemed by their clan; still there are few cases where torture is not applied to the captive as a means of extorting a higher ransom. But when bloodshed has once let loose all the diabolical passions which work in the human breast, prisoners taken red-handed in the fight are butchered in the most revolting manner. Often they bind the ankles and wrists together, toss the rope over the branch of a tree, and then while some drag their victim up and down, others burn him with incense sticks. But the most common way of avenging the death of clansmen is by cutting and mutilating a captured foe, withholding the merciful *coup de grâce* until the agony has been prolonged to its utmost limit. This kind of desultory warfare is frequently carried on for months together, not a single pitched battle being fought during the whole time. Occasionally other villages endeavour to mediate and re-establish friendly relations between the contending parties. The general reward of all such efforts is that the would-be peacemakers are themselves drawn into the vortex of war. In some of the Kwantung districts these petty wars have often been prosecuted until one of the parties became quite exhausted. The defeated party have then little mercy to expect: their village is laid in ashes, and all their families are rooted out; but the conquering clans have seldom much cause to rejoice, for the struggle brings their own resources to so low an ebb that they find themselves reduced to beggary.

The most singular feature in these contests remains to be told. The fighting-men are professional braves in the pay of the hostile parties, or we ought rather to call them freebooters, who are not above doing work of this sort for hire. These braves are a scourge even to those whom they are employed to succour, and a constant drain upon their resources, for if not actively engaged in warfare, they distribute their attentions impartially over the different villages, committing depredations when and where they please. Lawless bands of this type, when they gain sufficient strength and are not disorganised by opium, grog, and low living, extend their sway over entire countries, levying "black-mail" on all goods as they pass to the markets inland. The Government only interferes to put a stop to such abuses when it has become impossible to collect the revenues. The bandits usually place no obstacle in the way of the local tax-gatherer until he has filled his bag, and then they considerately relieve him of his burden and send him about his business. The mode in which the local government has been known to interfere at such a crisis is something in this wise. When the authorities conceive that there is a fair prospect of their putting into the field a force sufficient to cope with the gang they call out the military. This is the signal for the villagers of the district to desert their houses and flee to the mountains with all the goods they can carry, for they dread the visits of imperial troops no less than the raids of freebooters. Once on the mountains they dwell there in huts until the district has been cleared of robbers. But the Government rarely engages in an enterprise so costly and so unremunerative; a much cheaper expedient is to bribe the robber chiefs with money and a title. This offer the chief is fain to accept, although it involves the betrayal of his followers, for the bargain is not complete until a report can be sent to the central Government that the imperial troops have cleared the district of the gang.

The above details serve to show what was the actual condition of the peasantry three or four years ago in some parts of the south of China, where the natives are noted for their savage instincts and for their turbulent dispositions. But the characteristics thus disclosed must be understood to be purely local, confined to portions of one or two provinces at most.

As has been already pointed out in these pages, the general tendency of the race is to resolve itself into peaceful settled communities drawing all their sustenance from the surrounding soil. It is indeed the village life of China which is really the life of the people; it is the settled life of the industrious husbandman which best explains to us how the race has maintained its identity for so many centuries.

Other agencies have no doubt had their share also in preserving this unique type of the old world civilisation so perfect in all its details. Nevertheless it is the common people, the sons of the soil, who have proved most true to the tradition of their fathers, and have adhered most closely to the rules which the wisdom of their forefathers supplied to them in the remote ages of the past. It is the people who, when they had once acquired a knowledge, which to them was all-sufficient, of how to sow and reap, how to build needful dwellings, to clothe themselves, and to toil together for one end, have ever since been content to labour on without change, regardless of the rise and fall of empires and the struggle of contending dynasties. The poor peasants of China following their daily rounds of duty have uninterruptedly held their own against the fierce hordes that invaded and laid waste their land.

CHAPTER VI.

SOCIAL CONDITION OF THE PEOPLE.

Different races of China—The savage Yao—Puntis—Hakka, Hoklo, and Tanka of Kwangtung—Social ranks—Mental and physical characteristics of the Chinese—The condition of women—Births—Marriages—Burials—Beggars—Dress of the people—Gambling—Theatrical performances—Music—Opium—Food—Etiquette—Guilds and trades' unions—Coinage and commerce.

BEFORE proceeding to consider the condition of the people of China it is necessary to point out that the two great races of the empire, the Tartar and Chinese, may be sub-divided into a number of nations and tribes, either tributary to China or coming under the sway of the central government. Besides these, there are independent tribes of alien race, inhabiting the mountain fastnesses in the southern provinces, who are supposed to be the descendants of the original owners of the soil.

Great questions of race such as those involved in the history of the descendants of Genghis Khan and the different Tartar nations, cannot be dealt with here; they can only, so to speak, be indicated in outline. Tartars speaking different tongues, all of them more or less allied to each other, have spread themselves over a vast territory in the north and north-west of China proper. And so it is with the Chinese; the race seems to have sprung from one parent stock, but it has been broken up into great tribes, each speaking its own dialect. It is erroneously supposed that the people of China are all alike in appearance and attributes, that the Chinese in the north are the counterpart of their countrymen in the south—all cast in one mould and endowed with faculties that, through ages of repetition, have been brought down to one dreary uniform level. In reality the only points of true likeness between man and man in China, as revealed to the eye, are the uniformly straight black hair and dark eyes. There is, it must be owned, a more uniform type of man prevailing in China than in any other quarter of the globe of equal extent, at the same time it cannot be denied that no two Chinamen are alike, and the dialect spoken by the Cantonese is as little understood by the men of the adjoining province as is English by a Frenchman. This difference of dialect and of tribe may be more fully illustrated by taking the races of Kwangtung.

The mountains of this province are peopled by wild tribes, called Yao and Miautze, supposed to be offshoots and remnants of prehistoric settlers. A clan known as Tanka to the Cantonese, and said to be descendants of the savage Yao, who had escaped from the hills, took up their permanent abode in boats on the creeks and rivers where they are still found in the Kwangtung province. It was not until 1730 that they were permitted to dwell on land and have their names inscribed in the census. They were marshalled under their own chiefs, and set to till waste lands. Many of the customs of the Tanka, who are the boat people of Kwangtung, are identical with those of the Yao; they are, however, making progress in civilisation, and have already begun to learn the arts of reading and writing.

The Hakka of this province are another large tribe of northern origin, speaking a language unintelligible to the Cantonese. They are a poor, industrious, and prolific race of immigrants, who first occupied waste lands, and gradually increased in number and strength, until at the present time they possess some of the finest districts in Kwangtung. For a considerable time after their entrance into the province they were the hired servants and tenants of the Punti, the old masters of the soil, by whom the immigrants were treated as pariahs. The Hakka are humble, industrious, and courageous, as the Punti know to their cost. Almost their sole occupation is agriculture; nevertheless, in defence of their rights, they frequently abandon the plough, and prove themselves not unacquainted with the art of war. By hard fighting, and harder working, they have gradually taken possession of the soil.

The Punti of Kwangtung, a more polished, deceitful, and altogether less trustworthy tribe, are in many districts the owners of the land, also the dwellers in cities, and the students of literature and the arts. Supremely vain are they of their antiquity as a people, and of their language, which they maintain to be the oldest form of Chinese, probably the tongue spoken in the time of Yu, 2200 B.C.

The last division, the Hoklo, natives of Fukien province (who speak a dialect known as the Fie-chew, unintelligible to any of the surrounding tribes), are chiefly found along the river courses and on the coast. They are a maritime people, fierce, turbulent, and addicted to piracy.

In the island of Hunan, which forms a department of the Kwangtung province, the mountains are inhabited by tribes of savage Li, and the plains by Chinese.

Some of the Li are said to carry tails of a rudimentary sort with tufts of hair at the end. This story may be set down as of purely Chinese origin. Native writers have not scrupled to describe certain other barbarous tribes as possessing only a single eye in the forehead, and others as having hoofs in place of human feet. Very little is known about the Li. They are supposed to be allied to the Yao and Miautze, who in their physical appearance and customs bear a striking resemblance to the mountain races in the north of Indo-China and north-west of India.

Difference of race may to a limited extent be traced in the appearance of the Tanka, Hakka, Hoklo, and Punti. The Hoklo resembles most the typical Chinese, in the fair yellowish tint of the skin, the brown eyes set obliquely, features rounded, and (if one may use the expression) refined by ages of stereotyped civilisation and devoid of any great power of expression, black, coarse, and glossy straight hair, small hands and feet, well formed limbs, perhaps rather short in proportion to the body, and the muscles rarely so equally and fully developed as in European races. The other three types display fewer tokens of refinement; the skin is of a much darker hue, Chinese characteristics on the whole prevailing, the appearance of the face and figure being modified by the hereditary toil of each. The Hakka is the most slender, and in this respect bears some resemblance to the natives of India.

The Punti, or Cantonese, may be taken as the type of race prevailing in the north of the empire, as well as in the south, with modifications effected by climate and food. Chinese characteristics are continually spreading among alien races wherever the Chinaman is found in Asia, whether in Manchuria, Mongolia, Thibet, or in the British colonial settlements in the Straits of Malacca. The manners and customs, industries, physical characteristics, and religion of inferior or subject races are revolutionised. In defiance of war, pestilence, and famine, the Chinese appear steadily to increase with a celerity that must seem astonishing to those who are unacquainted with the fact that the Chinese emigrant, wherever he settles and alliance is possible, selects his wife, or wives, from among the people of the country. But enough has already been said regarding the population of the Flowery Land.

The constitution of Chinese society is so totally different from that of European countries that one is at a loss to determine what it is that divides the people into well defined ranks and classes. The Mandarins who hold civil and military office are systematically divided into grades as distinct one above the other as are the stores in a Chinese pagoda. Each officer carries with him the badge of his rank in the globular button which adorns his hat, and in the colour and decorations of his official robes. But in China there cannot be said to exist anything corresponding to our learned professions. There are no faculties of medicine, art, or science to confer degrees, nor is there the profession of the law. The only men who devote themselves to the study of law are employed by Mandarins to guide them in their decisions so as to avoid penalties imposed for maladministration. These quasi-lawyers have no recognised rank. In the same way the profession of medicine (if a profession it may be termed when the quacks engaged in it have no special training and hold no diplomas) confers no sort of social position on the practitioners, who dare not aspire to associate with men of letters who have made their mark or won their button. There is therefore a great gulf separating the governing classes from those governed. The lawyer is nothing more than a salaried unofficial retainer at the Magistrates' Court, with whom the Mandarin may, or may not, condescend to associate. The artist is a shopkeeper, and the physician a quack and astrologer, who, while he is supposed to study the stars by night, compounds his drugs and decoctions in the public highways by day. The man of science is a sort of popular magician, who, adding to a faint glimmering of the laws which regulate the physical world, and affect the health of communities, the grossest superstition, is called on to determine lucky sites for houses and graves. He, too, is found in some humble shop, or seated by the wayside; or it may be he wears the attire of the Taouist priest, and thus courts seclusion and a higher class of customer.

Hereditary aristocracy can hardly be said to exist in China. The aristocrats of the land are the men who have most distinguished themselves in literature. Education is the great power which determines fitness for office, and yet after all the Chinese are semi-barbarous. They have made no progress for many centuries, because their learning is not progressive. Competitive examinations for civil and military preferment are constantly held, and the men of the most distinguished attainments become in time ministers of state. But the subjects of examination are stereotyped. The knowledge of old classical lore and old modes of warfare, together with the possession of physical strength, have hitherto been held as tests of competency. Anything in the shape of modern knowledge, or of discoveries in the arts of peace and war, has not been included. Nevertheless the time appears to be approaching when Chinese students who would serve their country, must gather a store of knowledge from the sciences and arts of other lands than that of Confucius. There is something admirable in the Chinese system of preferment which throws open to the humblest scholar in the empire a prospect so **brilliant**; for all that it is extremely defective, in so far as the most scholarly men are not always the best statesmen, and the system from beginning to end is to cram the student with an unintelligent knowledge of classical writings of little practical value in the discharge of his duties as a civil servant **under** Government. Anciently education was esteemed the best means of disciplining and training the heart and mind, and developing and discovering the natural faculties of truly gifted men, in order that they might be chosen to aid the emperor. In modern times the ground to be gone over, and the number of writings and commentaries to be committed to memory by the student to enable him to write essays that will reflect the full lustre of classic lore, implies a task so burdensome as to undermine the health of thousands of competitors. Memory is indeed the chief faculty exercised in the civil competitive examinations. The greatest benefit which the examinations confer is in stimulating the people to encourage education.

The schoolmaster is abroad over the land, and there are few, even among the peasantry, who can neither read nor write. The popular instructors are, as a rule, poor broken men, who have spent their days and nights in study, in the vain hope of passing the examinations. They are found in the meanest hamlets, are poorly paid for their labour, although they are treated by their neighbours with deference and respect.

As a race the Chinese are susceptible of high culture. No better proof of this could be adduced than the aptitude with which coolies (labourers) employed in the foreign arsenals pick up the use of complex European machinery. In the schools of Hongkong, where European and Chinese children are educated side by side, it has been frequently remarked by the teachers that Chinese pupils are in no respect inferior to the children of European parents. An ambition which fills the heart of Chinese parents is to educate their sons. Daughters they consider are sufficiently difficult to manage without literary tastes and acquirements, which would only be misapplied and add a new pang of bitterness to the grief that heralded their entrance into the world. Ten daughters, they say, do not in any case equal one son. Confucius spoke of women as on the same level with slaves, and equally difficult to control. Even one of the few native female

CHINESE CHILDREN. Page 124.

writers of eminence impresses upon her sex the full sense of their inferiority, observing that they hold the lowest place in the human species. Dr. Morrison gave a curious quotation illustrative of the joyous reception of a boy at birth contrasted with the sorrow which accompanied the entrance of a girl into the world.

> "When a son is born
> He sleeps on a bed;
> He is clothed with robes;
> He plays with gems.
>
> . . . . . .
>
> But when a daughter is born
> She sleeps on the ground;
> She plays with a tile;
> She is incapable of either good or evil."

The lady authoress just referred to adds that when a female child was born, she was left for three days upon some rags on the floor, thus to indicate the contempt she was doomed to experience through life. But after the three days had expired, the family engaged in mock rejoicings. It is customary on the third day after the birth of a child to employ charmed water to wash the babe, in which artemisia, acacia chips, pepper, lichi, dates, walnut, and soap, have all been mingled. This is supposed, says Dr. Dudgeon, to remove the outer coating of the skin. The babe is also washed in water containing coins, chestnuts, dates, and silver, to secure riches, so says the nurse, who pockets the silver, fruits, and coins. As a preventative of future pain a huge plaster of artemisia and pitch is applied to the abdomen, while the albumen of an egg is smeared over the skin to secure a good complexion. Many other charms are employed, of which probably the most curious is beating the child on the hips with an onion to secure intelligence. This arises from a play upon the native character for onion, and not, as might be supposed, from any misconception as to the seat of intelligence in man.

After one month has passed over, the little head is shaved. This operation is conducted by some mother of male children.

The matron who can only boast a family of daughters is to be studiously shunned and excluded from many important ceremonies relating to birth and marriage.

The education of women, according to the best native authorities, ought to include nothing more than moral precepts and domestic training. She ought never to open a book, or at any rate never be able to read it when she forgets her position so far as to open it.

It has been argued that the aversion to female children is the chief cause of infanticide in China; but that custom does not prevail to the extent some writers suppose. The story of the cart going its morning rounds in Peking, picking up the bodies of infants, is perfectly true, but it is only to collect the bodies that have not reached the age that secures for them the rites of sepulture. The authorities show some token of humanity in thus removing them for burial, or at least conveying them out of sight. The bodies exposed are of both sexes.

Infanticide does prevail, and to a sufficiently

alarming extent in some parts of the **southern** provinces, where the people are excessively poor, under-fed, and where daughters born to parents probably exceed the sons in number; and in regions where females must be in excess, owing to the tens of thousands of male emigrants who annually leave their native shores. Boys are always spared, as they alone can be of service in conducting the burial of parents and in sacrificing to their spirits after death. This is not all; they are better fitted to engage in the hard struggle for existence that falls to their lot in China.

The Chinese are not devoid of natural affection. Parents love their children with a tenderness unsurpassed in any other land, and children are devoted to their parents. The pressure of want hardens the heart and freezes the springs of maternal affection, and so, having no fear of the great God who gave them their little ones, they destroy them to save the toil of providing food for their wants.

Marriage and its inviolability are said to have been instituted by Fouhi anterior to the reign of the first emperor.

The most suitable season for marriage is springtime, but this is settled by the parents of the bride and bridegroom, aided by the doctors of Feng-Shui or good-luck.

There is no period of courtship, no love-making, no serenading, no happy meetings and partings. No; the separation of the sexes is so strictly guarded, that a maiden, almost before she has passed the sunny years of childhood, must remain shut up like a cloistered nun.

Unlike Mohammedan ladies, her face is not veiled from public gaze, but she dare not walk abroad alone; she is carried in her closed sedan, and the only companionship she enjoys is among her female relations.

Old women, professional go-betweens, are hired to arrange a marriage, to find out a suitable match for a daughter, and the whole is carried through by the parents, without reference to the contracting parties. Engagements are not binding until cards are exchanged bearing the representation of the dragon or phœnix—the former for the boy, the latter for the girl. Engagements are made early. These cards are laid on the ancestral altars, inscribed with the names of the two families, and a brief account of each. A red cord is passed through the cards emblematical of union, a practice introduced during the Tang dynasty. The Feng-Shui man selects a lucky day for the ceremony. Wedding cakes and materials for the bridal dress are presented by the bridegroom's family to the bride. The bride cakes are small, and may number four or five hundred, each about the size of a quartern loaf. But they are not sugar-coated, nor have they gay ribands and towers of snowy whiteness. They are soft, sodden, grey-looking cakes, containing in their flabby hearts little bits of pork fat and sugar.

The young lady after her betrothal keeps more closely still to her apartment. For all that, she contrives to make herself acquainted with the movements of the outer world. Maid-servants and pedlars alike contribute to her store of knowledge, and at times she gets a glimpse of her future lord, who just before the wedding is capped by his father as an introduction to manhood. The furniture and belongings are paraded through the streets before the wedding-day. This is followed on the eventful day by the procession which carries the bride from her early home.

If the day has been properly chosen, and the omens attended to, all goes well, unless the newly-wedded pair should, in place of loving at first sight, hate each other, or dutifully determine to tolerate each other till death. It is a strange lottery, and yet with the practical Chinese it seems to answer.

The wife must be very submissive: at first she becomes the drudge of her mother-in-law, and should she show temper, or be given to talking too much, the law enables her husband to procure a divorce.

The husband enjoys far greater liberty and security; he may, if he choose, wed a second or third from among his female domestics, but the first remains by law his wedded wife.

A very curious part of the ceremony before marriage consists in passing the bride's clothes over fumes of charcoal to dispel evil influences, or the lady in person before leaving home is held over a fire.

The marriage ceremony, which is most tedious, is consummated by the couple pledging each other in small cups of wine united together by a red silken cord.

The poor dispense with all the expensive part of the ceremonial, and it not unfrequently happens that a father purchases a partner for his son, and has her reared in the family as a help. When she

K

has reached the mature age of sixteen marriage robes are hired and the pair united with all the pomp and splendour of which their lot in life will admit.

It must be extremely miserable for a woman to be thus disposed of for life. With her heart breaking beneath her jewelled robes she may be carried in her sedan to a doom worse than death. Who can doubt the secret misery which such marriages are likely to bring about even in a land where the men are noted for their evenness of temper? Love can seldom rule the household with its mild sway, or fill the hearts of women who are at the best only slaves.

The Chinese themselves assure us that domestic tempests are not unknown beneath the roofs alike of prince and peasant, and that the serene air of the Flowery Land is disturbed by ten thousand tongues of discord and discontent. Much of the strife which prevails in many Chinese houses is to be in a great measure accounted for in the concubinage prevalent among the rich.

The power with which the law invests the head of a family is almost absolute. He may punish wife and children as severely as he deems necessary, or even sell them to be the slaves of others as he would dispose of land or cattle.

Children must serve their parents during life, and even after death, in performing the daily worship at the ancestral shrine, and in making periodical offerings at the grave. But a wise father will prepare for himself his own grave-clothes, and a cool and comfortable coffin carefully fitted and polished, or a dutiful son will display his filial piety by present-

BRIDE AND BRIDEGROOM.

Page 130.

ing his father with as fine a coffin as he can afford to purchase. No gift could be more acceptable; it is received as a pledge of the affection with which his memory will be cherished after death.

The finest coffins are made of a very heavy, costly wood grown in Szechuan, called Shi-mu. If made of this wood a single coffin costs from twenty-five to sixty pounds sterling. There is a peculiar varnish, provided from a tree in the province of Kweichow, used for repeatedly coating the inside and the outside of the wood. When finished, the coffin is left at the house of the undertaker or carried to a temple to await the body of the parent. In the Chinese language this last resting-place is called "Longevity wood," suggestive of long life beyond the grave. The grave-clothes are made with red silk, lined with blue, and thickly wadded. Over these are laid the official robes, if any. These are all of them pawned or kept ready in the house for the event. A mattress and pillow are also used.

As death draws near a stretcher is brought, having a pall of black silk. The dying person is then dressed and placed on the stretcher to close his last moments. The notion they entertain is that if they wait till life is extinct, and then dress the body, the soul would appear naked in the next world, and the robes would remain on the body.

At Peking death is never allowed to take place if possible on the bed, as it is feared that the spirit would haunt it afterwards. If a female, the ornaments of gold are all arranged in the hair, her bracelets laid by her side, never worn, for fear the spirit of darkness would use them as shackles to bind her. For the same reason a Mandarin never wears his necklace.

Pillows in the north of China are usually filled with husks of small millet, but those for the dead with paper, because each husk represents a period of time which must elapse before the spirit can enter another body. On the deceased is a cover with some classical phrase wrought in gold to aid the flight of the soul to the Southern Heaven. The household gods and ancestral tablets are all covered, so that they may not impede the exit of the spirit; and for the space of one hundred days the family do not burn incense at the shrine, or perform any act of worship. In the mouth, between the lips, is placed a pearl wrapped in red paper. The poor use a little tea instead. This is supposed to preserve the body from decomposition. Furs or fabrics made of wool are never used in dressing the dead, in order to prevent the spirit by mistake animating the body of the animal from which they were taken. When everything has been prepared, the relatives assemble and utter a wail of distress. The hair of the sons and daughters-in-law is undone and shortened, the shreds are rolled together, and, if it be a mother, placed in her right hand, if a father, in his left. Next the Geomancer is called; the family having provided a sheet of white paper, he writes on it the day, month, year of the birth of the deceased and the date of death, as well as the days of life. From these data he divines the day and hour the spirit will quit its earthly tenement.

The paper is then placed over the breast of the

corpse, and a small mirror laid on the top of the coffin.

On the appointed day the paper moves, or a noise is heard which indicates the flight of the soul. In the room a table with tea, wine, and cakes is spread, whilst all around the ash of incense is scattered, and afterwards examined carefully to see if it has been disturbed by the exit of the spirit.

A funeral never takes place on an even numbered day of the month, as that would ensure the speedy death of some member of the household.

The mourning consists of very coarse white cotton or calico, white cord wrought into the hair, and white shoes.

Musicians sit by the entrance to announce the arrival of guests. If the stranger be a male relation, they beat a drum; if a lady, a trumpet is sounded. The guests all contribute money to defray the expenses of interment.

If a husband has died, the widow is supposed to kneel day and night at the head of the coffin. Priests, Buddhist or Taouist, chant prayers. The funeral procession is most imposing, infinitely more imposing and costly than the marriage procession. As the coffin is carried along on its canopied bier, attendants scatter mock paper money along the road, to arrest the progress of malignant spirits. Paper habitations, garments, furniture, and models of slaves are carried to the grave, where they are etherealised by fire, and transferred to the spirit waiting beyond the tomb. Beggars, the pests of Chinese cities, and a source of great annoyance at feasts and funerals, loiter about the grave, or get into it, and persistently refuse to make way for the dead until they have been properly bribed by the attendants.

These unfortunates, in cities and villages, are subject to chiefs or head-men, who have charge of the mendicants in their respective wards. In some places the office of beggar chief is hereditary, and receives a quasi-recognition at the hands of Government. This man has the power, in the absence of any municipal rates for the support of the poor, to levy a tax upon the people of his district for the maintenance of his ragged band. He is at liberty to make arrangements with special streets of shop-keepers, who combine, paying a certain fixed rate to rid them of the beggars. Those who do not subscribe are liable to be visited at all hours by the most loathsome class of mendicants, and they are bound either to pay or tolerate their offensive visits in order to escape the greater trouble and loss entailed by proceedings before the magistrate.

The attire of Chinese beggars varies according to the habits of their craft. Many of them find nightly shelter in tombs, whence, after reposing with the dead, they issue. When the morning dew lies heavy on the land, rising from their beds of straw, strewn over the dust of crumbled coffins, they effect their toilet. The toilet of a beggar, like that of a belle, is not unfrequently conducted with as great care and solicitude as if the fate of an empire depended upon its success. It may be that the wretch wears nothing more than a coat of mud, if so he is careful that the coat should be an attractive one, that will arrest the eye of charity and procure many an offering for its owner. He may by an ingenious use of paint mimic the most loathsome disease, and go abroad among men as if on the brink of the grave, to solicit alms to pay for his interment.

Some of them mutilate or starve their children, and wrapping the poor innocents in filthy rags and bandages, carry them through the streets moaning and wailing for the suffering they themselves have inflicted. An old hamper, sack, a fragment of matting, or a piece of tough paper, is all the clothing required by a beggar. Such are the mantles that descend from father to son, as the profession in many instances is hereditary, having its own peculiar laws, arts, and usages.

The dress of the industrial and governing classes of China is made up mainly of three fabrics—silk, cotton, and hemp. Woollen cloths are never worn unless in the form of rugs; in the north of China wool is also made into felt for hats and the thick soles of shoes.

The garments worn by the common people are made of cotton, dyed either dark blue with a species of polygonum (cultivated in the same manner as the indigo plant), or black, or left white for mourning. During the months of winter the dress of a peasant consists of a silk, cotton, or felt skull-cap, one or more jackets quilted with cotton, and so long in the sleeves as almost to reach to the knees, when not turned up for work. Cotton trousers, several pairs, stockings, and cotton shoes, with flat thick soles of felt faced with leather. Rain coats are made from hemp, or the leaves of the bamboo overlaid like the thatch of a cottage or plumage of a bird.

In the silk districts the small farmers produce, spin, weave, and dye silks for their own use. Silks, satins, and fur-lined coats are worn by the gentry during winter, and robes without lining in summer. But the cut, colour, and quality of the dress of the people are subjects of the gravest importance in China, and have engaged the attention of all wise emperors. The Chinese dress by law, as well as by usage; the imperial edicts regulate the style of their robes. So minutely are all things ordered by the Board of Rites and Ceremonies, that the colour of a single button on the top of the hat denotes the difference between a prime minister and his secretary, or a Mandarin and his domestic. The make of a gentleman's boots, too, denotes his social standing, so that literally "stepping into a dead man's shoes" has a very decided meaning in China.

If a Mandarin has won the love of the people, when he is leaving the city gate, after his term of office has expired, one of the highest tokens of public appreciation will be shown by a deputation of citizens, who, in place of presenting him with an address, make a touching appeal for his boots. The functionary, protesting his utter unworthiness, in his secret heart rejoicing, accedes to the request, and the boots will be borne back by the people in triumph and deposited in the temple of the city god.

Changes of fashion are confined to changes of temperature. When the emperor puts on his summer robes the Mandarins and people follow; and so with the ladies. There are no court milliners, who, with the changing of the seasons, turn bonnets and everything else upside down. No immaculate tailors, whose duty it is to cut, and carve, and pad into the form of men, and men of the period, the votaries of fashion. A good fur coat and silken robe may descend as an honourable covering from father to son, and if the son prove worthy, the cut of his coat can never seal his doom in so far as society is concerned.

All this is thoroughly in keeping with the social economy and genius of the people. It is a part of the patriarchal system, and displays the reverence with which children's children accept the guidance of their forefathers even in the minute details of dress.

Not many years ago a rich Chinaman who had lived and prospered under British rule sent his son to England for his education. The youth at length returned transformed into an Englishman in dress and manners. The father was aghast at the transformation, and fearing all the evils that might follow this act, arousing as it would the vengeance of a thousand ancestors, he sent the boy to China, where he soon fell back into the old ways in dress and habit, if not in thought.

The Chinese consider European male attire, if not indecent, as utterly barbarous. The commonest coolie views our cutaway coats and tight-fitting habiliments with disgust, however naked he may be, and would sooner dress as a Hottentot than disguise his nationality by wearing a single article of cast-off European clothing. The attire of a Chinese gentleman is much more gorgeous and picturesque than ours. His long loose flowing robes, held in at the waist by a girdle, conceal his whole person, and lend a certain dignity to his appearance.

The chief articles of dress are all of them similar in shape—long gowns, with sleeves hanging to the knees, which, when doubled up, keep out the cold. The outer robe of rich figured silk or satin has an upper cape and a stiff collar of blue. The hat and boots complete the attire.

The ladies follow, to a great extent, the fashion of their lords, but dare not aspire to the hat or boots. Any strong-minded maiden breaking out in such manly adornments would probably be treated as a lunatic.

The Mongol Tartar women do wear hats, and boots too, and probably find the latter useful as a stimulant to their lazy husbands. The costume of a Chinese lady is extremely modest and picturesque, but her graceful appearance is spoiled by the feet, which are, by a gradual process of bandaging, so contracted as to render her a cripple. The Manchu Tartar ladies do not cramp the feet or use cosmetics to so great an extent as the Chinese.

The latter employ powder and colour so plentifully as to induce the premature decay of the skin. Their peculiar mode of life no doubt has a great influence in blighting the beauty of matrons. The strict seclusion, the atmosphere of home poisoned by concubinage, care, and jealousy, wither the young cheek and furrow the brow. In vain do they seek to preserve their blandishments by the artful use of paint, so thickly applied that one would think a smile on their sad faces would fracture the enamel.

The outer robe worn by a Chinese or Tartar

THE SMALL FOOT UNBOUND.

Ningpo Woman. CHINESE FEMALE COIFFURE. Kwangtung Women.

Page 13).

lady displays some most beautiful **tints**, and is made of silk or satin falling in folds to the feet. The body and skirt are in one, and fall naturally and gracefully, unaided by hoops, springs, or any of the strange western devices by means of which female forms and **attire** are sadly disfigured. The robe overlaps in front and is buttoned across the right breast, the line of division being **marked** by a broad parti-coloured band of rich embroidery. A long jacket **or** cloak, also tastefully embroidered, is frequently worn over the robe, and has the usual long wide sleeves turned over at the cuffs, and lined with pale blue, yellow, or rose-coloured silk. This completes the outer and visible dress, **if we except** the delicately-tinted embroidered shoes and head-gear. But the latter is so varied and so attractive as to be almost worthy of a special word. The ladies manage somehow to make so much of their hair, and get it to stand in such varied and fan-**tastic** forms, that the difficulty of knowing where to begin to describe it is only excelled by the question of how and where to end.

There can be no doubt that the dressing **of the** raven tresses of a Chinese lady is a work of con-summate skill, and must be the labour of most artistic slaves. She is a treasure of a Chinese maid who can dress the hair of her mistress in three or four hours, so we are assured. Endless, indeed, are the modes and diverse the designs which characterise the female coiffure of China. In some quarters the hair is built up on the top of the head to imitate a vase stuck full of flowers; in others it is a bird with outstretched wings, the handle of a teapot, or it is parted in front and looped up in a huge bow behind, supported by a piece of bamboo so as to stand out far beyond the ears. But whatever form it assumes it is greatly aided in retaining its shape by the gum of a particular tree, obtained by soaking the shavings in water.

When the ladies have finished their toilets, and can steal an hour from domestic duties, it is often spent in gambling. If there are no lady visitors to join them in the absorbing game, they have at least their slaves to share in the favourite pastime. Gambling is, however, a common Asiatic vice, and one which in China is by no means confined alone to women. Everybody gambles, high and low; dice, cards, and dominoes are found everywhere. They are even brought to decide whether a labourer shall have a double share of dinner or none; whether he shall receive a large sum of money or part with one of his children to cancel debt incurred at the gaming table.

Lotteries and gambling in any shape are supposed to be prohibited; yet games of chance are constantly and even openly played. Lotteries are organised, although their promoters may be punished with death.

The connivance of the underlings in the employment of Mandarins procures immunity to the keepers of gambling dens and to the manufacturers of gaming tools.

Besides the gaming appliances already noticed, a revolving hand, on a table divided into sections which hold the stakes, is also used, although the commonest game is odd and even, played with cash. Drawing lots is also greatly practised.

Theatrical performances are a leading source of amusement in China. Actors nevertheless are regarded somewhat as they were by the Romans before the time of Nero, as buffoons, and are excluded from all polite society. They, indeed, with their descendants—unless they change their profession—are not allowed to compete at the literary examinations. Just as in England before the Restoration, actresses are unknown on the Chinese stage, men and boys taking the female characters.

The plays are for the most part dramatised histories, in which the unities are totally disregarded, and in which fragments of historic truth or legend are encumbered with a multitude of details, tragic, romantic, and comic, of the exploits of ancient chieftains.

These plays, which seldom inculcate the purest morality, extend over four or five days, and the poorest labourers frequently find leisure and unalloyed pleasure in sitting them out. The faculty of memory must be developed to a wonderful degree in the actors, as when called upon in private the chief guest exercises the privilege of choosing his play, which they must at once proceed to perform.

The exclusion of actors from the profession of letters and government examinations was not always so strictly observed in ancient times. There was a sort of Nero among the historic rulers who exalted men of this profession to the highest offices of State.

The experiment was unsuccessful. It proved so signal a failure that it has not been repeated in later times.

Plays are enacted in presence of the women of Chinese households, who are provided with private seats at great feasts and public gatherings.

Jugglers, story-tellers, musicians, Punch and Judy, marionettes, and peep-show men also figure at public and private entertainments, and form a source of attraction at the restaurants and city tea shops.

The wandering minstrel is also a native institution. He is often blind, and is led about from door to door by some faithful attendant, tuning his lute as he goes, and singing simple ballads to pleasant, plaintive airs. It cannot, however, be said, in justice to the Chinese, that they excel in music. They produce sounds in great variety, but sweet melodies are rarer than song-birds in their land.

Music from the earliest ages has been curiously mixed up with their history, political and religious. Officers were appointed more than 4,000 years ago to adjust the instruments. The cock and hen phœnix were supposed to produce the positive and negative notes of the scale. This discovery was made by a minister, Ling-lun, who flourished about 2600 B.C., and invented the first pan pipe, which was made of bamboo. No nation has accorded a more honourable position to music and its influence, and no people on earth have done less than the Chinese to develop music into an art of harmony and sweet sounds. It has always been in some way mixed up with State religion and politics, and is now under the special care of the Board of Rites and Observances at Peking.

There are at least fifty different kinds of musical wind and string instruments, made in wood, stone, and metal, besides bells and gongs. One of the most interesting is the Chin, or "Student's Lute." It derives its name from *kin*, to check, as its formation is to soothe the soul and subdue evil in man. It varies in size, some of the largest being about five feet long, and has seven strings of silk, which pass over a bridge near one end, and are tightened and tuned by wooden pegs.

In ancient times the measures of the tubes (bamboo) which produced the gamut were curiously blended with the measures of capacity and length. The length and capacity of the pipes for producing the various gradations of tone are given in so many millet seeds.

The Chinese theory of music bears a strong resemblance to that of the Lydians, who probably borrowed their system either from Asia or Egypt, its gradations corresponding in some measure to our major keys. They do not understand the chromatic scale, and their notes are written down in such a way as to render them very difficult to read.

Pieces are written for special instruments, and the character for each note is rendered extremely complex, as it is supported by a cluster of other characters, which, all taken together, give the note, time, position of the fingers on the instrument, and the chord to be struck.

Foreign music has no charm for the Chinese ear; it awakens no sentiment, touches no chord of the heart. The finest melody, sung by the sweetest voice, or the richest harmony of Beethoven, might only bring a smile to the face of a Chinese musician, who would be moved almost to tears by the shrill notes of a native fiddle. Foreigners, on the other hand, if gifted with a musical taste, cannot avoid feeling contempt for the best performance of a Celestial band. The coarse croaking of flutes and fifes that seem to be broken-winded and difficult to sound, the screeching notes of rude fiddles, the strumming of lutes, and the crashing of gongs and cymbals, produce a mingled medley of sounds more easily imagined than described.

Harmony there appears to be none; short snatches of melody may be heard for a moment and again lost amid the wild clamour of brazen tongues and pipes hoarse with groaning.

Music seems to have been better understood by the ancients at a period in history when wise emperors sought to soften the hearts of their subjects by soul-breathing melodies, and when it was the duty of the members of the Board of Ceremonies to instruct ministers in the airs and dance-steps required in the management of the affairs of State.

In those days music held a high place, from which, alas! it has fallen in modern degenerate times. It must have been an important institution in the hands of an ancient and enlightened government, and yet it would be difficult for us who pride ourselves on our advanced knowledge to determine what sort of music and dance step would be appropriate for a minister in introducing a bill into Parliament.

The Chinese of the present day, when they sing at all, produce, male and female, an unmelodious falsetto, holding it a defect in training to allow the voice to sink into its natural modulations. Music, with its array of scholarly lutes, has proved power-

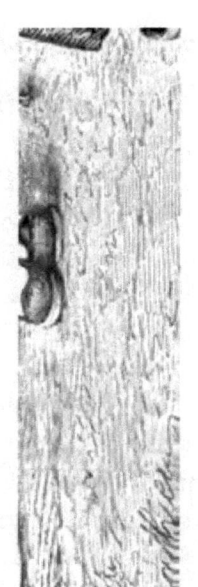

less to charm away the vices of the Chinese people, vices which are common to almost all Asiatic nations; yet if polygamy be excepted, and viewed more in the light of a national defect in the social system, the Chinese are not an immoral race. The social evils common to all communities, whether in heathen lands or in Christendom, are in China the subjects of repressive legislation. The evil effects which the intemperate use of opium has brought upon the people are too well known to require discussion here.

The better class of Chinamen, and many of those who have become the slaves of the drug, are opposed to the opium traffic. But it contributes a large share of the revenue to the coffers of the Government, who are directly interested, if not in the maintenance of the opium trade, at least in the maintenance of the imperial revenue. The Chinese rulers, therefore, if they earnestly desire to get rid of the evil, must make up their minds first to prohibit the growth of the poppy in their own dominions, and, further, to impose a much heavier tax upon the imported article, such as would greatly limit its sale and save many native consumers. If it were possible in this way gradually to destroy the market for the drug, the supply would diminish, and new and more remunerative industries would take the place of opium cultivation in India. But the opium question may be viewed as one of supply and demand, without touching upon the higher grounds which ought to regulate trading intercourse between Christians and heathens, whether natives or individuals. In the event of the Chinese proving themselves thoroughly in earnest by making a voluntary sacrifice, Great Britain would doubtless make similar concessions. But why not take the initiative and retire from the Government monopoly of opium in India, and thus withdraw the stimulus afforded for extending the growth of the poppy?

Indian opium has been imported into China for rather more than a century. In 1767 the quantity did not exceed 200 chests of 100 catties each. It was at that time used as a drug for the cure of chest complaints, dysentery, and diarrhœa. At the present time more than eighty-one thousand chests are annually imported, and the revenue to India from the growth of the poppy is over six millions sterling.

The Chinese Government have made great efforts to keep the Tartar soldiers from the vice of opium smoking, but it gains apace, and is secretly indulged in by men and officers.

It has been argued that the Chinese have found in opium the national stimulant they require.

This is not the whole truth, as they had their own alcoholic drinks and used them prior to the forced introduction of opium to the country. But the love which the Chinese have contracted for the pipe may be partly attributed to the low physical condition of the people, to their many hardships, to the unalleviated pain they have to endure, owing to ignorance of the proper treatment of disease. It is customary for the medical charlatan who fails to cure his patient to advise him to try the opium pipe, which affords relief from pain, probably aids recovery, and at the same time confirms him in the habit.

The smoker is thus described by a native: "Smokers while asleep are like corpses, lean and haggard as demons. Opium-smoking throws whole families into ruin, dissipates every kind of property, and ruins man himself. The youth who smoke shorten their days; those in middle life hasten the termination of their years. It wastes the flesh and blood until the skin hangs down in bags and their bones are as naked as billets of wood. When the smoker has pawned everything in his possession, he will pawn his wife and sell his daughters."

This picture is not too highly coloured; the writer has himself witnessed the ravages produced by the vice—the once highly respected member of society sinking down till the desire for the pipe became a passion consuming body and soul. The daily increasing pallor of the cheek; the glazed eye, with its cold, stony expression; the loss of self-respect—the slavish craving that drives the smoker to his pipe at certain hours of the day or night; the gradual development of the craving that is consuming his flesh, and the last stage, when his moral and physical nature implicitly obey the behests of the drug that, demon-like, hounds him to his doom.

Another native writer says: "The population of this vast empire has increased from year to year, but now the evil practice is spreading widely and checking this increase. All men smoke, the high and low, the old and young, and life is degraded and shortened. The substance of families is wasted, and the wealth of the land is passing away."

Natives may taunt us by saying, "Let your Christian missionary land in China with a ball of opium in one hand and a Bible in the other; he would find a ready market for the one, but the other would remain unopened, unless mistaken for a text-book on the cooking and smoking of the drug." The poor Chinaman, to whom the struggle for existence is a fearful reality, sees in the one a brief illusory heaven within his reach, albeit he knows that the respite thus purchased from the cares of earth is followed by a craving hellish in its intensity: in the other, the Bible, a far-off promise of future bliss, but he has his own experience of priestly promises, and he scornfully rejects it.

Here are a bland, pleasant poison and a Christian missionary both pressing for a welcome. The one, with its subtle soothing vapours, stealing into the soul, and slowly, almost imperceptibly, dragging men down below the level of the brutes; the other seeking by his pleading to win men over to Christ.

The Chinese, naturally stoical and proud of their own gods, are rendered doubly so by the fumes of the narcotic that impregnate the air of the Flowery Land, and may be tempted to inquire, "Can anything really good and true come out of the barbarous West?"

This is something like the view taken by Chinamen of western barbarians (if he happens to know anything at all about them). They are to him bold adventurers, traders in useful wares and opium, men whose whole energies are concentrated upon gain.

The office of the Christian teacher is little understood; when he travels into the interior, and assures the heathen around him that his boots and Bible are not lined with opium and other smuggled wares, he is viewed with distrust and scornful incredulity. They cannot conceive why men with trading instincts should travel so far, with no other motive in their breasts than the saving of men through the love of Christ. It is but few of them who can realise the simple truth that the knowledge of Christ and our higher morality fit us to become their teachers.

The medical missionary is a great power in China; as a healer of disease he wins the gratitude and confidence of the people, and none more surely than those whom he rescues from the slavery of the opium pipe.

There is very little of opium smoking or its effects seen by the casual observer in China. It is secretly carried on at home, and in private illegal opium dens, the existence of which is winked at by the officials. These resorts are found in obscure streets and alleys in all Chinese towns.

They are furnished with wooden benches, bare or covered with straw mats, on which the smokers lay themselves systematically out for the indulgence. They are usually dark, filthy, and filled with the most noxious atmosphere. Upon entering, an array of dim lamps on the benches reveals the prostrate forms of the smokers, with little more, many of them, than a ragged girdle round the loins. The action of the narcotic is beheld in all its stages. The youth whose cheek is still round, and flushed with the glow of health lies stretched out in a languid stupor, a smile playing over his face.

Yonder the middle-aged epicurean smoker, who vainly believes that he can never exceed a moderate dose, has carefully toasted his opium pellet over the lamp, and daintily placed it in the tiny cup of the pipe. His flesh looks flabby, and his face already bears traces of decay. But almost too loathsome to behold, a living skeleton, with eyes sunk deep in their sockets, is there stretched out, owning nothing but a filthy rag. He has sold everything, family, reputation, the very flesh from off his bones, to win the soothing fumes that inflate his shrivelled cheeks. He will be soon turned adrift to make way for others, to end his days by eating the opium ash.

The food consumed by the people and modes of preparing it are not unworthy of careful consideration. It has been frequently observed that the Chinese have the most unaccountable, and, withal, disgusting gastronomic tastes; that they will eat anything if cooked to their liking, and that they display a genius for cooking and rendering palatable animal and vegetable products such as we should esteem unfit for human food.

There is doubtless some truth in all this. It must in justice, however, be said that they are far from foul feeders. Their repasts, the simplest of them, are prepared with a degree of care and cleanliness from which the lower orders in Europe might gain instructive lessons.

The tables of the rich display many dishes unknown in other lands, where animal food may be had in greater abundance, as, for example, preparation of sharks' fins, land turtles, the **gelatinous** coating of swallows' nests, *bêche de mér*, snails, frogs, bamboo shoots, and a long list of indigenous fruits and vegetables. Vegetable **oils and** garlic are as commonly used for dressing **dishes as** in the south of France or Italy.

The Chinese cook is most ingenious and **skilful**; whatever may be the materials he employs, the resulting preparations are, as a rule, exceedingly palatable and nutritious. The *chef de cuisine* is found with his assistants **in** dwellings of the rich, in restaurants, and at the corner of every street ready to supply wayfarers with substantial fare and dainties at a trifling cost.

Groups of poor peasants **attracted by** savoury odours range themselves **round** his stall to partake of a cheap and toothsome meal. The chief ingredients which make up the food of the poor are pork, fish, **rice, and** vegetables. But these slender resources, added to sugar, water, and salt, are made to yield an endless variety of dishes and soups, **all** so tempting to the native palate that each is consumed with the **relish** which a perfectly new dish affords to a gourmet.

The Chinese, even the poor among them, are dainty eaters, and at the same time remarkable for the care they show **in** avoiding waste. The food of millions of tillers of the soil and boating people is of the poorest sort; it is simply rice, at best supplemented with preserved vegetables, salt fish, or pork.

A boat's crew, for example, entering upon a voyage up one of the rivers, engage a cook, and lay **in** a store of salt fish, rice, and pork. A small section of the boat at the bow is cut off for the galley, where an earthenware stove is set up for cooking. It is planned so that very little fuel is consumed in cooking; the fuel may be wood, charcoal, or a preparation of coal and clay cast into blocks.

The little galley is kept scrupulously clean. The cook sets to work by washing the rice in repeated changes of water, preserving the first washings, which are afterwards boiled down into a sort of soup or starch. He then places a large concave iron pan on the fire, filling it partially with water; when this comes to the boil a long wooden tub, having a sieve-like bottom, and containing the uncooked rice, is placed above the water, the sieve standing high enough to clear the surface. A lid is then fitted to the top of the tub, and the rice allowed to cook by steam.

When the rice has become soft by saturation, it is ready for serving, and is set aside to cool, while the fish or pork is roasted, or stewed in oil. Such meals are prepared twice or three times a day. When the men have finished the cook washes the bowls and bamboo chop-sticks, and gathers up every grain of rice, placing it in the sieve to be heated for the next meal. It must be gratifying to the cook to note how heartily the crew enjoy their simple fare, and to see the tender consideration each one evinces for his comfort. It is astonishing to observe the power of this simple food in building up bone and muscle, provided its effect is not neutralised by the use of opium.

In the northern provinces of the empire the diet of rice is supplemented by bread made of millet flour half cooked, and eaten in the form of tough dough in long elastic bands that may be pulled about like india-rubber. This is eaten **hot** and in enormous quantities by the peasantry. Such simple repasts are washed down by tea, or, when opportunity offers, by native wine. In the north a greater variety and abundance of animal food may be had; hogs' flesh claims the preference, although mutton is largely imported from Mongolia, and is sold at a very low price. Dogs, cats, and rats, or animal food of any sort, are eaten by the extremely poor, and may be seen exposed for sale in low neighbourhoods. The writer once brought home a plump rat, which he bought for a favourite dog. The dog, however, would not look at it, but a coolie from Hainan secured the prize, cooked it, and ate it.

The worst feature of a Chinese dinner, to the European, is the disagreeable noises made by the guests to indicate that they are full **to** repletion, and that they really could not venture to oblige the host by partaking of another morsel of his dainty fare. It is not agreeable perhaps to the foreign guest to receive from the host some choice morsel, held between the chop-sticks that have been passing in and out of his own mouth; but Chinese etiquette is very different from that in vogue with us. When the signal is given by the host, Chinamen unbend at table and talk naturally and freely. The conversation may be intellectual or humorous, but it might be more refined were it the custom **to** permit the women to dine with the men. Etiquette, so far as official intercourse is concerned, is fixed by the Board of Rites. In the presence of the emperor, and at state ceremonials, the master of ceremonies gives the time in a loud voice for the nine kneelings and the nine knockings of the head—ceremonies which, it might be mentioned, give rise to apoplexy and the untimely death of full-blooded officials. In official intercourse the most punctilious etiquette is observed, and strictly regulated according to rank. The keynote of the whole is a tone of mock humility, which begets insincere praises and elaborate acknowledgments of superiority from inferiors. Thus paying visits, receiving visits, and entertaining guests, all call for the exercise of courtly breeding, whereby the line is drawn inflexibly, although its bare existence is shaded off and illuminated by hollow phrases and posturing. This sort of thing is not altogether unknown in western lands, although, unless when vanity and egotism interpose, it is managed with less fuss and a greater show of manly equality.

The lower orders follow suit in China, transact their daily business, cheat and hate with a degree of polish wonderful to behold. Strangers meeting for the first time greet each other with speeches most elaborate. Europeans could not find leisure or patience to indulge in such idle questions as, What is your honourable title? Where are your great lands? Who is your honourable wife? How many honourable children have you? What is your honourable age? When did you come to our obscure neighbourhood? and so on. In framing replies all title to distinguished consideration must be studiously disclaimed and followed by the same list of interrogations. Children are early taught the forms to be used in addressing parents, superiors, and teachers, which are prescribed in the Book of Rites and Ceremonies.

In offering presents it is understood that a number of the articles ought to be declined, and they are not unfrequently given as bait to beget something better in return.

Guilds or trades'-unions exist in every town in China, and are largely patronised by merchants and handicraftsmen for the adjustment of all questions relating to work and wages, as well as for the regulation of the various local industries. The enlightened principles upon which foreign commerce are conducted, and the benefits which accrue to large trading communities from extended combination of capital and enterprise, have yet to be learnt by the Chinese. These advantages are being slowly realised by the native traders at the open ports, where insurance and steam navigation companies—one of the latter subsidised by the Chinese Government— have been formed, and are carried on with native capital and labour. It has hitherto been foreign to Chinese usage to unite private capital to carry out great enterprises, owing probably to the opposition of the local government to schemes which might in the end lead to political complication by the creation of a new class of men, wealthy and in no way connected with Government. In the interior provinces the restrictions placed upon trade, the bad roads, neglected water-courses, and the fluctuating nature of the transit dues, all tend to check native enterprise; the result is that moneyed men of the non-official classes are the exception, not the rule in China.

In these corrupt days money may, indeed, bridge

the social gulf, and obtain for its owner some subordinate Government post and a button. Men with capital, therefore, do not continue in trade.

Capital and credit occupy a very unsatisfactory position in the commerce of the country, unless at the treaty ports, where advances may be obtained on produce from the foreign banks at a comparatively low rate of interest. Loans effected by the Chinese from native bankers may be burdened by a rate of thirty-six per cent. interest per annum. No extensive banking companies exist in any of the cities; in place of them there are firms who negotiate promissory notes and bills of exchange, issuing notes in some cases for local circulation.

These notes are bound in books like ordinary cheques, and torn out across a certain line, but before removal from the book each note is signed by a clerk who has a flowing cypher, which it is almost impossible to imitate. The cypher runs into the part of the note left in the book, so that when torn out forgery may be detected by comparing the edges of the note and slip. As a further precaution notes are made payable only within a limited number of days from the time of issue, after which they must be renewed at the shop where they were issued. False notes are issued to a great extent, and sold for about a tenth part of the value of good notes. In Peking paper money is extensively circulated, and issued by small firms of shopkeepers.

The only native coin in China at the present time is the "tseen," or cash, the nominal value of which is one thousand to the tael weight of silver—about six shillings—but the value has fallen to about one thousand to the Mexican dollar. The value of the tseen varies in different parts of the empire, and fluctuates with the rate of exchange. Silver is the medium of exchange, and is cast in ingots of different weights and qualities, stamped with the style of the bank of issue. The purest ingots are forwarded to the imperial treasury, and must contain only about two per cent. of alloy. This high standard of purity gives rise to official peculation in the impost of a percentage above legalised taxation to cover the loss arising from nutting and purifying. The margin, by the malpractice of tax collectors, is made wide enough to cover the loss and supplement their meagre salaries.

Land taxes may be paid in silver of an inferior quality; salt duties in metal of a still lower standard.

The use of coins in China dates back from the earliest times. What are termed the kintaou coins, of which there are several kinds, are perhaps the most ancient. They vary in length from four to seven inches, and are formed of bronze, shaped like a knife, and inscribed with characters denoting their value; some have the characters inlaid in gold. About the beginning of our era, during the Han dynasty, coins of an oblong form, having an aperture at one end and a division up the centre, were in circulation. But the prevailing shape coined during the succeeding dynasties is that of the "tseen"—round, with a square aperture in the centre.

The art of counterfeiting is practised with great ingenuity by the Chinese, the Hong Kong or the Mexican dollar being imitated with a cheap white metal having the appearance and ring of silver. This is so cleverly done as not to be easily detected unless by the counterfeiter or some expert trained under him. Spurious dollars are also manufactured by cutting the coin in halves, and scooping out all the silver, excepting the outer skin, which is left intact, and re-united with cheap white metal in such a way as to deceive any one, save the educated schroffs, whose duty it is to examine dollars. These schroffs* are many of them trained by counterfeit coiners, and are employed by native and foreign merchants as clerks and treasurers.

The native tendency to imitate genuine and circulate spurious money has probably deterred the Chinese Government from producing coins of the precious metal.

* Cashiers.

CHAPTER VII.

ARCHITECTURE, ART, AND INDUSTRY.

Origin of Chinese architecture — Dwellings of rich and poor — Architectural geomancy — Interior of a gentleman's house — Graves — The art of painting — Enamelling — Porcelain — Carpentry — Wood-carving — Ivory-carving — Paper — Working in metals — Barbers.

THERE are no great architectural remains in China such as would enable the student to mark the origin and development of the ornate style of building which the Chinese have made so peculiarly their own. But, apart from the evidence which ancient structures might afford, were they found in any part of China, the modern temples and dwellings supply incontestible proof that the style is one of the most ancient in the world. The roofs, with their graceful curved lines drooping as if made of some soft pliant material, supplemented by fringe-like ornaments along the edges, their upturned corners decked with bells and tassels, carry us back to the remote ages when the first settlers pitched their tents upon the plains. It would almost seem as if the primitive nomad tents, erected at last on permanent camping ground, had become petrified, and that their simple outlines had been embellished and beautified by succeeding generations.

Some trace of the old way of setting up the tent remains, perhaps, in the practice of first raising the roof and then building the walls of a dwelling. In the south of China, when a builder begins his work upon a house, even before sinking the foundations, he elevates the roof on bamboo poles, and then commences to build the walls up to the roof from the foundation. Stories have been told (in support of the saying that the Chinese do exactly the opposite of Europeans in everything) about their building downward from the roof.

Everything is so thoroughly stereotyped in China, that this erecting of the roof first may come of the ancient practice of raising tents on poles. However it may have originated, it has the advantage of enabling the men to work under cover during rain. The first roof is always light and temporary, and is replaced by one of more durable material when the walls are finished. In studying the details of a Chinese roof, they will be found to closely correspond with those of a tent, not only in the outer curves, but in the supporting beams and framework. Iron nails are seldom used, and the joints are formed in imitation of a portable framework that may be taken to pieces by undoing ligatures, or removing long wedges. Ventilation of the interior is frequently effected by having an open space at the apex of the roof at each end of the buildings. Ceilings are only found in private high-class dwellings, and are made by constructing a light frame of squares, over which a sheet of white cloth is tightly stretched. In some cases the squares are filled by embroidered silk panels.

Beneath the eaves hang bamboo blinds, which may be rolled up or let down at pleasure to shade the verandahs. These and, indeed, the inner walls of the dwelling are adorned with landscapes and sylvan scenes, suggestive of glimpses of nature through the open spaces of the tent.

The bamboo holds an important place in the domestic architecture of the Chinese. In rustic abodes it not only forms the skeleton, but supplies the covering for walls, roof, doors, and windows, while in buildings of a better class the form of the stem is imitated in beams and pillars, water-pipes and gutters. In inner and outer decoration its graceful sprays, plumes, and pointed drooping leaves supply an inexhaustible mine of material for the artist.

The plan of a Chinese house is in miniature the plan of the palace or temple, and to the native mind it also affords some clue to the design of the dwellings of the just in their western paradise. But there will be no need of walls, bolts, bars, and locks in this paradise, for all the immortals are to be pure and just.

There are few Chinamen who would be happy in such a place, at least so some of them imagine when this picture is placed before them. No wall round any part of a house worth protecting is a notion they cannot comprehend. But then there are to be no women in their heaven, for before they can reach that thrice-happy spot they must be transformed into men. Such a change is not impossible to the Buddhist, who believes in transmigration, and many devout women wish to appear in a future state as men, and their erring husbands as women, that they may lord it over them. The wall to the Chinese on this side the grave, whether they be Buddhist, Taouist, or Confucianist, is a *sine qua non*. It must hedge round the entire abode, and is as thoroughly a national characteristic as ancestral worship. It is a social and political necessity that isolates the households and families of the population, and its moral counterpart is found in each individual breast of the millions. An adamantine rampart of politeness, polished hypocrisy, with a narrow doorway most difficult to find, through which the true inner man may reveal himself to his friends.

"The neighbouring walls have ears" is a Chinese proverb; the remaining four gateways of sense might have been appropriately added, as the wall round the dwelling is always strong enough to bar neighbourly curiosity, whatever shape it may assume. These outer defences of the family are for the most part built of brick of a grey colour, nicely pointed with lines of white cement, or plastered over, washed grey or white, and protected on the top by glazed tiles to prevent destruction by heavy rain. Were there no shops thrown open to the streets, a Chinese city would resemble a beehive in the multitude of its walled-in spaces, divided by narrow alleys leading to the different cells. The cells would be square, or oblong, and open at the top; as what the Malays call "Mata hari" (the eye of day), the sun, is the only eye that may gaze freely in upon the courts. Nay, not freely, for his hot glare must be shaded by carefully devised blinds and broad eaves to the inward and downward sloping roofs. In these human cells there are not wanting indications of distrust even of the blue heavens, in the shape of little dagger-like pieces of wood pointing downward at the angles of the roofs. These are designed to carry evil influences straight down to the earth, much in the same way as our lightning conductors. It is not the subtle electric flash that is dreaded, but certain influences intimately connected with the celestial dragon and terrestrial tiger, monsters who may raise a plague by merely wagging their tails at an unpropitious moment. So say the geomancers, who determine the positions of the walls and dwellings, exercising a sort of astrologo-architectural censorate over the work of the builder. This deep-rooted superstition wields its power over all classes of society, and accounts not only for the position of the house in reference to the sun, but also for many curious details in domestic architecture.

These geomantic details, viewed by those unacquainted with this phase of popular superstition, would be set down as useless and cumbrous ornaments, whereas they have a deep and vital significance. The reader must guard against condemning the Chinese for their implicit belief in geomancy applied to the erection of edifices. When it is properly understood, it will be found less barbaric than the practice still in vogue in some parts of Scotland of nailing a horse-shoe to the door to secure good luck. Admitting that Chinese "Fengshui" (for so it is called) is in the main contemptible, it nevertheless performs valuable functions as a sort of rudimentary natural science, in selecting suitable and healthy sites for cities and human habitations.

But as this subject will be further considered in its proper place, the reader is now invited to enter within the walls of a typical abode. If left alone in the narrow street he would be apt to wander up and down, seeking in vain for the porter's lodge, or the front garden with its iron gate, or the willow pattern bridge spanning the lotus pool that conducts to the front pavilion. The street is hedged in on both sides by a high brick wall, pierced at long intervals with unobtrusive doorways.

We enter one of them cautiously, armed with a stick to ward off the dogs, and with a red visiting card about a foot long. In front of the entrance, about two or three yards from the doorway, there is a brick or wooden screen set up to conceal the front court, and check the ingress of evil spirits, or defunct poor relatives. In spite of the feeling that our guide has brought us in at the back door, and that we may at any moment be seized for trespass, rest assured that getting over the wall would be the less dignified, and only other mode of entering this mansion. Summoned by the howling of the dogs an attendant appears, and with grave ceremony assures us that we are welcome.

Behind the screen is a paved court, adorned with a profusion of flowering shrubs, set in pots on ornamental stands, and at one side in a small pavilion are the family chairs or carriage—cart rather (a clumsy vehicle without springs). The front hall facing the entrance is raised two or three steps above the court. Beyond this hall is a second court, similar to the first, but surrounded by the apartments of the male members of the family; it has at the inner end a pavilion for the reception of select gentlemen friends and relatives. Here, enjoying the usual repast of tea and cakes, we look around upon walls hung with scrolls, pictorial and literary: for the Chinese delight in displaying texts written by men distinguished for literary skill; the characters of the language being also largely used in ornamenting interiors. From this pavilion the court presents the aspect of a landscape garden in miniature. There is a fish-pond, marble bridges, and quaint rockeries decked with dwarf trees, ferns, temples, and pagodas. The third court, or women's quarter, is the innermost of all, and may be described as a repetition of the second; only the apartments around are sacredly guarded, and may not be entered even by the most intimate male relatives of the family. Here the women and children spend their days smoking, gambling, and gossiping with their female friends and slaves. The children, and they are exceedingly pretty many of them, dressed in bright-coloured silks, are at play among the rockeries, or watching the gambols of favourite fish in large earthen water-jars.

The courts are paved with marble, or red earthen tiles, while the dwelling-rooms are built of grey brick, having only a ground and upper floor. Communication between court and court is established by covered passages, and through a series of doorways, never placed exactly opposite to each other, in order thus to intercept the progress of evil spirits that are supposed to be only capable of travelling in straight lines. The buildings which divide the courts have generally under and upper verandahs, supported on substantial polished teakwood or brick pillars, having ornamental wing-like brackets, but no bases. The lower verandah is open to the court in front, and at the back closed by carved hard-wood partitions containing windows, by which the interior is lighted. These windows are composed of wooden frames carved into an open-work of curious geometrical patterns, the spaces being filled in with pure white paper, or with thin slices of oyster shell.

The upper verandah differs from that beneath in the fringe-like row of glazed tiles along the eaves, in the carving on the rafters beneath the eaves, and in its exquisitely carved, painted, and gilded balustrade between the pillars. The effect of the whole is exceedingly picturesque, although it must be admitted that Chinese notions of grace, harmony, and fitness do not accord with our own, nor would such houses, the very best of them, were they placed in any part of our metropolis, be at all likely to find tenants. The partitions are too thin, and the rooms have no fire-places other than those used for cooking. The Chinese, however, do not sacrifice comfort to appearance. The bed-rooms, ranged round the court, are, in good houses, protected from winter cold by walls thicker and superior to those of our modern London abodes; the windows are also smaller, and better fitted to keep out draughts. Fires are dispensed with during winter, thickly-padded clothes being worn, and hand-braziers carried about, as in some parts of Spain.

The interior of the dwelling is severe in its geometrical uniformity and symmetry. Geometrical design prevails in the richly-carved dark-wood partitions, in the arrangement of the scrolls and sketches on the walls, as well as in the furniture and flooring. Chairs are never very numerous, and are always arranged in rows to suit the social rank of visitors. At the best they are neither tempting nor comfortable-looking seats, their square-carved backs and carved-square arms precluding the notion of ease, while the cold marble seats are suggestive of rheumatism.

The native craving for articles of virtu manifests itself in a display of ancient bronze tripods, porcelain, stone screens, vases, and coins.

Bed-room furniture appears to our luxurious taste extremely defective. The chairs and couches are all angles, the bed is like a house in miniature, and is built of hard wood, or, in country inns, of brick, with a fire-place beneath. It has a heavy ornamental wooden canopy, fringed with embroidered silk, carrying felicitous texts. The sleeper reclines on a level board, covered in summer with a straw mat, and in winter with a mattress so thin as to yield no relief to aching bones. The pillow is a block of polished wood, a piece of basket work, or silk stuffed with millet husks. The bed-room has usually a massive well-stocked wardrobe, and toilet stand.

The sleeping-rooms of the ladies and children differ only in minor details from those already described. They always contain a toilet case, fitted with a bright metallic mirror, combs, false hair, paint, powder, and cosmetics.

Screens or poles, stretched from wall to wall, carry clothes that are being aired in an atmosphere charged with domestic odours not unknown in the nurseries of our own land.

The Hall of Ancestors, or simply the shrine, has its place in every abode. Among the poor it occupies some obscure spot, some niche or shelf on which the ancestral tablet, a simple piece of wood, inscribed with the name and rank of the deceased, is placed upright on a stand.

In an establishment such as the one described, the Ancestral Hall, however small it may be, is adorned with lanterns and costly ornaments, and has its tablets ranged in chronological order, each generation in line. "It is, indeed, to the Chinaman what the chancel of a parish church is to the English squire."

The tablets are objects of daily worship, the eldest son acting as high priest of the ceremony.

In quitting the four walls of this fortified dwelling, supposing the season to be spring, we might observe the household, each member dressed in coarse sackcloth, repairing to worship at the ancestral tomb. The ordinary tomb is supposed to be a local habitation, or sort of country seat of the spirit, to which it resorts at certain seasons to receive the homage of the living. The spot chosen is frequently remarkable for its sylvan beauty, on the side of some hill, whence the spirit may sit when the trees are budding, and view old familiar scenes.

But departed spirits are supposed to be existing, and to require substantial fare and homage from the living, and to have their abodes repaired and put in order at least once a year. Men, women, and children all engage in the worship; the tomb is swept and mended, food, wine, and paper-money are brought and laid at its door.

Incense sticks are lit, and the members of the family kneel and koutaou (bow) nine times. After which they make offerings to the god of the locality, and to the manes of the poor. Before leaving the grave long pennants of paper are fixed to the tomb to show that the posthumous rites have been duly performed, as the neglect of these for two or three years would render the grave liable to destruction by the original owner of the soil.

The Chinese are lovers of their own school of art, and are proud of its antiquity. They have their ancient masters, who furnished the time-honoured designs for tripods and vases in bronze and porcelain; the originators of the quaint landscapes and figures that have passed down from age to age as the classical ornaments for their native ware.

Perhaps the most ancient examples of the application of art to manufactures are the bronzes, some of which are reputed nearly as old as Chinese history. More modern are the specimens of the painter's art on porcelain and earthenware vases. These, although they display a conventional style of drawing, and some knowledge of colour, cannot be taken as the best examples of the art of any period in Chinese history. They were probably executed, many of them, by artizans, such as are employed at the present day in the native potteries, while works of the highest class were painted on some perishable fabric such as silk.

The oldest silk paintings prove the decadence of art, and in this we are supported by native tradition. Many curious stories are told about the old masters who flourished during the reigns of enlightened monarchs, many centuries ago. Thus, for instance, in the third century, Tsaou-Puh-Ying painted a screen for the Emperor, and with a few dashing touches of the brush added flies to the surface; some dressing their wings, others ready for flight, and all so real that they deceived the potentate. Great was the joy of the limner to see His Majesty raise his scarf to brush them away.

Hwan Tseuen, who lived about nine hundred years ago, introduced some pheasants into the decorations of one of the halls of the palace. Some envoys, who had brought with them falcons as tribute, entered the hall, when the birds of prey made a dash at the pheasants on the wall, more to the detriment of their heads than the satisfaction of their appetites.

An Arab author, who visited China during the ninth century, says: "Of all God's creatures the Chinese are the cleverest as regards design, arts, manufactures, and every kind of handiwork, nor are they surpassed by any other nation in such matters. In China a man will do with his hands what would seem beyond human power. When he has finished such work he takes it to the Governor, who exhibits it for twelve months outside his palace door. If during the interval no one criticises it, the artist receives a reward; but should any important defect be pointed out, the work is condemned." He goes on to say that, "a man made a painting on silk, a perfect masterpiece—a sparrow perched on an ear of corn—which was exhibited to the admiring public gaze; at last a hunchback passing exclaimed, 'Every one will admit that a sparrow cannot rest on an ear of corn without causing it to bend, the artist has drawn the ear of corn quite erect.'" The remark was considered just, and the artist was dismissed without reward.

Although Chinese art, ancient or modern, will not bear comparison with that of Europe, there are old pictures carefully preserved in the collections of the rich, which are far from contemptible.

They can never be said to display the sublime in conception, yet the composition is not unfrequently characterised by tenderness, dignity, imaginative power, and surprising accuracy in drawing.

Perspective was never clearly understood: nevertheless, in many old works, distance is rendered by atmosphere as well as by well defined gradations of altitude in the objects of a landscape. This knowledge of perspective may probably be traced to the teaching of the Jesuit missionaries, who, during Verbiest's time, published a number of works, in Pekin, on drawing and mechanics.

The historical records inform us that portrait painting is an art most ancient. In the fourteenth century B.C., the Emperor dreamt that God had sent him an able minister; on awaking, he described to the court-artist the person he had seen in his dream. The description was so accurate, and the execution so perfect, that no sooner had the portrait been painted and circulated over the empire than the original was discovered and brought to court. In those days art was not so much used in discovering ministers sent by heaven to aid the government as in recruiting the royal harem. When a beautiful woman was discovered her portrait was painted and forwarded to the palace, to be frequently followed by the original.

The artists of the present day pride themselves on the excellency of their portraits; it is, however, difficult to make out on what grounds they base their claims. The works they produce are not unlike the sitters. This much may be said of them, they are mere charts of humanity, revealing nothing but the outlines of the face or figure. There is no attempt to pourtray character, to idealise the subject, and hand down to posterity the tokens of the higher nature that shine through the human face. No ; a Chinese portrait is geometrical and orderly. It must be a full front vacant stare upon the world, so as to prove to future generations that the head of the family had the regulation number of organs— two eyes, two ears, and so on. The arms must be placed with the elbows at right angles, and the legs to correspond, while the folds of the dress must fall in a limited number of straight lines, the whole recalling the axiom, " Things that are equal to the same thing are equal to one another."

At the coast ports are Chinese photographers, whose productions are characterised by the same angularity, the same broad stare, symmetry, and pairing of the members. Painting shops also flourish in seaport towns, their chief patrons being foreign sailors, who bring out portraits of Polly or Susan to be enlarged by John Chinaman. Labour in such establishments is minutely divided. The artistic genius (after the canvas and photograph have each been divided into an equal number of squares) proceeds to lay in the features, another paints the hands, a third the ornaments, and a fourth the dress. The resulting picture is aflame with bright robes and jewels, which afford a cheap delight to the "blue jacket," unless his instinct revolts against the barbarous drawing and hideous colouring. These shops are full of rejected pictures hung around, forming a sort of gallery of horrors.

The work of the Chinese ivory-miniature painter is worthy of special notice, as this is a branch of

CHINESE ARTIST, HONGKONG.

Page 172.

art in which some really excel. Painting in oil is comparatively new, and owes its introduction to Europeans. Chinnery, a foreign artist, who resided for many years at Macao, has left his impress on native art. Lumqua, his pupil, produced some good works, which are imitated by the painters of Hong Kong and Canton, who never venture upon any original composition.

Canton painters enjoy a certain spurious fame for their paintings on rice paper, or more correctly pith paper. Many of these painters are very clever and characteristic; the colouring is remarkably good, but the figures and landscapes are badly drawn.

Artists are found among the educated classes in large cities; some of them display great ability in sketching flowers and birds, and in dashing off types of native character. These are frequently done in black and white, with the finger nails, finger, and thumb. The nails are used for fine lines, as one would a quill, the fingers and thumb for laying in broad shadows.

It is astonishing the extent to which painting is used for decorating dwellings and articles in daily use, such as fans, japanned cabinets, trays, and the cheapest sort of wares. But what is much more astonishing is, that art should have been practised so extensively, and for so many centuries, without showing any signs of that progress upon which Darwinian philosophers base their theories. We are told that man is a progressive being. Chinese history affords a striking example of what spontaneous development does for Chinamen, when fairly put to the test. The knowledge of the modern Chinese is derived from ancient sources, from men who were physically and intellectually their superiors. There is scarcely any art they practise that is not a spurious imitation of something older and better. Why should this be when the immutable laws of progress are constantly acting? Perhaps they do not apply to the Chinese and other retrogressive Asiatic nations.

The art of enamelling was better understood some centuries ago than it is now, as practised in Peking. The art was introduced during the Ming dynasty, but the finest enamelled vases are said to have been made during the reign of the Manchu Emperor Kien-loong, about the middle of the eighteenth century.

There are now two or three establishments in the metropolis where enamelling is carried on, but the modern work is inferior to the ancients in quality and design.

The first part of the process consists in forming a copper vase of the required shape. The design for the enamelled flowers, fruits, and figures is then traced over the surface, and afterwards all the delicate lines replaced by strips of copper soldered hard to the vase, and deep enough to contain the enamel. The materials used in soldering are borax and silver, which require a higher temperature for fusion than the enamel itself. The design is next filled in with various coloured enamel powders, mixed with water into a thick paste.

The receipts for preparing the powders are kept secret, a fact which probably accounts for the enamellers having lost some of the finest colours.

Boys are chiefly employed in filling in the designs, or persons who have not been thoroughly trained to manage with artistic skill this important branch of the work.

The elements are fused in small earthen furnaces set up in the centre of an open court. They are then examined, and defects filled in with powder, after which they are again placed in the furnace for fusion. The vase, if it be round in shape, is then fixed on a small foot lathe, and ground down with sandstone, until perfectly smooth, after which it is polished, and finally gilded or electro-plated with gold.

Porcelain, commonly called China ware, was first manufactured by the Chinese, to whom we are still indebted for many of the finest specimens in our cabinets. When this delicate ware was first brought to Europe, it was supposed to be made of egg-shells, fish-glue, and scales, while its resemblance to the iridescent nacre of sea-shells led to its receiving the Portuguese name "porcelana."

This article, as already stated, is largely manufactured in the province of Kiangsi, at a place called Kingte-chin, where upwards of a million workmen find constant employment. The factories were established by an Emperor of the Sung dynasty, 1004 A.D.

The material used, "Pe-tun-tsz," is decomposed granite, or felspar, and "Kau-ling" (Kaolin); the latter is similar to that found in Cornwall, composed of silica and alumina. The fineness of the porcelain depends on the proportion of the Pe-tun-tsz, admixed with kaolin. A substance called "hwa shih," supposed to be the English soap-rock, is largely used in place of kaolin, and produces an article of very fine texture, and well adapted for receiving colour. These materials, when reduced to a fine state of division, are moistened, mixed, and kneaded into a paste, which is spread over the surface of large slates, and exposed to the action of the air until it acquires the requisite tenacity. It is then fashioned on the potter's wheel, after which it is fired, painted, and glazed. The labour at each progressive stage is minutely subdivided, even the painting of the designs which adorn a single cup is the work of many hands, trained each to perform, machine-like, its allotted task. The quaint paintings, which look as if printed from the same block, are all the handwork of men and boys, who are poorly paid for their labour.

The porcelain after painting is again baked and glazed. The firing is managed by placing the finest ware in earthen cases filled with sand. These cases are placed in the furnace and raised to a red heat. After which the fuel is withdrawn, and the contents of the oven are allowed gradually to cool. A large quantity of the Kingte-chin ware receives only the first baking, to prepare it for exportation to other provinces, where it is painted, fired, and glazed.

It is evident to collectors of China-ware that the modern porcelain is inferior to that of the Ming dynasty.

The graceful forms of the vases, together with their colour and delicacy of painting, have secured for the manufacture of that period a place in all the finest collections of Europe and Asia.

The superior quality of the old ware may be accounted for by the encouragement held out to manufacturers. A splendid imperial reward awaited the artists who produced the finest specimens of porcelain, or who introduced some new and graceful design. Imperial patronage has long been withdrawn, and skilful artists find more congenial and lucrative occupation than in modelling and embellishing vases.

The increasing demand for a supply of ware in the foreign markets has led to a corresponding decline in quality and beauty. Division of labour has been introduced to cheapen the cost of production, and the skill of the artist has been substituted by the toil of the poor labourer, who earns his pittance by repeating the old designs. Thus it has come about that the delicate China cup as well as the fragrant China tea are the result of unremunerative, unromantic toil.

When gazing upon the curious pictures while sipping the aromatic draught, one imagines that the Chinese, to whom we are alike indebted for the cup and its tea, are differently constituted from ourselves; that their country is a sort of vast tea garden interspersed with lotus pools and pagodas, and fragrant with the tea flower (tea is never allowed to bloom, unless for seeding); that the people are like those depicted on the cups, the women lame, with their "lotus lily feet," and the men leisure-loving opium smokers — short, plump, sensuous-looking persons, who wake from their drugged slumbers to cross marble bridges and view their wives and children gathering in the harvest of ripe tea leaves.

A single day in the land itself dispels our crude notions and strange imaginings. We find that the

Chinese are our true kinsfolk in all the attributes that pertain to humanity; that the vast empire is full of scenes recalling familiar spots in our own land; that the men are not wholly devoted to opium smoking and watching their wives at work, being themselves busily engaged in diverse occupations; and that the prevailing atmosphere is more suggestive of decay and density of population than of the fragrance of flowery fields or of lotus pools.

A branch of industry in which the Chinese may be fairly said to excel is carpentry. The native carpenter abroad is one of the most ingenious and useful of men. Freed from the trammels of conventional Chinese carpentry, he puzzles over and masters the foreign art of furniture making, upholstery, and even house-building and decoration. He appears, above all, to be endowed with a latent genius for constructive art, which, when it finds free scope for development, is by no means confined to servile imitation. A carefully executed plan or design soon becomes intelligible to him, and when he has grasped its full meaning, he may be trusted in putting into practice the knowledge he has acquired. In the Straits Settlements there are many instances of poor joiners who, after a few years spent among foreigners, have carved their way with their simple tools into the position of contracting carpenters and builders, and who at the head of large establishments do their work cheaply and efficiently.

In China the carpenter is content to saw and chisel and plane in the same groove all his days, rarely seeking to rise above the humble position occupied by his ancestors, unless during his early years he displays a genius for literature, and strives to compete for his country's honours.

His shop, if he is a master, is similar in all respects to what it would have been had he lived in the days of Confucius. There is the same tendency to abide by old custom. He makes and mends, just as his forefathers did, for families who have flourished in his neighbourhood for many generations. His shop sign, it may be, is "The pavilion of celestial repose and cheap couches." A sign which confers an ancient fame, a sort of escutcheon he fears to stain or dishonour by adopting any new-fangled notions, or by making any article that has not, so to speak, run in the family. He is careful to do his proper work well, so as to sustain the old name, and he pays his daily homage to Lo-Pang, the god of his craft.

There is something admirable in the life of such a man, and in his simple contentment. He is never actuated by nervous ambition, an insane desire to tread down his fellows in the struggle for gold. His way of life is settled for him, as it is for millions of his countrymen, and he lives it calmly. There are no wasting cares and heart-breakings that are the offspring of overstrained energies.*

The workmen and masters of this, and nearly all other handicrafts, meet at their guilds or temples to feast and discuss the condition and prospects of their trade in the third or fourth month of the Chinese year, and at other times to settle disputes by arbitration. The expenses of such trades'-unions are defrayed by fines inflicted on

* It is indeed a singular fact, that heart disease, so common in western lands, is almost unknown in China.

defaulting members. Disputes frequently arise between native guilds, and are not always amicably settled.*

Chinese joiners' tools, although coarse, and not so well tempered as our own, resemble those used in Europe, and include planes, augurs, bits, drills, chisels, saws, and axes. The bench is a low inclined plane of wood, on which the workman sits astride, using his foot for a clamp to steady the plank he is dressing.

The plane has two handles. The ordinary saw is a ribbon stretched on a bow-like frame. Augurs and drills are fitted to a long wooden handle, with a revolving end, which is set in motion by a drill-bow. The turning lathe is driven by a treadle, to which a rope is attached. The rope, passing upward, is twisted one turn round the wooden spindle, formed by the block to be turned (carried between two iron centres), and is fixed at the upper end to a bamboo spring in the roof. The spring keeps the rope tight. By depressing the treadle, the spindle makes a revolution in one direction; as soon as the pressure is withdrawn, the motion is reversed by the spring coming into action, and so on back and forward goes the lathe, the workman getting a bite at the wood with his chisel every alternate revolution.

The work turned out by means of these primitive appliances has not, as a rule, the finish of similar products in Europe, if we except the exquisite carving of the Chinese. The carved work of native furniture, panels, partitions of dwellings and shops,

---

* CANTON, *October*, 1875.—The feud between the weavers' guilds has not yet been settled. Your readers will remember that during the recent fight a boy was accidentally killed.—*Daily Press*, Hong Kong.

could not be executed at such trifling cost in any other land.

Many of the designs are so chaste and beautiful, as to make one imagine that toil so artistic must be highly paid; but the men employed in such labour are hardly so well paid as an English female cook. The art of the wood-carver is only excelled by that of the worker in ivory, who with unsurpassed patience produces wares that rival lace in delicacy. The carved-ivory fans of Canton are the finest specimens of this class of skilled labour; but the great ivory ball, having nine or ten balls one within the other, is an astonishing piece of turning and carving. This article of Kwangtung workmanship is still viewed as a sort of Chinese puzzle. All kinds of speculations have been advanced as to the manner in which the balls are cut and carved. The vulgar notion is, that the whole is built up of a multitude of fragments fitted together, and fixed with some hard cement. But the truth is, they are made out of a solid block of ivory, first roughly cut round, and then fixed into a lathe and turned, until quite spherical. The ball is then marked off for the regular positions of the holes, after which the holes are drilled from all the points to the centre, each aperture increasing in diameter towards the outside. One of the holes is then centred on the lathe, and a tool inserted, bent to a right angle at its inner extremity. This serves to turn a groove near the centre of the ball; hole after hole is in like manner centred, until all the grooves are cut, and meeting each other, the innermost ball falls into the centre of the sphere. This inner ball is then moved about and carved with long tools passed through the holes, after which the bent chisel is again brought into play to cut out the next ball; and this is repeated until all the balls have been released and carved.

Having noticed some of the native uses of wood and ivory, this section of the work may be rendered more interesting by the addition of a brief account of the uses of the bamboo, one of the most valuable and graceful of grasses, for it is a species of grass, whose stout stems tower to a height of sixty or seventy feet. It is grown in all parts of China for its wood, fibre, and leaves.

Its waving plumes of pale green may be seen everywhere shading the dwellings, and hedging them round as if with a fence of iron. But it is not alone its beauty and strength which charm the cotter; it forms no small part of his worldly possessions. His hut is built of its wood and thatched with its leaves; the simple furniture of the interior, everything excepting the rude table, is made of bamboo: water-jars, grain-measures, buckets, mats, his fan, pipe, the paper he writes upon, and the pen he writes with; his hat and rain coat are, all of them, made from the same plant.

There are said to be sixty varieties of bamboo in China, some used in paper making, a finer sort for pencils, those with large stems for furniture and house building, poles, ribs of sails, shafts of spears, and waterducts. Besides this it supplies various instruments of torture, and the imperial rod, so largely employed to improve the tone of society.

Paper is said to have been invented by the Chinese during the reign of Wanti of the Han dynasty, in the second century B.C. Up to this period bamboo leaves, the bark of trees, and tablets of stone had been used for the purposes of writing. The most ancient records of the empire were engraved upon slabs of bamboo, and the characters filled in with a durable varnish. It is recorded that the paper of the Han dynasty was made from bamboo pulp, and the step seems a natural one from the use of thin sheets of bamboo to the manufacture of thinner and more flexible sheets from fibres of the same plant. So intimately, indeed, has this plant become associated with letters in the minds of the people, that its graceful sprays are the classical emblem of literature. It supplies paper and pens. To it may be traced the origin of the phrase, "Forest of pencils."

The finest bamboo papers are made in the Fakien province, where they may be had in great variety, pure white and extremely fine in texture, tinted and water marked for note paper, strong and coarse for packing, or compact and smooth for the use of gold beaters, in place of parchment. Certain varieties of bamboo are specially cultivated for this industry. The paper, which is remarkable for its beauty, strength, and durability, is manufactured something after the following manner:—

The labourers repair to the mountains where the plant is grown, and selecting the most suitable stems, cut them down in lengths of six or seven feet, and place them in a tank cut out of the ground. The tank must be kept full of water by laying down a series of bamboo ducts connected with some mountain spring, so as to act as feeders and prevent the water draining off. The bamboos must soak for the space of one hundred days, after which they are taken out and beaten with a mallet, and the outer fibrous coating separated to form the pulp, which is placed in a cauldron containing a mixture of water and lime, and is boiled for eight days and nights. It is next subjected to a further boiling and bleaching with wood ash, and finally mixed with rice starch. When the pulp has been prepared it is placed in a vat, into which a workman lowers a square-shaped sieve or board and covers it with a thin coating of pulp, allowing the water to drain off; this is afterwards placed between boards to press out the water, and finally stuck upon a plastered wall to dry, partly by the heat of the sun, and partly by aid of a flue which runs the whole length inside the wall, and is heated by a fire.

The Chinese are skilled in the use of metals, in the manufacture of domestic utensils, mechanical and agricultural implements, musical instruments, and jewellery. Nearly, if not all the most useful metals are found within the limits of the empire, although they are not produced in quantities sufficient to meet the wants of the natives. This is owing to the prevailing ignorance of geology and of the art of mining, and to the restrictions placed upon mining operations by the authorities. Metals of the most precious and most useful kinds do exist in enormous quantities in the mountainous provinces. Iron and coal are found almost side by side in Kwangtung. The former was worked for a short time about the beginning of the seventeenth century; but the mines have long been closed, and the supply for Fatshan, the Sheffield of China, is nearly all imported.

Fatshan, in Kwangtung, is a town of metal workers, whose trade consists in making knives, scissors, teapots of a white cheap silver metal or alloy, and basins of brass and copper. The white metal spoken of above is often used to make a solid lining for earthen teapots, finely turned and polished inside. It is difficult to make out in what manner the lining is introduced, unless it is cast inside the pot or the pot moulded over the lining.

The most valuable Chinese alloy is the gong metal, which has yet to be discovered in this country. The two metals employed are said to be copper and tin; this the writer is unable to confirm by personal observation; but the art of producing metals yielding clear ringing tones has been known to the Chinese from the earliest times. The writer, when in Pekin, was shown a very old bronze bell with a series of knobs outside, which, when struck in succession, rung out a sort of chime.

The oldest bronze tripods and vases, dating as far back as 1760 B.C., are made of a kind of bronze that cannot be imitated at the present day.

Five hundred years ago the Chinese cast astronomical instruments of bronze, having enormous circles finely divided. These have been constantly exposed to the action of the outer air, and may still be seen beneath the walls of Pekin, almost without blemish.

The five great bells cast during the reign of Yunglo, of the Ming dynasty, one of which now hangs in the bell tower of Pekin, each weighs

120,000 lbs. avoirdupois. These bells, notwithstanding their enormous weight, are perfect castings, even to the sharp outlines of the raised inscriptions on the surface.

The coppersmiths of Foochow-fu take full advantage of the ductility of the metal with which they work, by beating it from flat sheets into the most varied and complex forms. No less remarkable are the gold-beaters, who, with the aid of bamboo paper, placed leaf and leaf between the sheets of the precious metal, succeed in beating out the leaves so thin that they will float like feathers in the air.

The Cantonese show considerable ingenuity in the manufacture of gold and silver filigree work, displaying that phase of native industry which delights in the elaboration of minute and intricate details.

Many of the appliances used in China handicrafts appear to have been originally designed for portability, so that the journeyman mechanic might take his kit upon his back and march from town to town.

This seems to point to the dim past when, under the sway of some nomadic chieftain, camps were suddenly pitched and as suddenly struck to seek new pastures or places of security. Perhaps in no other land do equal facilities exist for having all sorts of work done at one's doorway. The wandering workers of China are no shabby tinkers, persons always extremely poor and often depraved, who can do a little of everything, and very little indeed in the shape of making a decent living. No; the Chinaman who takes to the road with his tools may be a highly respectable and independent member of society, a carpenter or blacksmith. Take the latter; he has a most ingenious outfit for his journeys, just the sort of appliances that would be required by the armourer attached to an ancient army on the march. Genghis Khan, the great conqueror, it is said, started as a poor Tartar blacksmith, and ended by forging the chains that made empires captive. So the blacksmith, even in China, need never be ashamed of his craft or the music that rings from his anvil in front of some humble doorway. We have seen him on the roadside, his cheerful face lit by the ruddy flare of the forge, and his muscular arms moving in strange harmony as he strikes and fashions the hot iron. But how, it may be asked, does he manage all this on the roadside? Where are his forge, and fire, and bellows, and all the little etceteras of this curious picture? Let us suppose he has received an order for a pruning knife; he has none in stock, and undertakes to make one on the spot. He lays down his materials and tools, which are carried by an attendant coolie in two baskets slung on a bamboo pole. The coolie proceeds to dig a hole in the ground, and when deep enough builds his fire there; he then scoops out a connecting canal, in which he places a longish pipe to act as a flue, and covers it up. Next a long, square, box-like air-pump is laid down and joined to the flue. This takes the place of bellows. In two or three minutes therefore the forge fire is in action, and is fed by a steady blast from the pump. The anvil and hammers are placed in readiness. The iron is next heated and beaten into shape, and a fine edge of steel is welded on to the blade. This done the knife is dressed with a sharp hard chisel fixed into a two-handled iron bar; it is then tempered, and lastly edged on a block of sandstone.

Humble and yet indispensable is the trade of the barber in a land where millions of human heads have to be shaved every morning, where an Atlantic cable of queues has to be combed out before sunset. The barber's is an out-door occupation in China, and the typical professor is always a sleek, well-fed, respectably clothed personage. In the latter attribute he differs from many of his customers, who, if we except a narrow cloth round the loins, wear nothing save the queue, which they coil up round the head to be out of the way. His operations are soothingly and gently performed, and he has a way of telling strange stories, winning popular favour, and getting well paid for his work. His paraphernalia is wonderfully complete, and consists of a small charcoal furnace for boiling water, a brass basin, and a chest of drawers, which serves as a seat for his client and repository for razors, combs, and cosmetics. He first applies a hot wet cloth to the head and face, and shaves the whole bare surface including the face and ears, and trims the eyebrows. Next he inserts a small bone instrument into the ear, and prepares the tympanum for daily duty. The eyes are then cleared of much of their lubricating mucus, a proceeding which, no doubt, is a fruitful source of ophthalmic diseases in China.

CHAPTER VIII.

RELIGION.

State religion—Human sacrifices—Confucianism—Taouism—Buddhism—Mahometanism—Christianity—Feng-Shui, or Chinese geomancy.

THE religion of China is a subject which must be briefly dealt with. Could it be treated *in extenso* the reader would still be left in doubt and perplexity as to what, after all, constitutes the faith of the Chinese. Although they worship strange gods and follow the creeds of Confucius, Laoutsz, and Buddha, the emperor as high priest offers periodical sacrifices to the Supreme Ruler of Heaven.

The altar of heaven in Peking, a circular triple terrace of pure white marble erected on sacred ground, is the scene of the great state ceremonials which are a remnant of the most ancient form of Chinese religion. The simple altar devoid of covering, on which the finest produce of the soil, together with animals carefully selected and prepared for burnt sacrifices are offered, bears an affinity to the ancient patriarchal worship of the Jews.

This State religion, this worship of "Shangti," the Supreme Ruler, is nevertheless strangely mingled with elements of Paganism. The spirits of deceased emperors, the material principles of nature in heaven and earth, the sun and moon, the gods of agriculture and of industry, all share in the rites prescribed by the code of the empire.

"The State religion," says Dr. Williams, "has been so far corrupted from its ancient simplicity as to include as objects of worship with the heavens, gods terrestrial and stellar and ghosts infernal, flags and cannon, as well as idols and tablets, the effigies and mementos of deified persons."

It is impossible to determine the time when the worship of Shangti became associated with that of the host of inferior spirits. It was probably anterior to the commencement of China's reliable history.

In the "Canon of Shun" it is recorded that the emperor* "sacrificed specially, but with the ordinary forms, to God; sacrificed purely to the six honoured ones; offered appropriate sacrifices to the hills and rivers, and extended his worship to the hosts of spirits." This occurred about 2000 B.C.

Since the days of Shun, emperors and sages have been deified and canonised so largely as to render the objects of State worship limitless. The preparation of the hierophants for this worship has perhaps been less subject to innovation than the rites they practise. They are required as of old to purify themselves by fasting, ablution, and temporary withdrawal from society.

It would appear that in after times barbarous rites were introduced. Human sacrifices were offered at the burial of the dead, as anciently with the Egyptians and Hindoos. History enables us to trace the origin, development, and final condemnation of the custom. In ancient times bundles of

---

* Dr. Legge's Chinese Classics.

straw were made to represent men carried to the grave, and buried with the dead as attendants upon them. Next, during the Chow dynasty, painted wooden figures were in vogue, and finally came the practice of burying living persons with the dead, which Confucius thought was an effect of this invention, and therefore he branded the inventor.

At the funeral of Chi-Hwang-ti, of the Tsin dynasty, the imperial wives and concubines who had borne no children, and the workmen employed in the construction of the tomb, were buried alive.

No such revolting cruelties have been practised in China for many centuries.* The writings of the sages and of Buddhism have each had their share in uprooting these barbarous customs.

The three national religions of the Chinese are Confucianism, Taouism, and Buddhism. The first of these systems has always been accorded the preference among the governing and literary classes, while the last two forms of faith are most deeply rooted among the lower orders of society, although the nature of the philosophy of their doctrines and dogmas is as little understood by the priesthood as by the people.

Confucius was the greatest sage of Chinese history. He lived in the sixth century before Christ. The legendary accounts of the personal appearance of the " Great Teacher " make him out more monster than man. As a child he presented "an extraordinary appearance, with a mouth like the sea-ox's lips, a dragon's back," and so on. As a man he was

* An imperial edict was issued in 972 A.D., prohibiting human sacrifices. See Bowra's "History of the Kwangtung province."

about ten feet high,* and of a swarthy complexion.

There is, however, nothing legendary about his character, which stands forth clearly and boldly in his own writings, and is described minutely by his disciples. The scenes of his life, his habits, actions, and personal influence upon the rulers of the petty states, and even something of his personal aspect, are all known to us. Although the accounts have been carried down through so many centuries, they are more minute and satisfactory than our own chronicles of some of the great geniuses of the Elizabethan period.

The disciples of Confucius, in describing the domestic life and daily occupation of the sage, have completely raised the illusory veil, viewed through which an ancient philosopher becomes a sort of demi-god. We are told in regard to his meals he had likings which he was careful to gratify. He did not eat largely, but daintily. That his food was prepared and skilfully cooked, and cut like that of other mortals who are not sages; that he was courteous, charitable, and thought it no degradation to order his domestic affairs with discretion; that, unlike the great geniuses of western lands, he neither disdained to dress well and becomingly, nor did he seek in any way to disguise or conceal his ordinary humanity. He studiously regarded outward appearance and manners in order that his example might benefit society.

* "It is allowed that the ancient foot was shorter than the modern, but it must be reduced more than any scholar (I have consulted) has yet done, to bring this statement within the range of credibility."— Dr. Legge's Chinese Classics.

It is not recorded that as a great man he had his eccentricities which society good-naturedly tolerated, or that the profundity of his learning prevented him fulfilling the ordinary duties of life. No; Confucius, although he was a man of an extraordinary stamp, and a great reformer of men and manners, was not worshipped during his lifetime, nor even appreciated by the majority of his own countrymen. The influence of his labours was not felt for two or three centuries after his death, until the beginning of the Han dynasty (194 B.C.), when literature was honoured after the burning of the books by Chi-Hwang-ti, and the emperor visited the tomb of the sage and offered an ox in sacrifice to him. About the beginning of our era commenced the practice of conferring posthumous titles on Confucius. At first his worship was limited to the state of Loo, but in 57 A.D. it was decided to sacrifice to him in all the chief schools of the empire.

In the temples of Confucius—there is one in every great town—the ancestors of the sage and his disciples have their tablets or images. Twice a year, during spring and autumn, sacrifices are offered in these temples in honour of the sage, whose spirit is supposed to be present in the tablet on the sacred shrine. The emperor in person presides at these ceremonies in the metropolis, when, after the reading of an eulogy to the spirit, animals, fruit, fabrics, and wine are offered in sacrifice.

The sacred Edict of Kanghe, the second emperor of the present dynasty, is one of the text-books of the learned sects, by which they seek to maintain their influence. It is supposed to be read publicly twice a month in presence of ministers and people. The text consists of sixteen maxims amplified into discourses on morality and industry treated as the groundwork of national prosperity, and appears to recognise no power in heaven or in earth higher than the emperor. Obedience to the imperial Government is the focus towards which all its arguments converge; obedience to parents form important converging beams; while isolated self-interest, subject to moral and political law, constitutes the converging luminous rays of the whole system embodied in the sacred text. Reading and explaining the laws to the people is a practice instituted in China about three thousand years ago.

The Confucian morality teaches that man's nature was originally pure, bestowed by Heaven, and that evil came from the union of the soul with matter, and from the existence of the passions. Conscience leads man to a sense of the duty he owes to his own higher nature and to society, or to "the three relations and five constant virtues." The three relations are prince to subject, father to son, husband to wife; the five virtues are, benevolence, honesty, good-breeding, learning, and fidelity. The exercise of the virtues, however, is to be reasonably adjusted. Neighbours are not to be loved without sufficient cause, or hated unjustly; everything is to be nicely fitted to meet the wants of the social relations peculiar to the land; but the Confucian code of morality, with its obvious defects, rests upon a broad basis of truth, and its maxims are those contained in our own moral laws. Had it been otherwise, the system could not have stood the test of so many centuries. Its greatest defect is that it embodies no conception of God as the Creator and Preserver of all things. Its tendency is to deify mind and the material agencies that are at work around and above us.

Confucius is worshipped as the "Great Teacher," education being held in the highest estimation by all classes; the members of the *literati* are, however, the chief worshippers, and the graduates who hold the highest official rank, the priests of the temples.

In nearly every schoolroom throughout China the worship of the sage is performed on the first and fifteenth of every month by the pupils, who bow before an inscription dedicated to Confucius. From all these facts, and from the high moral tone of his writings, some notion may be gathered of the influence of this single life and its labours on so great a section of the human family as that contained in the Chinese empire.

Laoutze, the founder of the Taouist sect, was a contemporary of Confucius, who, although he had met and conversed with him, and extols the doctrines of the rationalist philosopher, says little or nothing about the man himself.

Laoutze sought to attain perfection by secluding himself from the commotion of the world, by subduing the passions of the human heart and cultivating that absolute calm which is supposed to secure immortality **for** the soul. His was not unlike the philosophy of Zeno, who placed man's chief happiness in being conformable with nature and reason. The sage of Cyprus was unsuccessful in purifying his attendants by the application of simple reason. The rod was found necessary as a valuable adjunct. When a servant was being beaten for theft, he exclaimed, "'Tis my fate to be a thief." "Yes, sir," said Zeno, "and to be drubbed for it too."

The followers of Laoutze, at least those of modern times, never attain to that perfect bliss so vainly sought by the philosopher himself by searching after the Taou-le—the ultimate reason—which is the beginning and the end of all things. They vainly continue to study astrology and geomancy, trusting by the aid of these occult sciences to discover the hidden secrets of heaven and earth, of time and of eternity. Perhaps the purest types of the Taouist are the hermits—and there are many of them—found dwelling in mountain caves in the Upper Yangtsze, or in the most romantic spots of the mountainous provinces of China. The writer well remembers having seen one of these recluses marching up and down on a ledge of rock in the front of his cave cut in the face of a precipice high above the waters of a deep river, his white hair flowing in the wind, and wearing on his brow a band of silver inscribed with the symbol of his order. But the majority of Taouists imitate the Buddhists in their monastic life, and rear their monasteries close to or amid the haunts of men, as they depend for sustenance upon the geomantic and astrological rites they practise at births and burials.

Laoutze was a thoughtful, though a misguided man, and wrote his books with a good measure of sincerity. But Taouist priests as they are known now-a-days are not intelligent. They are ignorant and selfish characters many of them, who do not as a rule write treatises on the philosophy of their religion because they do not understand it. They recite their rituals because it pays to do so. Some are no doubt intelligent and sincere, but many have drifted into the priesthood because it offers an easy and not unpleasant way for lazy, low, and cunning men to gain a living.

Quite another sort of being was Chwang-tsz, an ancient disciple of the founder of the Taouist faith, who did more even than Laoutze himself to diffuse rationalistic views. Others have added to the literature of the sect. Dr. Medhurst quotes one who eulogises Reason thus:—

"The venerable prince (Reason) arose prior to the great original. . . . He is spontaneous and self-existent, produced before the beginning of emptiness" (whatever that phrase may mean), "prior to uncaused existences, pervading all heaven and earth, whose beginning and end no years can circumscribe."

Laoutze was supposed to be one of three impersonations of this power. Their incarnations bear some resemblance to the avatars of Vishnu, with this difference that only three incarnations of Reason are mentioned in place of the nine of the Hindoo god, but the attributes of the Indian trinity are all combined in the Chinese Reason. The doctors of Reason exercised great power in ancient times, and their modern followers wield even a greater influence on the people of the Flowery Land. Not that the principles of these doctrines are intelligently understood, but blindly followed as superstitious practices.

One of the most dangerous early pretensions of the Taouists was the possession of certain charms to prolong life beyond the ordinary span. This attracted many votaries, and among them more than one emperor, who, seeking earthly immortality, drank the nostrums which they prepared. These were not always harmless; they were stimulating to an extraordinary degree, but the reaction which followed gradually weakened and wasted the frame. It was also held by this sect that a fountain of immortality existed on some fabled spot, a garden on a sacred hill, whose flowers ever bloomed and whose fragrance fanned the leaves of the tong tree at the gate of heaven. It was the immortal life-giving water from this mythical spring that the priests feigned to bestow or to imitate.

Taouist and Buddhist ceremonies are strangely mingled in all the superstitious observances practised by the great majority of the people of China, and yet the advent of Buddhism is comparatively modern. It was unknown to Confucius, and according to popular tradition owes its introduction to an imperial dream (the Chinese have always had great faith in dreams and omens). During the first century of our era the Emperor Mingti, in obedience to a vision, sent ambassadors to the West to bring thence a new god who had appeared among men. The results of the pious expedition were the image, sacred books, and priests of Buddha. The priests sought zealously to propagate the new faith, but several centuries elapsed before it became permanently rooted in the empire. Its followers were alternately patronised and persecuted. The doctrine of transmigration of the soul after death through the bodies of inferior animals and its ultimate perfection and absorption in Nirvâna became at last a fixed belief. Temples, monasteries, and shrines were erected, and sacred relics of Buddha, in the shape of a tooth, a footprint, even a hair of his head, were eagerly worshipped by the people. So far as the people were concerned, the Buddhist found virgin soil overgrown with the rank weeds of Taouism. The worship of Confucius belonged mainly to the State and to the *literati*. The people were prohibited under pain of death from practising the rights or taking part in the ceremonials of State worship. It would be folly to say that the new faith was readily embraced by the masses, who were then, and remain to the present day, wedded to their ancient superstitions. The attractive ritual and visible tokens of the Buddhist religion, after the lapse of generations, supplied a want, and the new faith was engrafted on the old in a form modified and adapted to the national prejudices.

In Chinese Buddhist temples the Hindoo divinities are relegated to very inferior positions. They guard the temple doors of Buddha and his disciples, and receive no part of the worship. The supreme power is assigned to Buddha.

In Thibet alone there is a Buddhist hierarchy invested with political power. The Grand Lama is the Pope of the Church, the living Buddha, who is supposed by the people to be incarnate in him. The spirit of Buddha is believed to animate a human body perpetually; when the body fails and the spirit ceases to breathe an infant into whom the sacred spirit passes is selected by the priests. Subject to the Emperor of China, the Grand Lama rules Thibet. In China the priests are not only invested with no political power, but as an order they are viewed with contempt by the literary and governing classes.

There are two great divisions of Buddhists, the northern and southern. Those in Siam, Cambodia, Ceylon, and Birmah have their sacred books in the Pali language, while the works in China and Thibet are translations from the Sanscrit. In the latter also there are certain fables and deities introduced which have no place in the literature of southern Buddhism.

In Peking several large monasteries of Mongolian and Thibetan Buddhists are supported at the expense of the Government. In many other quarters of the empire similar establishments are endowed and maintained by the rents and produce of imperial lands. But by far the greater number of temples and monasteries are upheld by voluntary offerings from the people, and by the mendicancy of the monks and bonzes.

Shâkyamuni Buddha, the great founder of the sect, who lived about a century before Confucius, died at a ripe old age, after having gained many disciples. His remains have become so sacred that the dust of his feet, if it could be found, would be enclosed in some magnificent shrine and receive the constant adoration of thousands of his followers. Pagodas in China are believed by some writers to have been erected over relics of Buddha.* Pagodas are now set up simply as ornaments in temple

---

* This opinion is not confirmed. Pagodas, in most instances, have been placed on the banks of rivers, in such positions as to command an extensive view of the windings of the stream, as well as of the country. This is notably the case in provinces anciently exposed to invasion. They may, therefore, have been intended as watch-towers.

BUDDHIST PRIEST.

Page 200.

grounds and gardens, and the ancient structures of this sort are superstitiously regarded as objects which ward off evil from their vicinage.

The sacredness of Shâkyamuni will be understood when some of his antecedents are pointed out. Before his advent on earth as the Hindoo reformer he was no stranger to our terrestrial sphere; he had appeared at least five hundred times in forms as varied as the number of his visits to earth. Sometimes he basked in the sun as a snake, a plant, or butterfly; his later births made him acquainted with the brute creation, and after countless ages he became man in the person of Shâkyamuni Buddha. It is related that he was even in early life given to solitude and contemplation. The efforts of his father to win him from his lonely meditations, to take a part in the affairs of the kingdom, were unavailing. He finally left his home for the deep recesses of the forests, where he elaborated that ascetic religion which has since borne his name. Here he learned to conquer all the passions, which he recognised as the sole cause of human misery, and steeped in profound meditation great peace filled his soul and he emerged from the wilderness perfectly purified to preach his new faith. Among those moved by his fervour were women, but for a long time he refused to admit them as his followers. There can be no doubt that either Buddha or his disciples relented, as women at last became nuns of the order.

It must be said, in justice to the founder of this faith, that its progress has been marked by degeneracy. It has lost much of its primitive purity by the addition of absurd dogmas and by the use of images in the temples. Buddhism was a reform of the old Hindoo Church, which sought to abolish caste and render all races equal before God. It is the Lutheranism of the Hindoo Church, and its moral code is indeed of a very high order.

The tenth law, totally disregarded by the Buddhists of China, is, "Thou shalt not have in thy private possession either a metal figure (idol), or gold, or silver, or any valuable thing." There are idols in every temple, and avaricious men among all ranks of the priesthood. Like the Taouists, the bonzes are unintelligent, and their ranks are recruited from the lowest orders of the people; they spend their days in idleness, unless when exorcising spirits, burning incense, counting charms for the cure of the sick, or repeating litanies over the dead. The most imposing Buddhist ceremonial, such as may be witnessed morning and evening at the Mongol Lamasary in the metropolis, is a performance without any definite object. Those who engage in it are the priests only, who have nothing else to do, and who, after the chanting is over, seem not unwilling to repair to their private apartments to gamble or to smoke.

The Buddhist priest of Southern China wears a long yellow robe with very wide sleeves, and carries a rosary round his neck, which enables him to keep a daily reckoning with Heaven; his head is shaved, and his features are those expressive of weakness of character, or something decidedly worse. No foreigner would care to trust him out of sight with a coin, far less with the future welfare of his soul. There are, however, exceptions—men who are intelligent and devout—but they are far from numerous.

Buddhist monasteries are pleasant resting-places; many of them are built among scenes the most romantic and beautiful, perched on precipitous rocks in richly wooded ravines, gay with the bloom of azaleas and the graceful leaves of gigantic ferns. But the beating of gongs and drums, ringing of bells, and smoke of incense at early morning and at intervals during the day, detract from the charm of a lengthened sojourn with the monks.

In order to form some impression of the outward aspect of Buddhism in China, let the reader imagine he is entering a Buddhist temple near to the highway. The building is of the ordinary Chinese form, having a portico supported by wooden pillars adorned with sacred texts; the roof resembles that of a tent, is beautifully tiled and ornamented with rampant dragons along the central ridge. The gateway is spacious and inviting, and flanked by stone lions seated on pedestals. These are emblematical of the moral power of Buddha. Resting in the cool shade are groups of half-naked mendicants, among whom may be seen one or two lepers. Nothing can be more revolting to a human sufferer than to be imprisoned in such bodies. To see and feel the slow death paralysing and destroying their members one by one; the fingers that ever responded to the slightest wish crumbling into dust; the feet stiff and palsied with decay so slow, so bitterly slow, yet so certain, works the canker that many a poor wretch in utter despair ends his days by suicide.

Within the temple gate, looking out with a calm benignity that may soothe the misery of the motley crowd of beggars, are the clay images of the incarnate Buddhas—sometimes three, sometimes five. They are painted and plated with gold that sparkles in the dim light of the inner shrine. On the right and left, close to the doorway, stand the guardians of the faith. These are Hindoo deities of gigantic proportions, supposed to be posted round the sacred Mount Meru. The central shrine has an altar placed in front of the holy ones and covered with offerings and incense vases. Before this the priests kneel to invoke the favour of Buddha for themselves, or pray that some soul that has passed on its way may gain a free entrance to the paradise of the West. It may be a poor peasant has entered to consult his fate in some difficulty that is casting a dark shadow athwart his life. He places an offering of sweet cakes, and lights the incense stick that fragrant odours may fill the nostrils of the gods, and, devoutly kneeling, he bows before the images; stretching his eager hands towards the altar he seizes two pieces of bamboo, each flat on one side and round on the other, these he tosses into the air, allowing them to fall to the ground, and the positions in which they lie determine his fate. Sometimes in order to bribe the idols he will offer them spirits, as he has a faint notion they were once mortal.

Many saints and demi-gods figure in the Buddhist magiarchy, whose effigies are scattered over the courts and chambers of the temples and monasteries. The largest establishments, unlike the one described, have many courts and halls, and are built after the plan of the ordinary dwellings, the place most sacred being reserved for the holy ones. Kwan-yin, sometimes a male, sometimes a female divinity, is greatly worshipped among the northern Buddhists. She is commonly called the Goddess of Mercy, and her attributes are not unlike those accorded to the Virgin by Roman Catholics. The spiritual watchword of the Buddhists of China, Dr. Eitel remarks, is "Westward, Ho," for this very sufficient reason, that, mixed up with the notion of Nirvâna, or ultimate absorption into nihility, they have the dogma of a blessed immortality among the gods in the pure sunless western paradise; a region filled with lakes with golden sands, gigantic lotus flowers breathing fragrance around, enchanting harmony of tinkling bells, and birds more musical than the nightingale, dazzling light and purified immortals. But the vulgar notion of this realm of bliss is not so transcendently refined; the popular belief gives prominence to the torments of the hell or purgatory which finds a place in the Buddhist creed. The doctrine of transmigration is viewed by the lower orders as the means which shall secure them against a repetition of their sufferings on earth, and an entrance into a sort of China beyond the grave, where they may possibly exercise the power and secure the emoluments of a Mandarin. The poor will even sell themselves as substitutes to suffer death, provided before the hour of execution they are fêted and attired in the robes of a Mandarin, believing that they will wear them in a future state.

The other religions of China are in no way mixed up with the three national systems, and their adherents appear to have a more intelligent knowledge of the faiths which they profess, as they seldom take part in rites of systems other than their own. Of these the Mohammedans are most numerous, more especially in the northern provinces, where they exist in such numbers as to threaten the imperial power with their frequent and bloody rebellions.

The most recent Mohammedan rising which ravaged the north-western regions of the empire and spread into Turkestan has only been suppressed within the past five years.

So thoroughly aloof do the followers of Islam keep from the Pagan Chinese that the latter look upon them as people of a different nationality, with whom they even refuse to intermarry, and who are known to them as Hwei-hwei. They are supposed to be descended from a tribe of Tartars who aided the Chinese in quelling a revolt during the Tang dynasty, and afterwards settled in the country. Independent of these northern Mohammedans there are numerous native converts to the faith scattered over the central and southern provinces.

The native Roman Catholics of China are said to number more than a million.

Protestant missions have not met with so great a success. The Roman missionaries boast that theirs is the pure primitive form of the Christian religion, and this is not without its effect upon a people whose reverence for antiquity is unparalleled in any other part of the world. But they also hold the door of their Church wider open that all may enter, from whatever motives they choose; or, to take a more moderate view, they are not so strict in the examination of their converts, and in determining whether they have really an intelligent and honest belief in Christ. It is not necessary that the convert should absolutely discard all his own faith in "Feng-Shui," and in the power of images. At his new shrine he is introduced to the Virgin carrying the child, whose appearance and attributes are so similar to those of his own Kwan-yin—the Goddess of Mercy—that in his ignorance he may suppose the new faith after all is but a modification of the old.

It would therefore seem, if the true significance of conversion be taken into account, that the number of converts set down by zealous Roman Catholic missionaries may be largely overstated. It cannot be denied that the priests, many of them, are self-sacrificing, earnest propagandists. They expose themselves to great dangers in travelling through the interior of the country, and accordingly observe the strictest secrecy in regard to their movements. Unlike the majority of Protestant missionaries, it is their custom to adopt the native tonsure and dress—a very questionable policy, as the deception implied is apt to engender distrust and suspicion in the minds of the Chinese. Their mission stations are found scattered over almost every province, and their small chapels, under the control of ordained native priests, are very numerous, and are decked inside with pictures, images, and such adornments as appeal to the senses of a superstitious people. They have also many schools and establishments for the rescue and training of female children, who in time become the wives of the converts.

The Roman Catholic cathedrals which have been erected in one or two of the chief cities are viewed with disfavour by the authorities, as their towers rise high above the most sacred edifices of the country and dwarf the dignity of the loftiest palaces and other State buildings. Theirs is a system which presents to the heathen something visible and tangible in the form of the objects of its worship; ours, on the other hand, depends for its diffusion not only on the faith and zeal of the teacher but also upon his power to present great truths of Christianity in an acceptable form to a people who are not without culture.

An intimate acquaintance with the language and literature of the Chinese, as well as with their peculiar phases of thought, ought to be acquired by the missionary before he ventures upon his task of evangelisation. A scholarly and uniform translation of the Scriptures, such as that completed by Bishop Burdon, and a uniform rendering of the name of God such as would be recognised and used by all denominations of Christian missionaries, would also prove of the greatest service in spreading the knowledge of our religion among the literary and governing classes of the empire.

Everything in the form of division or sectarianism ought surely to be discarded, and the truths of Christianity presented broadly to a people whose forms of faith have been established for so many ages, and whose religious literature has made them familiar with the titles and attributes of all their own divinities. The Chinese themselves are not remarkable for simple uniformity of belief; their ethical systems are by no means the same in different quarters of the land. The Buddhists are divided into sects more or less orthodox in their belief, that is, in conformity with the primitive dogmas of the Church.

The Confucianists are an **exception**; they practise the same rites and ceremonies everywhere, and this renders them, as a class, less accessible to the influences of western religion and more liable to ridicule its teachers when they perceive that they are not of one opinion in regard to the doctrines they advance. The shades of Christian belief are not so important that they should be displayed and insisted upon so much abroad, where their existence is apt to weaken and paralyse the efforts of the missionaries.

The deep-rooted superstitions of the Chinese are well illustrated in the following dialogue on the subject of "Feng-Shui," or "Geomancy," between an European and an intelligent native:—

Foreigner—" May I ask what geomancers are employed for?"

Native—" Geomancers* are employed to examine whether a house or piece of land is suitable or otherwise to the person wishing to buy it. They are called in also to determine whether in repairing a house, in building at cemeteries, in moving an old grave or opening a new one, in executing a wall, or in doing anything involving the displacement of earth, any hindrance exists to the work being proceeded with. Sometimes when faith in geomancers is not very strong, their aid is not sought in such a simple matter; but in everything connected with graves the universal custom is to employ them, hence there is no region without its geomancers."

* Called in China "Professors of Feng-Shui."

F.—"What do the geomancers examine into, and wherein do they guide those who hire them?"

N.—"They examine into the good or bad luck of a place, and they guide their employers to the attaining the one and avoiding the other. In examining the 'Feng-Shui' of a house or piece of land, the first thing done is to inquire for 'the eight characters' of the applicant (*i.e.*, the two characters indicating respectively the year, month, day, and hour of birth), and then to see if they agree with the position (also indicated by eight characters) of the house or land. This is done according to the male and female principles of nature and the five elements. Besides this, the feng-shui of the house or piece of land is determined by itself, without reference to any individual. The four points of the compass, the eight points of the position, the ten celestial stems and the twelve horary characters (which are all marked on the Chinese compass invariably used in this operation) are each associated with lucky and unlucky deities, the latter being the more numerous. If through ignorance any one should offend against these it would be difficult to avoid calamity. The one most to be afraid of is Fei-Shui, the god of the year, who is very malignant. If he be offended, calamity must ensue; hence the proverb often applied to a bad tempered and tyrannical man, 'Don't move the earth at Fai-Shui's head.' There is a host of deities of this kind, and as they change from year to year, from month to month, their different positions cannot be ascertained without the most careful examinations and calculations.

"With reference to houses and lands, there are many other points that must enter into the geomancer's calculations. In the case of houses the most important are, that the principal house,* such as dwellings of Mandarins, be lofty, and the other buildings, those of the people, low; that neither exactly opposite the outside site, nor on either side of it, shall there be a temple of any kind; that the private drains be arranged according to geomantic principles; that a certain number of doors follow each other in succession, never exactly in line, and that the windows be on certain sides of the houses; the differences in the height of the ground must be taken into consideration, and the neighbours' roofs must be examined lest there be anything thereon to interfere with the feng-shui of the house in question.†

"In the case of land, the secret influences‡ that come and go, the height and evenness of it, on which side the hillocks are to be raised, the low

---

* The Chinese houses of the better class consist of a collection of buildings arranged around courtyards in the form of a square, the principal house being that which faces the south. The side houses, which are smaller, face the east and west. In large houses there are many courtyards of this kind, extending one behind the other.

† The houses of the Chinese are so arranged that chimneys are never needed. Foreigners, however, in the north of China, can no more do without chimneys than they can do without fires. Hence the Chinese (in Peking at least) shun, as much as possible, living next door to a house occupied by a foreigner, the roofs of which are dotted with chimneys, built simply with a view to comfort and convenience with a reckless disregard of all the laws of Feng-Shui.

‡ These influences must be very "secret," one would think, to the geomancer, and to everybody else; for the literal translation of the terms used to express them are, "The Coming Dragon, the Departing Pulse, the Breath of the Earth, and the Power of the Earth."

parts filled in, in what direction the water is to flow off, and how the trees are to be planted, &c., are all points that are intimately connected with the Feng-Shui of the place.

"In the case of cemeteries much more has to be attended to, such as how to find the dragon, how to point out the spot to be opened for the grave, how to determine which shall be the back and which shall be the front, how to lay out the sacrificial ground; in burying, the day and hour of breaking ground and the day and hour of burial must be carefully regulated according to the character of the position of the cemetery, the eight characters of the deceased and those of his surviving relatives. If no obstacle is found to exist, then, and then only, can the interment take place.

"Changing the place of burial is a much more troublesome business than fixing upon one in the first instance. The position in a geomantic sense of the temporary grave being different from that of the permanent cemetery, the peculiar character of the year (also in the same sense) may not allow of the change being made. In consequence of this it frequently happens that parents cannot be permanently buried for many years after death.*

---

* Instances of this are constantly occurring among rich men who can afford to waste money on the professors of Feng-Shui, who seem as clever at getting hold of the money of such individuals as some of our own lawyers in Chancery. A story is told of a certain rich man who died, leaving a large property to his two sons, between whom it was equally divided. After some time the sons began to look out for a piece of ground for a cemetery, and one was bought for the purpose. The professors of Feng-Shui allowed thus far, but no further. In the erection of buildings on the cemetery no agreement could be come to; those proposed by the geomancers employed by one son being invariably rejected by those employed by the other. Years passed; money

"Even cemeteries that have actually been bought and put in order for permanent use are sometimes abandoned at the word of the geomancer. Something goes wrong in the family; a geomancer is called in, he makes inquiry into the state of the family cemetery, and finds its 'position' or its buildings unpropitious, and he recommends another piece of land with better geomantic influences. The land first bought is abandoned, and, though interments may actually have taken place, the coffins are all moved to the new cemetery. Is not this a piece of folly? But, after all, it is only rich fools who, without any understanding of true philosophy, take this stupid method of seeking good luck and avoiding bad luck."

F.—"Is there any result of all this talk of the geomancers about good and bad luck?"

N.—"This is a thing that cannot be determined. It depends altogether on how a man likes to think about it. If after calling a geomancer a man's family keeps in health, his property in peace, and he meets generally with success in his undertakings, he attributes it all to the merit of the geomancer, and says

---

was all the while being frittered away on the erection and the changing of buildings, and the only result of all was that both sons were brought to beggary, and the corpse of their old father was still unburied. This case can occur, of course, only among the rich; but every one, rich or poor, is more or less under the influence of this wretched superstition. It is, moreover, a melancholy fact that China contains nothing within itself to counteract it. The more educated a man is in China (as education goes in this country), the more is he under the power of the belief in Feng-Shui. Whatever attempt (and it is a very feeble one) is made at literality in the conversation given in the text, is due to the writer having been long in the employ of a foreigner, and to his writing this paper for foreign eyes.

it is owing either to the change rightly made on the gate or to the proper building of his wall. If any of the family is successful at the examinations, or obtains office under Government, the geomancer again gets the credit, and the luck is attributed to the good influences of the cemetery. If, on the other hand, after the geomancer's visit sickness or trouble come upon the family, it is laid at once either to the malice or to the ignorance of the geomancer, and another is called in. If trouble still continues, it is attributed to something wrong about the cemetery. Such people, however, are ignorant of what really governs the actions of men, and know nothing, and believe in nothing but Feng-Shui. Although it brings them no profit, they cannot shake off their belief in it. Is not this a case of self-deception?"

F.—"I see that most of the people of China believe in Feng-Shui; if there is really no good to be got from it, why should so many believe in it?"

N.—"People do not believe in it for any good that is to be got out of it, but simply because it has become a custom. If, as is the universal belief, such a malignant demon as Fai-Shui exists, who will venture to risk offending him? It is better to believe, if thereby you may avoid calamity, than to suffer from want of faith. And so the common saying is, It is better to believe that these things exist than to reject all faith in them. Every man naturally shrinks from calamity, and if the whereabouts of unlucky demons is plainly pointed out to us, who will venture to run right in their teeth? Hence in China believers believe in Feng-Shui, and unbelievers believe in it; every one thinks like his neighbour, and thus a custom is established. Although a man may be fully convinced that calamity and prosperity are not necessarily connected with this, yet it is impossible not to comply with the custom. If a reformer were to arise to expose the folly of Feng-Shui everybody would say he was mad, and would regard him as a foreigner. Custom, then, rather than any benefit obtained, is the foundation of people's faith in Feng-Shui."*

* The true "foundation" of Feng-Shui lies in the ignorance of the Chinese of the origin of matter, or of the laws of physical science. Pantheism is, in fact, the true source of this superstition, and until right views are instilled into the minds of the Chinese about the Creator, and the laws by which He sustains the universe, there is little hope of change. Foreigners may laugh at Feng-Shui and all its rules and fancies, but it is a real power in China, and so long as it exists, progress is hardly possible. England is interested in the development of trade in China; Feng-Shui, however, stands in the way.

CHAPTER IX.

AGRICULTURE.

Rice cultivation—Terracing hills—Irrigation—Agricultural implements—Tea culture and manufacture—Black teas—Green teas—Tea season—Sugar—The mulberry—The silkworm—Silk—The loom—Silk embroidery.

THE genius of the Chinese displays itself conspicuously in the perfection to which they have brought the cultivation of products grown in different parts of the empire, especially the cultivation of rice.

Rich harvests are gathered, not only in the low-lying fertile plains, but on the high-lands and hill-sides, which are terraced, tilled, and sown with cereals to an extent unknown in other lands. Terraces cut on a steep declivity are ingeniously faced with stone to prevent the soil breaking down with rain. The stone facing economises space, and enables the farmer to carry tillage to the extreme edge of each terrace, leaving spaces between the steps not wider than the ordinary furrows of a field. No toil is spared to render the hills productive by irrigation and manuring. In some instances the water is led from higher springs by a series of bamboo ducts, which may be readily withdrawn when the ripening crop requires dry soil.

The success of the rice crop, upon which so many millions of Chinese depend for food, is owing in some measure to the native system of irrigation, which supplements the natural or tidal rise of the rivers. The most productive regions are nevertheless those directly dependent upon the overflow of the great streams, such as the Yangtsze and Hwang-ho, which performs the twofold function of fertilising the soil by depositing alluvium and flooding the fields with the water necessary for the early growth of rice.

The Chinese have a number of different contrivances for raising water, which are in constant use when the streams have fallen unusually low. One of the most ingenious machines is the chain-pump, which bears some resemblance to the Spanish Norea, although it is less primitive and more serviceable. The Chinese chain-pump consists of a long straight wooden gutter with an axle at its upper end round which a chain revolves. This axle is fitted with three or four spokes that serve as treadles for the feet of the labourer who sets the pump agoing, or with two long handles attached to cranks. At the lower extremity of the gutter is a roller, over which the endless chain is passed. This chain supports an array of diaphragms fixed at intervals of about one foot apart, these diaphragms fitting loosely into the gutter. The pump, when in action, is placed slanting against the bank of the canal with its lower end in the water, so as, when set in motion by the man stepping on the treadles, to force the water up by the action of the diaphragms. A continuous stream thus flows into the fields on the higher level. At first it is puzzling to see men at work on these machines; one is astonished, when following some footpath through the fields, to descry in the distance a number of naked savages, dancing up and down like a troop of bushmen preparing for an attack. One is apt to imagine that the Chinese, after all, find in dancing not an insane foreign amusement, but an agreeable national pastime, as sounds of mirth float upon the wind. Closer inspection dispels the illusion. The men, though they laugh merrily, are clinging to their bamboo rails, busily at work upon the little treadmills, whence the water flows over the fields already green with the blades of young rice.

These rice-fields have been carefully prepared before seed-time. The irrigation canals by which they are intersected have been robbed of their deposit of alluvium to spread over the surface.

Most ingenious are the devices resorted to in order to replace what the soil has lost by the last crop. After harvest the stubble is ploughed up and gathered into little mounds, over each of these the farmer builds a furnace of sods in which to burn roots and refuse, and afterwards ploughs the ash into the soil. But he has carried his economy further; the paths through his fields are dotted with little shelters for the comfort and convenience of wayfarers who may care to add to his store of manure. Not far from his hut is a deep pit securely hedged round with stone. The filling of this precious pit swallows up all the farmer's spare capital and leisure. His poor dependents scour the surrounding villages in search of dung to fill it. Garbage, offal, old plaster, dust of dwellings, the shavings of the human head and face, are all eagerly bought and consigned to it to ripen for his fields or vegetable gardens. It thus happens that the atmosphere of Chinese farming life is far from fragrant. In traversing the country, indeed, it becomes necessary to study the wind, and give a wide berth to the youngest and most promising grain.

Rice culture, as practised by the Chinese, is an occupation laborious and often unhealthy. It is customary to soak all kinds of seed before planting, and rice forms no exception to the rule. After soaking until sufficiently swollen it is sown broadcast in richly-manured beds, after which the ground is flooded with water. The seed is then ploughed in, harrowed and hoed, the labourers toiling all day long through the mud and water, exposed to the hot sun. The result is that fever is very prevalent during spring in the marshy rice-growing regions, and the poor, who depend upon their toil for bread, are exposed to great privation and suffering. Medical missionaries in such lands would find many to care for, and would win such gratitude as the Chinese ungrudgingly bestow on those who befriend them. More than that, they would open the way into many a true, simple heart for the love of the greater Physician. Day after day the poor husbandmen toil, falling by the malaria from the soil. When the rice stands about six inches above water, the plants are removed and bedded out in the fields, which have been transformed into huge basins knee-deep in mud. It is surprising how deftly the planting out is managed, and how regularly the rows are set in the soft mud. Water is again led on, and retained in the banked-up fields until the rice has attained nearly its full height, when the water is allowed to drain off and evaporate. The first harvest is reaped, after which the soil is again turned over for sowing the second crop, which is gathered in October.

The implements used in husbandry are of the simplest construction. The plough has no coulter, and only one handle, and with the exception of one piece of iron on the share, is made entirely of wood. When the soil is stiff, as many as four bullocks, or a pair of donkeys or mules and a pair of bullocks, are yoked; but as a rule one or two animals are sufficient for each plough. The old story that the farmer yokes a donkey and his wife to the plough is a clumsy fiction, as the women can be much more usefully employed in weeding, hoeing, or in domestic duties. A simple harrow, on which the labourer rests his weight, is used to break the sods. Two or three varieties of rakes, hoes, reaping hooks, and knives make up the tools employed in preparing the land and harvesting.

Thrashing is effected by treading out with oxen, or by the flail, similar to that still used in some parts of England. Husking is done in a hand-mill, composed of two circular stones placed horizontally one above the other. The upper one, pierced with a large hole through which the grain is passed, is roughened on its under surface, and made to revolve above and in contact with the lower stone.

Rice is reduced to flour in granite mortars, having granite pestles attached to long wooden levers placed horizontally and worked by the foot; or where water-power can be obtained, the mortars are ranged in rows and set in motion by a main axle furnished with a series of short arms. Mills driven by water, in which large stones are employed similar to those in use with us, are not unknown in China.

Enormous quantities of rice are grown in the southern provinces, and partly shipped to the north, where the supply of millet is insufficient. When the supply falls short of the demand, as has frequently happened in modern times, large quantities of rice are imported from Siam and Cochin China. But the island of Formosa alone contributes annually about 20,000 tons to the mainland.

The cultivation of the tea plant and preparation of the leaf forms the chief industry of the people in certain districts in China. These are, however, limited in extent when compared to the vast area over which the plant is now grown as a product of secondary importance.

China no longer monopolises the trade. The fragrant leaf is grown in Assam, Japan, the island of Formosa, and indeed far beyond the geographical limits originally assigned to it. For all that, tea seems still to reach its greatest perfection, and to yield the beverage most delicately aromatic, when reared amid the romantic scenery of the Bohea Hills, in the north of the Chinese province of Fukien. When planted on the low-lying plains, however carefully tended, the leaf degenerates, becomes coarse, rank, and unprofitable.

A Chinese tea plantation, as the writer has witnessed it among the hills of Fukien, presents a scene at once striking and picturesque. The hills, covered with the vivid green of the spring leaves, slope gently down to valleys where the morning mist lies, or, raised by the passing wind, is swept upward, crowning bamboo-clad heights with wreaths of white vapour. In the distance can be descried, down through an open glen, the dim outlines of rice-fields lying partially under water. On the left a Buddhist temple rears its brightly coloured roof beneath the shade of a grove of bamboo, and close at hand stands the rustic abode of the planter, whose old straw thatch, like a neglected grave-mound, is covered with patches of grass, moss, and weeds. The cotter and his family are out tending the tea plants. There has been a heavy fall of dew, that lies like beads of glass upon the leaves.

There are no flowers on the ordinary tea plant; it is grown simply for its leaves. Special plants are reserved for seeding. Two varieties of the tea-shrub exist in China, *Thea Bohea*, and *Thea Viridis*, from each of which the black and green teas of commerce are manufactured.

It may be said of tea culture, as of nearly all Chinese industries, that indications of its vastness and commercial importance are difficult to discover. The farms are invariably small, and the ground devoted to the shrub is frequently that which proves unfit for the growth of rice. The planters dwell in rude huts, and labour with their hands over their modest holdings.* There are no vast estates and imposing tea factories owned by millionaires and blackened by the smoke of engines. The whole process, from planting to packing in chests, to supply two-thirds of the world with this

---

* The largest plantations are found at the Peeling Hills, near Foo chow-fu. They are said to be owned by Cantonese compradors in the pay of foreigners.

chief of modern luxuries, is managed by hand labour, and in this respect is purely Chinese.

The plant itself is small, rarely exceeding four feet in height; the fields in which it is bedded, as a rule, form part only of the soil tilled and tended by each family. Even in provinces which supply the bulk of the annual crop, this industry seems to be altogether of secondary importance. The system pursued, when it is understood, throws some light on the economy of the people. The peasant portions out his soil to suit the nature and rotation of his crops, making the most of every foot of farm-land under his care. He is equally careful to portion out his time so that the mulberry, bamboo, tea, and rice, may each be turned to account at the proper season without interfering one with the other.

His old-fashioned methodical way enables him to get more out of his farm and his servants than could possibly fall to the lot of any foreigner, aided by the whirr of steam and the science of manuring. There is no fuss about his management; a mutual traditional understanding exists between farmer and farm-land, between master and slave. The ground is tickled and coaxed with the smallest of ploughs and gentlest of harrows, it is fed with all sorts of dainties in the shape of manure, and it yields a bountiful return in its own good time.

The first tea leaves picked in the early spring are the finest, and are reserved to make the tea used in China by the rich to bestow as presents, or to infuse for their favoured guests. The second and third pickings take place about the end of

April. After the leaves have been gathered and partially sun-dried, the farmer repairs with them in baskets to the village fair, where they are sold to native brokers. Or it may be he has in his necessity accepted an advance on his crop, which has to be paid off, or the entire stock is handed over to the moneyed dealer. When the broker has collected a sufficient quantity from the growers, the leaves are all mixed together and prepared for firing. The cooking is varied according to the sort of tea to be produced. Difference in quality is also obtained by studying the time of picking, the oldest leaves making the coarsest tea.

Black congou tea is most largely exported. It is produced by exposing the fresh leaves to the action of the sun and air for about two days, after which they are turned over and again exposed for two hours. The juice is then partly expressed from the leaves to prepare them for the first firing, which lasts about twenty minutes. This is effected in iron pans about four feet diameter, built above a brick oven, and set in a slanting position towards the labourer, who keeps constantly turning over the leaves with his hands. This operation is sometimes effected by the grower before disposing of his crop to the manufacturer. The factories are built in the tea regions, or at the ports where the teas are finished and packed for exportation. The leaves are subjected to a series of short firings, picking, sifting, and rolling in the hands. They are also sorted into qualities by winnowing. The heaviest and best twisted or most compact leaves make the finest congou.

Women and children are employed in picking or

removing stalks, inferior leaves, and refuse from the finer qualities of tea.

Black teas are dried for packing in bamboo baskets over charcoal fires, and are weighed and placed in the well-known lead-lined dragon bedizened chests, while still hot. It is of the greatest importance to have the leaves made perfectly dry to the core, to prevent fermentation during the long voyage.

All the black teas of commerce are prepared as described, with differences slight but important in the details of manipulation. Oolong, for instance, is not exposed to the sun before firing.

Pekoe is made of the young leaf-buds, and after repeated firings is subjected to a short charcoal drying.

Special aromas are imparted to teas by scenting them with the flowers of the *Cloranthus inconspicuus* and *Gardenia florida*, &c.

Green teas are manufactured from the same leaves as the black; but they are roasted in the pans over a brisk wood fire immediately after they have been gathered. After five minutes' firing they are removed from the pans and rolled into balls by hand, slight pressure being applied to get rid of some of the juice. The leaves are then unpacked and spread on bamboo trays, after which they are again roasted above a slow, steady fire, the leaves being kept in constant motion by the hands. Again they are rolled, twisted, opened out, and finally fired for the last time. The leaves have then a dull green colour. During the last firing it is customary to add colouring matter made up of gypsum, Prussian blue, and turmeric, to give a facing to the leaves.

Gunpowder teas are differently treated in rolling. The globose form which characterises the finished leaf is obtained by rolling with the feet upon a brick floor.

A quantity of leaves are wrapped tightly up in a hempen bag, so as to form a ball of about one foot in diameter. This ball is tossed and rolled beneath the feet of a workman, who supports himself by hanging to a cross-bar above his head. The bag gradually loosens, and has to be twisted tight at the neck, and again rolled under foot until it becomes perfectly hard and compact. It will then be found that the leaves have become pellet-shaped, and are ready for sifting and assorting according to size.

Tea prepared for exportation is sold in "chops," or parcels of various quantities, containing some of them fifteen hundred or two thousand half chests. These parcels are made up to suit the wants of foreign merchants, and differ in quality and price as well as in quantity. Some of them contain fifteen hundred or two thousand half chests. The weight of a single chest is about 90 lbs., half chest about 45 lbs., and quarter chest 21 lbs.

The opening of the tea season, which takes place generally in May, is an event of the greatest importance to native and foreign merchants. It is then that the former are eager to sell, as they may have bought beyond the limit of their capital, and the latter quite as anxious to buy. It is the opening transactions that rule the market; the Chinese, patient and unimpulsive, bide their time, holding on for high prices, and frequently getting them. The guild merchants combine, and by a display of

CANTON TEA MERCHANTS.

Page 226.

leisurely unconcern defeat the foreigners, who, sanguine of ultimate gain by being first in the home market, at last yield and buy. This, however, seldom happens until the **Chinese** holders have modified their prices, and made some show of compromise.

The tea trade is a very speculative one; not so much so now-a-days as it used to be before China was linked to the telegraphic system of the world. The arrival of the mail carrying the news of the opening of the London market after the arrival of the first shipments of new seasons' teas was an event waited for with terrible anxiety, and one which decided the fate of many who had been toiling for years on the shores of China. The difference of a penny a pound one way or the other would decide whether the long-cherished vision of a competency and a snug home in England was at last to be realised, or to be postponed indefinitely.

According to our English notions of propriety, sugar should always be mixed with a cup of tea. The Chinese look upon this as a most barbarous practice, as it spoils the delicate flavour of the infusion. They cannot understand that the flavour is too pungent for English palates. But to them the use of milk or cream in any way whatever by persons out of arms is equally incomprehensible, more especially as this food of babes is used by foreign nations to nurture fierce, full-grown, turbulent men. Sugar, although it is not used in tea, is extensively grown and manufactured by the Chinese in some of the southern provinces of the empire and in the island of Formosa. It has become recently an important article of commerce at Swatow, Amoy, and Takow.

The mode of cultivating the cane, although fairly successful, falls short of that practised by the European planters of Province Wellesly in the Malayan Peninsula. Chinese crushing-mills are rude and comparatively costly. The mill consists of two upright granite rollers placed closely together on their axles, and driven by cog-wheels set agoing by a team of oxen. The mill-owners of Formosa are not the poor growers of the cane; they are capitalists to whom the farmers pay half their stock of canes as the price of crushing. The result is that the mill soon pays its original cost.

Notwithstanding the rude nature of the tillage and milling the cane, the process of refining the sugar is, if possible, more primitive still. In the Kwangtung province the mill is usually erected on the centre of the plantation, and rented by the grower, who crushes his own cane and refines his own sugar. Others, again, of the small farmers dispose of the cane to manufacturers just as they would tea leaves. The price paid for cane as it stands in the field is about a penny for as much as will produce a pound of the finest sugar, to which has to be added cost of manufacture. Raw brown sugar is sold wholesale for about three farthings a pound.

The cane juice, after it has been boiled and crystallised, is partly refined by what is called the claying process. It is placed in conical earthen jars. These are inverted on other vessels, and left to drain, moist clay being placed round the base and renewed as required. When the jars are removed, the cones of sugar are found to consist of three or four qualities, the top being coarsest, and the base white and crystalline. The molasses drained off by claying is collected and reboiled to form common brown sugar.

Much of the saccharine juice is lost by imperfect crushing. The canes still retain a quantity of juice after passing through the stone rollers, after which they are used as fuel in the boiling process. For all that, the cultivation of sugar in China pays. Swatow alone exports annually about a million piculs* of sugar gathered from many plantations and many mills, each of the latter producing not more than two or three hundred piculs a year.

The cultivation of the mulberry and the production and manufacture of silk have been known to the Chinese from the earliest times. It is recorded that when the Prince Shun, who lived about four thousand years ago, made his tour through the tributary states, the articles of tribute included "the three kinds of silks of different colours suitable for robes." Coming to the more reliable history of Yu, it is stated in the "Shooking" that "the mulberry ground was made fit for silkworms, then the people came down from the heights and occupied the ground below." Various additional notices in the "Classics of Ancient History" prove that the Chinese under Yu, their first emperor, were not only skilful husbandmen, but were acquainted with the art of weaving silken fabrics for clothing. The fame of discovering the cocoon and introducing silk is claimed for the queen of a sovereign named Hwangti, who reigned in China 2600 B.C.

* 1 picul = 133½ lbs.

The queen also had the silk woven into royal robes. The reign of Hwangti, who it is said sat upon the throne for a century, may be relegated to times prehistoric. If we are to believe that he survived the malaria of a marshy country for so long, we have no reason to reject the graceful tribute paid to his queen, a maiden born among the rude strife of feudal states. Let us hope, too, that the fair inventor of silk, Yenfi (for such was her uneuphonious name), who conferred such a priceless boon upon her sex, lived to a good old age, the loved companion of the centenarian ruler.

One can picture the care with which Queen Yenfi watched and fed the worms with mulberry leaves, while they, grateful for her ministry, spun their silken shrouds that were to deck her fair form. At last she discovers the thread of the cocoon, compares it with others, and the truth flashes upon her mind with the inspiration of true genius.

The rude looms used to weave the hempen robes were at length adjusted, and the first lustrous fabric woven from the shroud of a worm. There is a true moral in all this: Yenfi, stooping to learn the habits of so mean a creature, at last rose a wiser and a better-dressed woman.

Although the mythical element which characterises the Chinese classics is not altogether wanting in the above record, there is yet a germ of probability about the tale which tempts the impartial writer to rank Queen Yenfi as one of the greatest women of antiquity.

Whoever may have discovered the secret of the worm and its cocoon, there is something startling in the magnitude of the results of the simple discovery. The worm that must have been regarded as worthless and destructive has proved a source of enormous and abiding wealth to the Chinese as well as to other nations.

The importance of the silk industry has been recognised by the Chinese Government from the earliest times, and made the subject of special legislation.

During the Chow dynasty the inspecting officer who adjusted the price of horses and cattle forbade the people to rear the second brood of silkworms in one season, because, according to astrology, the horse belonged to the same constitution as the silkworm, and they were therefore considered of the same origin. The notion is sufficiently absurd, yet it shows that the attention of State had been drawn by some astute astrologer to the superstition which was supposed to affect the production of silk. Two thousand years ago it was the custom, as it now is, of the empress and her ladies to prepare themselves by fasting, to lay aside their ornaments, and during spring engage in picking mulberry leaves and in feeding silkworms. This was done as an example to the people, who were commanded to cultivate the mulberry trees; and when the cooing doves and crested jays were observed alighting on them, they were to prepare for work—to bring the trays, frames, and baskets for the purpose of gathering leaves for the worms. The empress also prepared the sacrificial robes of silk, and the silk to be used as burnt offering.

Many Chinese works, ancient and modern, are

devoted to the mulberry and silk. The best treatises contain most minute and curious instructions, both regarding the treatment of the plant and the care to be bestowed on the worm. They display, indeed, an exhaustive knowledge of the best modes of cultivating the mulberry; the kind of soil most suitable for its growth, the influence of sun and shade, pruning, grafting, and manuring, as well as the economy by which every twig and leaf, and the wood of exhausted trees may be turned to account. The habits of the silkworm receive, if possible, greater attention at the hands of the authors, who discover in the little toiler the strangest instincts, likings, and aversions, which must be studied by its owner, so as to develop its full energy in spinning the cocoon. The finest qualities of silk are produced in the provinces of Szechuan, Hupeh, Chekiang, and Kiangsi. The Hupeh silk is probably as fine as any produced in the world, but the primitive mode of reeling renders it inferior to that obtained in the south of Europe.

An attempt was recently made by a Chinese silk merchant in the province of Kwangtung to introduce the foreign method of reeling, but he was forced to fall back upon the old plan, as the introduction of an extra wheel or spindle to a machine was the signal for a whole village of reelers to strike work.

Rearing the worm is an operation which must be attended with the greatest care. In a dissertation by a writer named Tseu-Kwang-ki it is stated that when the worms are hatched they must not be touched with anything save the leaf of the mulberry, to which they will instinctively cling, and may thus be placed on the feeding hurdles. **But the leaves** used in lifting the worms must first be heated in the bosom of the woman who tends the grubs. The leaves for early food must be finely shred and spread over rumpled paper, as the grubs object to feed on a plain, smooth surface. But just after hatching, the cards with the young must be inverted above the heated leaves, when the worms, scenting them, will descend; those of them that cannot be induced to leave the card must be condemned as unfit for toil. The apartment in which they are reared has to be fitted with a number of stoves to distribute a uniform heat. It is necessary also that the woman who feeds the grubs should only wear a single garment, so that she may determine by her own feeling how to adjust the temperature to the worms that are not yet robed in silk.

Hatching-time is about the middle of April, and March is the best season to obtain eggs for exportation.

As the worms increase in size, they are distributed over a greater number of bamboo feeding trays, and require leaves less finely shred.

After hatching the worms continue eating for five days, after which they change colour from black to white; when this transformation is effected they again feed on an increased supply of leaves, until they change to a green hue. Their food must again be diminished, and they become yellow, losing appetite; then arrives the first sleep, or torpor, which lasts for two days. When they awake their appetite is not so good, still they feed, and change from yellow to white, from white to green, from green to white, and at last from white to yellow.

After the first torpor they generally eat for four days, and again sleep for two days. The periods of eating and sleeping are repeated four times, when, having gained full strength, the worms proceed to spin their cocoons.

The task of spinning lasts from four to seven days. Long white cocoons yield the finest silk, while those of a dull greenish tint produce a coarser quality.

While the little workers are feeding they display tastes the most fastidious, appearing to be endowed with a delicate perception of smell. The poor silk cultivators are, therefore, compelled to forego, for the time, dwelling in the mingled atmosphere of native perfumes which pervades their dwellings.

The worms sicken under the smell of Chinese cooking, of garlic, opium, or incense. They even strike work and die if they detect their keeper eating ginger or beans. They detect sounds of grief, strife, or any unseemly noise; neither can they suffer wanton conversation, or any taint of uncleanness in their apartment. Free ventilation must be maintained, and the rays of the western sun excluded. Strangers should not enter the apartment, as the worms are apt to leave their hurdles.

Many directions are given as to the best modes of reeling from the cocoons; the common practice is to reel after the worms have been killed, but the best results are said to be obtained while they are yet alive.

The worms are destroyed in three different ways—by exposure to the sun, soaking in salt, and steaming. The latter is the simplest and best method practised in China.

The wages of the reelers is about fourpence a day, or sixpence for every reel of silk wound. Reeling is effected by first finding the ends of the threads of a number of cocoons, passing each thread through a hole in the perforated ladle, with which they are held in position in warm water. The ends are then fixed to the spindle of a simple winding machine. Training is necessary to enable the workmen to reel without damaging the threads by breakage and varying the strain on the cocoons. It is believed, could the Chinese be induced to adopt foreign reeling-machines, the value of their silk would be increased about fifty per cent. One great obstacle stands in the way of the general adoption of such innovations, that is the costly nature of foreign machinery and the poverty of the silk producers. Many of them are peasant farmers, whose capital is laid out in tillage. Rearing the worms, and all the operations connected with producing the raw silk, furnish employment to the women and younger members of the family. Mulberry leaves for feeding are obtained from rows of trees, or shrubs planted between fields where rice or millet is grown. A great part of the silk brought to foreign markets is bought up in small quantities from the farmers at the country fairs, and made up into bales and cargoes by Chinese brokers and merchants. The greatest quantity of raw silk is exported from Shanghai. Some notion of the value of the trade may be gathered from the fact that, in 1873, from Shanghai and Chinkiang alone silk to the value of *Tls. 26,241,405 was exported. The vast importance of the trade to China and Japan will be better

* 3¼ Taels = about 1 pound sterling.

understood when it is known that, in 1875, 85,109 bales of silk were shipped to England and the Continent from the two countries. This leaves out of account the quantity taken by the colonies and America, as well as the enormous supply raised for home consumption in the attire of the men and women of both China and Japan.

There are in China a number of varieties of the mulberry, but the plants most largely cultivated for the food of the silkworm are known as the northern and the southern mulberries. The former is a shrub propagated by bending down the branches, and planting them while still attached to the parent stem. In process of time the suckers strike root, and may be detached to form independent plants. The southern variety takes the form of a tree, and is raised from seed when the berries are ripe; they are washed in water and the seeds dried in the sun, after which they are sown about twelve feet apart along the banks of rice or millet fields, or in rows, so as to admit of millet being planted between. This saves valuable space and shades the young trees. It is said that if the berries are first eaten by a duck, the seed reserved for planting will yield the finest trees.

In three years the plant, if properly manured and tended, will produce useful leaves. After fifteen or twenty years the trees lose their vigour, and must be replaced. The wood is then used in the manufacture of carts, saddle-trees, bows, and agricultural implements. Further economy is observed in manuring the trees with the litter of the silkworms and with ash obtained by burning the prunings and refuse of the trees.

The Chinese loom is simple and ingenious. It is made almost entirely of bamboo, and notwithstanding its imperfections, it enables the weaver to imitate almost any pattern placed before him. The native damasks and flowered satins afford, perhaps, the finest examples of the weaver's skill, although the delicate crapes and soft pongee fabrics of Shangtung display excellences peculiarly their own.

The silk embroiderers of Canton must not be forgotten in our brief review of this most beautiful textile fabric—they who with their nimble fingers so ably supplement the work of the loom. In the city of Canton there are entire neighbourhoods of poor families employed in embroidering the costly robes, breastplates, and backplates of Mandarins and ladies of rank.

The choice fans, screens, furniture covers, and slippers, so largely introduced into our luxurious English homes, are many of them the result of highly skilled and poorly paid Chinese labour. The shops of the embroiderers and the simple cotton dress of the women and children who so deftly ply their needles, form a strange contrast to the brilliant hues of the work that grows under their hands. The streets where they pursue their toil are always narrow, dingy, and many of them so filthy as to suggest the idea that the flowers of the embroidery owe their growth and beauty to the atmosphere of surrounding decay. Pale faces, worn fingers, and scant fare are too often common to those whose exquisite needlework calls forth our warmest admiration. But these poor people take the place of the machines of our own country, many of them repeat the same patterns from childhood to old age, until their eyes grow dim and their hands become palsied at the work.

The designs are beautiful, the colours, too, are so fresh, and the flowers look so real—none the less real that they have been watered with tears that stood upon their petals like summer dew.

The remark has often been made unthinkingly, "It is astonishing how cheaply and cleverly these creatures can work." It is quite as astonishing, and not so satisfactory to inquire, How can they live? They don't live very long some of them; they wither and die, and their places are filled by others. There are plenty of them, and they are never missed beyond the narrow circle of their homes.

Many of the embroiderers are most accomplished imitators. Place before them any picture or design, and they will reproduce it with marvellous fidelity. They manage all this without having enjoyed any advantages of art training, and are infinitely worse paid for it than we would pay the commonest out-door labourer.

Cotton, another Chinese product, is grown most extensively in the regions bordering the great rivers, and is partly exported in the raw state, and partly used to supply the native looms. It is said that the plant is not indigenous, but was introduced for the purposes of manufacture about the year 1000 A.D. from the Tartar province of Sifan.

Hempen garments were used by the peasantry before cotton was brought from the West. Its cultivation must have spread rapidly, as the plant and the mode of dealing with it are described by a native author of the eleventh century thus: " It is planted in the second and third month, and after the shoots appear the field requires to be weeded three times a month. During autumn the plant throws out a yellow flower, and matures its seed-vessels, of which, when ripe, the rind bursts open on all sides disclosing its contents, in appearance like floss-silk."

The ground selected for its growth is usually manured with the mud of rivers and canals, and the seed is sown broadcast about the beginning of May, after which it is trodden into the ground by the feet. The young plants are carefully hoed and tended until about a foot high, when the tops are cut to make shoots.

The Kiangsi cotton, from which the Nankeen cloth is made, is the finest. It is now more extensively exported in the raw state since Manchester goods have found their way into the markets of the maritime provinces, and to a limited extent to the marts inland.

CHAPTER X.

THE GOVERNMENT OF CHINA AND CHINESE POLICY.

Form of government—Central government—Provincial governments—The Peking Boards—Political divisions of the empire—Official responsibility for the crimes of subordinates—Chinese aristocracy—Punishments of crime—Official corruption—Weakness of the central government—The Yunnan mission—Signs of progress.

CHI-HWANG-TI, when he destroyed the power of the vassal princes and established his despotic sway throughout the whole country, founded the form of government which has prevailed since his time, and secured the absolute supremacy of the reigning monarch.

In reviewing the deeds of this great potentate, one cannot fail to remark evidences of genius mingled with childish weakness. He extended his dominions; and while he aspired to the empire of the world became the dupe of sorcerers, and died with their cup of earthly immortality at his lips. He drained the cup in quest of life, and exhausted the resources of his empire to build the great wall, a barrier designed to maintain the integrity of his dominions throughout all generations. But he died, leaving as the last of his dynasty an only son.

The wall is now nothing more than a stupendous monument of misdirected human toil. Internal strife, treachery, discord, and the withdrawal of troops from the passes neutralised its effect. The north-western provinces were thus exposed to the constant inroads of the Tartars, who at last, in 1644, conquered China and founded the present dynasty.

This brief recapitulation of the events which marked the reign of Chi-Hwang-ti is given to show the abortive nature of the mighty plans which he conceived and carried out for the permanent expulsion of the Tartars; to show, also, how he conferred an actual benefit on the Manchu Tartar sovereigns by founding an absolute monarchy, which supplied their invaders with a model for their government, and thereby aided them in the maintenance and extension of their power.

There can be no doubt that the system of government is well adapted to the genius of the people. It is purely patriarchal. The emperor stands in relation to his people as a parent to his children, and is supposed to exercise his sway by Divine prerogative. He is the vicegerent of Heaven, and is worshipped accordingly. The person of the emperor, thus held sacred, is hedged round with mystery. When he is carried abroad among his people they retire to their houses and bar their doors, as they may not look upon him and live. It becomes, therefore, a sacred obligation on the part of the people to render implicit obedience to the emperor thus chosen by Heaven to rule over them.

It is the emperor alone in whom the power is vested of appointing Mandarins of all grades, and whose edicts, issued from the dragon throne and signed by the awful vermilion pencil, pass into law. The people know nothing of their imperial ruler, further than that he is the "Holy Lord," protected by the "Five-clawed dragon." Perhaps they picture him in their dreams seated astride of this mythological monster, who is transporting him through the clouds to survey his central kingdom. Although popularly believed to be possessed of Divine power, the real duty of governing devolves upon his councillors, men who, in the picturesque language of the East, are his hands and feet, ears and eyes. The senses of hearing and seeing are cultivated and exercised to an almost incredible extent in an universal system of espionage. All the officers of state, from the highest to the lowest, are secretly watched in the discharge of their duties, and are liable to be reported, and doomed to suffer the severest penalties for the crimes of their subordinates. The imperial power, ostensibly sustained through filial piety, is despotic to the last degree, and is upheld by no loftier feelings than widely diffused jealousy and distrust.

The Government is divided into central, provincial, and extra-provincial. In the first division must be included all holders of high office in Peking; and in the second the governors of the eighteen provinces of China Proper, and the three provinces of what is loosely called Manchuria, the country to the north-east of China; in the third section are the Residents, in the vast regions known as Inner and Outer Mongolia, in the country between Mongolia and Thibet, and lastly in Thibet itself.

The Great Council, in which is vested the real power of the central Government, is an excrescence on the regular establishment introduced soon after the foundation of the dynasty. It is composed of members chosen, not on the recommendation of the departments of State, but by the emperor himself, or, being a minor, his regents. There is no fixed number of members; at the present time there are only five.

The chief court of the regular establishment, which confers upon its members the highest civil rank, is the Nêi-ko, or Grand Secretariat. Membership of this court does not render residence at the capital obligatory. Distinguished provincial governors are often rewarded by a seat in it, the total number remaining always the same. Next in degree to this office, and of far more practical importance, are the six Boards for the administration of the Civil Service. The Board of Finance, of Rites and Obligations (including Public Instruction and State Worship), of War, and of the Army and Navy, of Criminal Law, and of Public Works. The chief officers of each of these six Boards we should style Presidents, of whom there are two to each Board—one Manchu and one Chinese. Of these appointments the Ministers of the Tsungle Yamen possess a fair proportion.

The Tsungle Yamen, or Foreign Office, was one of the important results which followed the Treaty of Tientsin, as already stated.

In the provinces the civil and military establishments are more distinct than at first sight they appear to be in the metropolis. Each province has commonly over it a governor, in two instances a governor-general, but the title so translated is in six other instances borne by individuals ruling two, and in one case three provinces, having under them a governor in each. Thus a governor-general rules Kiangsu Nganwhui, and Kiangsi, and another

Kwangtung and Kwangsi. The governor-generals and governors have each of them a small force at their disposal, but they do not command the forces, naval or military, of the province. On the coast and frontier provinces there are permanent Manchu garrisons, under Manchu officers of very high rank; the Chinese force being under a separate general officer, below whom is a series of subordinates of a number of denominations corresponding with those of our own army, if we count from ensign to major-general. These all draw pay. The troops or constabulary assigned to them exist chiefly on paper. The system of placing permanent camps in the large cities, introduced by the Tartars, is still in vogue. The Manchu army was originally divided into four corps of bannermen, and afterwards into eight, each corps distinguished by the colour of its banner. The large cities, such as Peking, Nangking, and Canton, were divided into the Manchu and Chinese quarters; the former being allotted to the bannermen as a permanent camp, the latter to the Chinese citizens. At the present time there is little to remind one of this military arrangement. Poverty prevails in the Tartar quarters, and the men have lost almost all trace of the fierce, warlike nomad. They are neglected and underpaid, and as a rule are too proud and indolent to work. Nevertheless, in front of their houses they still retain the colour of their respective banners in the shape of paper lamps set up before the doorways.

After the governors come a host of officers—Superintendent of Finances, Provincial Judge, Collector of Salt Tax, Grain Collector, Intendant of

Circuit, Prefect of Department, and so on, down to the unattached graduates.

In like manner each province is divided and subdivided into circuits, **departments, and** districts (the latter about the extent of an English county), portioned out for the purposes of administration. The divisions of this political network are gradually further reduced until the patriarchal government is represented by chiefs of villages, who are held responsible for the conduct of their clans, and finally by the heads of families, who in like manner are responsible for the conduct of their children. The power of the emperor is thus felt by the meanest of his subjects. Filial **piety** tends to maintain law and order as the **Chinese super-stitions** and natural regard for parents beget obedience and love in children.

Liability to suffer for the crimes of others is not confined alone to the family or clan, it extends upwards through all ranks, civil and military, to the members of the Supreme Council of State. An instance of its application occurred quite recently in Canton. "Since the San-Shui Lekin Tax Station was attacked by pirates, the Viceroy of Canton ordered two head-men of the Peh-Kong coast-guard junk, named On and Yen, to prosecute search for the robbers; they, however, failed to find any of them, and the Viceroy has sentenced them to forty blows with the bamboo each, and threatens them with dismissal if they do not arrest the robbers in a month's time."

This system leads to endless abuses, to condoning crime, torturing supposed criminals to obtain convictions against them, to bribery and rascality.

To such a degree is this carried on that the Mandarins, many of them, leave their entire salaries in the hands of the treasurers to meet fines imposed for the malpractices of themselves and subordinates.

Illegal imposts and squeezes yield an income at least ten times as great as their nominal pay from government.

Civil and military office is obtained by competitive examination; the former by the knowledge the student displays of all that the ancient sages said and wrote. These sages spent their days in teaching morality, and their numerous modern disciples know all their moral maxims by heart, but they do not put them into practice. It seems strange that this very high-toned wisdom should qualify a man to cheat and oppress his fellows. If the mantle of Confucius has fallen upon his followers, it seems only to hide their sins from the people. China is a Godless land full of gods. What can be said for its system of competitive examination? It was originally good, but unlike old wine it has not mellowed and improved by reason of age. It still affords an incentive to all classes to make the most of early opportunities, as the prize of the poorest student may be a seat next the dragon throne. Nay more, the emperor can confer a title which will not only ennoble the living but the dead. Thus the obscure student may become the founder of an ancient aristocratic line; his rank will go backward through generations of ancestors. But it is necessary here to say a few words on Chinese nobility. From the most ancient times there have been five degrees of honour to which men have been raised for distinguished services, with remainder, as we should say, to their heirs male, the latter not succeeding, however, without renewal of their patent, and even then, as a rule, succeeding to a title one degree less honourable than that borne by the immediate ancestor. So that were such a usage in vogue with us a duke would become a baron in five generations.

The Manchu family which now rules China, or all those within a certain degree of the imperial line, have no less than eighteen orders of nobility, liable, like the old system spoken of above, to gradual extinction, except in a few special instances, when the patent ensures the title in perpetuity. Prince Kung received such a patent in 1865.

Civil and military rank is frequently held by the same individual. Thus Li-hung-chang commands the forces in the north, and is, at the same time, governor of Peichihli. But the Mandarin's duties, whatever be his rank, are of the most diverse character. An officer of the fourth rank in the provinces may at one time be called upon to act as judge, at another to take the command of troops raised to crush a rebellion. He is also certain to be consulted on the general government of the province, and to supervise the postal administration. His Yamen is at once a General Post and Inland Revenue Office.

There are no judicial functionaries distinct from civil officers. Civil and criminal suits are brought before the same magistrate, who has power to exercise summary jurisdiction, with the important reservation that the litigants may appeal to the higher courts, and finally, it may be, refer the case to the Supreme Court of the metropolis.

A Chinese district judge acts as tax collector, commissioner of police, sheriff, and coroner.

According to native law a man cannot be convicted until he has confessed himself guilty of the offence with which he is charged. It therefore becomes expedient for the magistrate, when a crime has been committed in his district, to find criminals, and if need be, to extort confession with the rack or bamboo. He is tempted to this course to save his own position. Thus it happens that many unfortunate innocents, tortured with maddening pain, are constrained to plead guilty, and go to their doom with a lie on their lips. A Chinese court presents many revolting scenes of cruelty; but the people, naturally indifferent to the sufferings of others, look on unmoved. Human life is lightly esteemed—so lightly that a drowning man in a river can scarce hope for a rescue. His struggles will only afford a moment's enjoyment to many impassive spectators on the bank, who will recount with glee how funnily so-and-so ended his life by drinking too much water.

Punishments inflicted on criminals all imply bodily suffering, and not a few of them torture most refined. Beating with a bamboo rod is a mild form of admonition, which leaves sundry weals, sores, and bruises to remind the petty thief of his crimes.

Carrying the cangue, a huge, heavy, square collar of wood fixed round the neck of the delinquent, and inscribed with the particulars of his guilt, is, perhaps, a punishment less severe, as it appeals more to the moral sensibilities of the prisoner, who is exposed with this badge in the public highway. The worst type of punishment is, perhaps, the bamboo cage, constructed so that the felon, bound hand and foot, stands in an upright position, and may either rest on his toes, or hang by the neck. Exposed thus in the open street or some market-place he is left to die of hunger and delirium. When the crime is capital, death by strangulation is the most honourable form of punishment, decapitation the most common and ignominious.

Reformatories, where erring men and women are taught useful trades, and where by good conduct they may at last win their way back to society, do not exist in China. Convict labour is unknown unless at the foreign settlements.

Banishment and terms of imprisonment also figure in the penal code; but to be confined in a Chinese prison must be worse than death itself. The writer has seen miserable diseased wretches, in foul dens reeking with filth, glaring out through the bars more like wild beasts than men, envying the lot of others who were crucified outside the prison gates. In the rocky pass of Nankow, beneath the shade of the great wall, he has come across felons who had been sent adrift into the wilds heavily ironed, some lying helpless by the wayside, too weak to carry the fetters that had fretted the flesh from their bones. Convicts such as these depend in a great measure upon the charity of travellers for food. There is, however, one way in the "Flowery Land" of obtaining commutation of punishments so terrible as these, and that is by money. Gold, like the magician's wand, will cause the fetters to drop from the felon's limbs. But the quality and quantity of the coin must first be nicely adjusted to clear the guilty. If a capital crime be committed by a poor man justice is satisfied with a small recompense, while the rich must yield up treasure tenfold, till indeed the nicely poised balance kicks the beam. The balance is not always held by clean, impartial hands; false weights are freely used to determine the fair market value of crime. In other words, this particular phase of Chinese administration opens a way for the practice of the most flagrant abuses. It is well known that in the south of China, at any rate, the assassin may purchase a substitute to suffer death in his stead for about twenty pounds sterling. For further details on this subject the reader is referred to Meadows' "Notes on China." Official corruption is a sort of recognised Chinese institution, arising partly from the inadequate pay of Mandarins, and the system of espionage already spoken of, and partly out of the mode of collecting and administering the revenue. Taxes are paid in money and in kind, each province retaining sufficient to meet its local expenditure, and remitting the balance to the imperial treasury. Those are the legitimate taxes; but the evil lies in the irregular manner of collecting the illegal supplementary revenue, which is entirely raised by petty officers attached to the establishments of Mandarins. It is these small functionaries who work the local mines, so to speak, for their employers; who manage, against law, to attach themselves permanently to the Yamens; and who, by a system of extortion, provide suitable salaries for themselves and their masters.

The importance of the duties which these men perform will be gathered from what Mr. Meadows says in speaking of the extent to which Mandarins' salaries are augmented by unlawful means. "For instance, one of those in the receipt of about twenty-two pounds sterling legal income, once complained feelingly to me about his poverty; and on hinting that his post was, after all, not a bad one, he protested, with some earnestness, that his whole income did not exceed 7,000 taels (£2,333)."

The legal incomes of Mandarins fluctuate with the harvest, as the funds in the treasury are greatly affected by the outturn of the crops, and the success or failure which attends the collection of the land-tax. This fact affords a clue to the importance which the rulers of China have always attached to the cultivation of the soil, and to the tenure of lands held under the crown, subject to an annual quit-rent in money or kind. It also accounts, in some measure at least, for the way in which Mandarins have been driven to trust to their wits to find pay to meet current expenses, and leave a margin ample enough to take the place of a retiring allowance.

The funds of the imperial exchequer have been brought low by a tide of adverse circumstances in the shape of rebellion and foreign wars, which have laid waste vast tracts of fertile land; at the same time they have weakened the power of the central government, and led to results alike detrimental to national prosperity and opposed to the maintenance of satisfactory relations with foreign powers.

Among the people, commercial morality is observed to a notable extent, but commercial law seems never to have been deemed worthy of the consideration of their rulers. The exchange of commodities, anything in the shape of trade, must be subject to a sliding scale of taxation, whose fluctuations will adjust themselves according to the necessities of the inland customs officers. A tariff of legal customs-dues does exist, but it is supplemented by vexatious illegal imposts, the nature and extent of which are never clearly understood. When we say there is no commercial law it is meant that magistrates rarely, if ever, attempt to subvert the rules applied by the powerful guilds to matters of trade. This is a constant source of trouble to foreign merchants, as some of the rules are put in force in a way highly advantageous to the Chinese trader. The guild merchants make it a point by every means in their power to support and protect their members or *protégés* under any circumstances. Thus, for example, native brokers may engage to take large quantities of foreign goods, and pay a small sum as bargain money. Should the market fall during the time given for delivery they cancel the transaction, leaving the foreigners small chance of redress.

Irregular taxation of foreign goods passing into the interior is another source of grievance. Imported articles are subject not only to the regular duties leviable, as in other countries, at the port of introduction, but subject to further burdens at every stage of their journey inland. The result is the restriction of foreign commerce to the narrowest limits, goods being so heavily taxed as to be greatly increased in cost and thus rendered unsaleable beyond a certain distance from the coast. At the port of Amoy, for example, the imperial tax on cotton fabrics is first paid by the importer, and afterwards supplemented by an impost, called "Lekin" (a tax levied to meet the war expenses in 1858), nearly double the amount of the imperial tax. The goods are bought by native traders to carry inland, where they are subjected to further taxation at numerous customs barrier stations. It is impossible to determine the exact extent of the imposts, as the tariff fluctuates and adjusts itself to the resources of the merchant or the rapacity of officials.

The duties are frequently heavy—so heavy as to stimulate smuggling, bribery, and corruption of all sorts. Contraband trade has indeed become a most ingeniously managed native institution, which is strictly suppressed by the authorities when it suits their purpose to do so.

While all this is going on, pressure has been applied to the central Government; they have been requested to amend their ways, to lay down a fair tariff of taxation on imported articles, to abolish Mandarin squeezes, and in brief to abide by their fair promises embodied in the Treaty of Tientsin.

The question arises, Have the rulers of China the power, assuming that they are actuated by the desire, to do all this? Are they prepared for such large measures of reform as are implied in dealing liberally and fairly with foreigners and their wares The Mandarins, and they are a most formidable body, have reason to be satisfied with affairs as they stand, and would to a certainty oppose measures that threaten their personal interests. Much of their revenue is drawn irregularly, leaving a fascinating uncertainty as to the value of their appointments, and the wealth that may be accumulated during terms of office. Again, would the long-suffering people willingly consent to have their own merchandise, or that which they themselves import, taxed immoderately, while foreign goods are granted free passes into the interior of the country? If the Government is to be forced at once to face and reform such contingencies, they must look to the safety of the dragon throne, and seek close intimacy and powerful alliances with the West. But viewing the tide of events from a distance, there seems to be a cloud rising to dim the lustre of the Tartar dynasty. An infant emperor is on the throne, empress dowagers are regents; there is no vigorous, responsible head of the administration, and Li-hung-chang, a true son of Han, of pure Chinese descent, chief of a large army, promoter of arsenals, is guardian of the young Manchu sovereign. During the last emperor's minority and brief reign, Prince Kung and his associates in office maintained peaceful relations with European powers.

Recent ominous events, however, have cast a dark shadow over the future. A growing hatred to foreigners has openly manifested itself, and ended in the murder of Mr. Margary, her Britannic Majesty's representative travelling on a special mission to Yunnan, armed with the credentials of his office and an imperial passport. The fair promises of the speedy punishment of the assassins have yet to be fulfilled; while the Chinese, under the direction of Li-hung-chang, still pursue the task of perfecting their defences and arming themselves with modern weapons.

The British Minister at Peking has wrung tardy concessions, one by one, from the central Government. Not the least important of these are freer intercourse between representatives of foreign courts and the high officials of State, together with the publication for the first time, in the *Peking Gazette* (the imperial organ), of some of the treaty rights of foreigners. An English commission, consisting of a member of Legation and two consular officers, has been dispatched to Yunnan to investigate the particulars of the outrage. Should the mission reach its destination in safety much will remain to to be done in sifting evidence to secure the punishment of the guilty. It is reported that a number of men implicated in the crime have been seized and await execution. Let us hope that these are the real malefactors, and not unfortunates brought forward to screen men in high position, the instigators of the outrage.

Besides unsatisfactory foreign relations, abuses have crept in under the waning power of the Manchus, which have spread discontent among the Chinese. Superior culture and mental attainments are no longer the only passports to civil office. Rank may be bought by persons who have accumulated their wealth by more than questionable means, who have had no literary training, and who speculate in office as they would in the shares of a gold mine. The quartz is the people; it requires crushing, but its yield is constant. Again, the unfair proportion of lucrative appointments allowed to Tartars is naturally a source of grievance to

Chinese officers, who, with Li-hung-chang at their head (he is said to be a loyal subject of the Manchu monarch), backed by his army, might sweep their Tartar conquerors from the land. It appears, according to the most recent statistics collected by Dr. Eitel, that the Manchu banner corps of the empire amount to 150,000 men. This is an approximate calculation based on information derived from Chinese sources, and cannot be taken as representing an effective Tartar army of such numerical strength; part of that army exists only in documentary form. A number of the corps are armed with foreign-made rifles, but the majority are archers, mounted or on foot, matchlock, and gingle men. The chief fighting army of China is called "the Five Camps"; it is distributed in minute divisions over the whole empire, and is strongest at the points deemed most important for the defence of the country. It comprises regiments of the line, cavalry, marines, and sailors, and is about 700,000 strong. Like the Manchu garrisons, the men of this standing army carry foreign breechloaders, bows, arrows, and matchlocks. The officers, from the rank of general or admiral down to ensign, number 7,157. About ten per cent. of this number are Manchu bannermen, with a sprinkling of Mongols. The army may be said to be almost purely Chinese, a fact by no means favourable, one would imagine, to the internal peace of the empire, or the long continuance of the Manchu dynasty. It is, however, more than doubtful that the Chinese contingent so far outnumbers that of the Manchus. Money is drawn for its maintenance, and it figures in official documents, but in many instances does not really exist. In Formosa, for instance, where there is supposed to be a standing army (part of the five camps) there are two or three hundred personal retainers of the Taotai of the island, who, in case of war or inspection by a superior officer, are swelled into a numerous force by rapid levies on the riff-raff of the towns. It will be seen that by distributing the men widely over the provinces of the empire, the difficulties of intercommunication render it impossible to assemble speedily a large Chinese force at any given point. Thus while order is secured all over the provinces, a general rising of the Chinese army is carefully guarded against, as quarterly army and navy reports are sent to Peking, and the movement of troops regulated by the Manchu officers and governors-general. Perhaps the largest force assembled in China at the present time is that under Li-hung-chang in the province of Peichihli, supposed to be made up of about 100,000 troops, well armed many of them, and accustomed to foreign drill.

The navy consists of numerous small river-boats, a fleet of gun-boats, and several ironclads. The gun-boats and one or two iron-plated vessels, constructed after foreign models, have been built by the Chinese themselves, and the work is so well done as to bear the strongest testimony to the mechanical skill and boundless resources which a wise government would find in the constructive skill of the people. These vessels carry Krupp and Armstrong guns, and crews of marines and sailors armed and clothed as in an European navy.

It is impossible to predict with any degree of certainty what may be the future policy of the

Chinese Government, or how many years or centuries may elapse before the empire regains her old position as one of the most civilised and mightiest powers of the world. Within the past ten years the Chinese have shown signs of progress, but chiefly in founding arsenals and perfecting their means of defence. They manufacture their own guns, small arms, shells, rockets, and torpedoes after the most approved models. Forts have been erected along the chief rivers, and a school of torpedo engineers established, so that when the time comes they may sink the ships of their enemies to block their river channels in place of their own war-junks.

It is with infinitely greater satisfaction that we perceive signs of change in other directions: the introduction of the study of foreign sciences into the Peking College, which is a feeder of similar institutions in different parts of the empire; the determination of the Government to follow to some extent, picking its way daintily along the shallows, the plunge which Japan has taken into the unfathomed depths of a new civilisation. The Chinese Government has subsidised a line of native owned steamers on the coast, and employed steam vessels to transport the grain tribute, which became so mysteriously diminished when sent along the Grand Canal. It has boldly entered the money market to negotiate a loan; not that the prospect of contracting a national debt affords any proof of advancing civilisation; but it shows that the rulers of China are gradually forsaking their ancient traditional policy.

As a further evidence of progress, Chinese youths

are now being sent abroad, at the expense of the central Government, to receive their education. After fifteen years spent at foreign universities they will return to China to fill posts under Government. It has also been proposed to appoint native consuls to foreign countries, and possibly accredited ambassadors to reside at the capitals of Europe and America.

The Imperial Maritime Customs, under the able administration of Mr. Hart and other European officials, have done something to open the eyes of the Chinese Government to the advantages which accrue from the honest and intelligent management of this important branch of the revenue. If the same system were diffused over the empire, and responsible and trustworthy officers appointed to all the Customs stations, it would tend greatly to decrease the abuses that may ultimately destroy the Manchu dynasty.

However hopeful the present aspect of affairs may be in so far as good omens are concerned, the past history of China would lead one to believe that her progress will be slow. The people have gone on for so many centuries under their own and alien emperors; they have sought only to be left alone, to live as their fathers lived, tilling and sowing, spinning and weaving, and at last to die and mingle their dust with that of a long line of ancestors. Foreigners have come and gone and dwelt among them, teaching their customs, usages, arts, science, and religion, but still they remain unchanged.

They are still the same Chinese in their arts and attributes. Take, for example, Canton, where foreign intercourse has been most intimate and long-continued, what do we find there that is not as purely Chinese as it was before the first foreign ship ascended its river? Where is the effect of all our civilising influence? Every Chinaman, from the governor-general to the coolie who paddles you to shore, wears the same dress as of old, speaks the language spoken in the time of Yu. Pidjin-English is a sort of baby jargon employed among the lower orders in conversation with the much-despised foreigners, while among themselves they use the loftier strain of their own tongue. There are no public buildings unlike the ancient edifices; no parks or pleasure grounds for the people; no churches, concert halls, monuments, promenades, or wider streets; no horses or carriages; no greater liberty to women, who are still the slaves of their husbands.

There is, indeed, nothing in the social condition of the people, or in the appearance of Canton city, to tell of the presence of foreigners.

The Chinese borrow nothing so readily as money, and that only when it can be had cheaply, from the outer barbarian. It may be said they have borrowed new modes of business, new ships, and new arms. The first two help to make money, and the last to protect it when it is made. But they heartily despise our barbarous tongue, and go-by-steam civilisation.

When the island of Hong Kong was ceded to the British Crown, it was thought that in a few years the English on that once piratical rock would stimulate progress in China—that it would be the remotest outpost of our civilisation, a sort of beacon that would flood the Flowery Land with new light.

Our just laws and our splendid institutions were to supply the models for reorganisation. The darkness that brooded over the great land of Confucius was to pass away before the dawn of life, light, and liberty. The effect of our little enlightened colony has been strangely disappointing. Like sunlight on the Sphinx it has only made all the more apparent the outlines of the old civilisation gazing with stony eyes over the barren wastes of centuries. The splendid city of Victoria, with its churches, schools, hospitals, and prisons—yes, prisons!—all of them full, is viewed by the Chinese as a sort of asylum for the scum of Kwangtung; a place in which a ruffian may find shelter and congenial society after his presence has become undesirable among native circles on the mainland.

A large class of lawless wretches have drifted to this British possession to be experimented upon, and the result is not always so satisfactory as to tempt the Chinese to alter their own summary way of dealing with such criminals. They prefer their own laws, and the flail-like discipline of the bamboo, by which they separate the chaff from the wheat of humanity.

The other foreign settlements which have grown up at the treaty ports must, one would think, have led the Chinese to appreciate the energy and enterprise of western nations. The little English island of Sha-Meen, at Canton, stands isolated close to the banks of the river, separated from the land by a narrow creek. This little stream might be an impassable gulf, so completely does it divide the old-world civilisation from the new. Sha-Meen is purely European in its houses, gardens, and society, while the other is as purely Chinese.

Shanghai, in Kiangsu, which has not yet been noticed, has taken the lead of all the settlements in winning the favour of the Chinese, and affords a splendid illustration of the value of municipal government—a system quite unknown to China. The wonderful prosperity of the place and the nature of the administration, which rests in the hands of the people, must present a curious problem to thoughtful natives. No spot of Chinese owned and Chinese managed ground presents so many tokens of wealth and perfect order as Shanghai foreign settlement, and nowhere in the richest part of the empire can one find so many merchants living in princely style. Those of the natives who reside within the municipal bounds must feel the protection afforded by a well-organised body of police, and appreciate the absence of Mandarin squeezes. Whether they realise the advantages or not, they prosper under them, using steamers and telegraphs in competing with foreign merchants. But for all that they retain their native habits of body, mind, and attire. They are only known to and by foreigners in business, and many of them, when they have made their money, flee from it gladly, as from a plague-stricken spot, back to the beaten paths of ancient custom.

An attempt will soon be made to lay the first railway in China, along the banks of the Woosung at Shanghai. Let us hope that this enterprise successfully accomplished may lead to the laying of iron lines through the vast regions of China, and thus bind the provinces securely together under a liberal and enlightened central Government.

CHAPTER XI.

THE CHINESE LANGUAGE AND LITERATURE.

THE Chinese assign to letters a place of the highest importance. The god of literature has his shrine in every village, while Confucian temples are found in every town of the empire. The spirit of the sage receives imperial homage, and the worship of millions of human beings to whom his sayings have become household words. The political system of the Chinese is based upon the classical writings, and a knowledge of ancient lore alone points the way to wealth and fame. Men of letters form the aristocracy of the land, many of whom have risen by their scholarly attainments from the humblest positions in life to wear the robes of mandarins or ministers of state.

From these causes everything connected with the art of writing is held in the highest estimation; paper, pens, ink, and the marble slab on which the ink is reduced, are called "the four precious things." Scraps of paper inscribed with the characters of the language are collected in the streets and byways to be burned as votive offerings before the god of letters.

A passage from a Chinese drama strikingly illustrates the proud position of the literati:—" If you are successful in trade, from a little money you make **much**; but if you study letters, your plebeian garments are changed to a mandarin's gown. If you compare the two, how much superior is the literary life to that of the merchant or tradesman."* Although the Chinese are pre-eminently a literary people, their ancient and modern writings are in a great measure barren of interest, at least to those familiar with the wealth of western literature. The genius of the people, together with the written language in which it finds expression, seems to have been arrested at a certain stage of its development. A period of great literary activity, culminating in the writings of Confucius and his disciples, appears to have marked the limit of the intellectual progress of the nation. The sage set the example to his followers of referring everything back to the writings of the ancients as the accepted standards of knowledge. Confucius thus moulded the mode of thinking which remains to this day.

The characters, indeed, in which they found a suitable vehicle of expression display tokens of advancement with which native thought has hardly kept pace.

To those unacquainted with the Chinese veneration for antiquity, and the inflexible nature of their language, the poverty of their literature must appear unacountable. The language is copious, and capable of expressing the most minute shades of meaning, and in this latter respect falls in with a peculiar phase of the national mind. Its characters are like algebraic signs, or the lines and angles of geometry, more capable of representing facts obtained by subtle processes of reasoning than the

* *Chinese Miscellany*, p. 43.

flight of fancy or fire of imagination. But it must be borne in mind that the Chinese are remarkable neither for imagination nor genius; of this we are assured by the most distinguished sinologues. They have enjoyed at least three thousand years' training, and their spirit, like that of a restive horse, has been thoroughly broken. The period is lost in the dim past, when they settled down to the respectable mediocrity which characterises their whole civilisation.

To recur to the simile, they submitted to the yoke as useful hacks, and have steadily continued to drag the lumbering car of old-world lore down through the ages. A retrospective glance across the level and monotonous past reveals millions of able men spending the best of their days in the dull toil of compiling matter-of-fact histories, classical commentaries, or mystical treatises on astrology: in amplifying the false theories of the phenomena of nature bequeathed to them by their sages, hoping to discover the light of truth in the darkness of their primitive philosophy.

This ponderous car, this Juggernaut of Chinese learning instituted by Confucius, has crushed beneath its wheels the originality and inspiration that betoken human progress in more favoured lands.

The nature of the written language, the difficulty of acquiring a scholarly knowledge of the characters, and the isolation of the race, have in some degree tended to retard progress and development.

It might have been expected that the invention of printing from blocks in the eighth century would have given a powerful impetus to the literature of the country. But the facility of acquiring knowledge thus afforded resulted mainly in the advantage derived by fixing the characters and the standard styles of writing. The ideas and mode of expressing them remained much the same.

The invention of the earliest written characters is attributed by some native writers to Fouhi, by others to Hwangti—the first and third of the "Five Sovereigns" mentioned in ancient history.

Fouhi commenced his reign about five thousand years ago, and is said to have discovered iron, agriculture, clothing, and marriage. Hwangti was no less remarkable as the first worker in metals, constructor of waggons, and builder of brick houses. He was, above all, the husband of queen Yenfi, who was the first to robe her form in a silken fabric. .

Fouhi, it is supposed, may as fairly lay claim to the discovery of letters as any other ancient potentate, and from what little is known of him and his remarkable discoveries, he might almost claim the credit of inventing the type of physiognomy peculiar to his race. Unlike most modern Chinamen, Fouhi must have possessed a vivid imagination and a creative genius of the first order. He was the first worker in iron and wearer of silk; he taught his people to till the soil, to sow and to reap; as a prince he ruled wisely, and as high priest he is said to have instructed his subjects in their duties to God and to each other. He studied the heavens, and established times and seasons, and sought to obtain social and political harmony by the judicious use of instruments of music.*

---

* Music still holds an important place in state ceremonials, and as the recognised means of expressing joy and grief at marriages and burials.

It therefore seems not unnatural that Fouhi should have discarded the rude method of recording events in vogue at the time by knotted cords; that he should have invented symbolic writing as the means of handing his deeds and discoveries down to posterity. He had probably no faith in oral tradition, knowing the tendency of the Chinese mind to diverge from the truth, and no confidence in the courtly fingers that might, at will, manipulate the knots on the classic cords. Fouhi was driven, therefore, as were the ancient Mexicans and Egyptians, to recording notable events by rude pictures or hieroglyphics.

Be the discoverer whom he may, it is known that the legion of Chinese written characters which contributed so largely to the intellectual growth of the nation had their origin in rude pictures of natural objects. The sun was represented as a disc, ⊙; moon, ☽; field, 田; mouth, 口; child, ♀, and so on. The earliest ideographic characters were such as these, a horizontal line denoting continuity, or placed at the base of a hieroglyph indicating the ground, at the top heaven, or roof, and in the centre standing for anything indefinite. Lines repeated one above the other came to represent 二, two; 三, three, &c.

Other characters, by their position, repetition, or inversion, were adopted as ideographic symbols. Above was pictured thus, 上; beneath, 下; from top to bottom by a vertical line, 丨; division, 八; crossing or communion, or ✕; entering, by the outline of a wedge, and unity, by a triangle. It is singular that this trinity of equal angles should be the symbol of unity.

Native philologists divide the characters of the language into six classes. The first is called "Sianghing," or those which carry a likeness of the object they are meant to represent. Dr. Williams says they were among the first characters invented, although the 608 placed in this class do not include all the original symbols. The rude symbols above have been so modified by the progress of writing as to render it difficult to trace the resemblance between the primitive hieroglyphs and their modern equivalents, as will be gathered from the following examples :— ancient, 首 modern, a head ; ancient, 矢 modern, an arrow; ancient, 斧 modern, an axe ; ancient, 禾 modern, grain.

The second class, called "chi-sze," numbers only 107 symbols, and is made up of two signs, so combined as to convey ideas to the mind from the relative, or independent, position of their parts.

The third class, "hwui-i," consists of a list of more than 700 characters, each made up of two or three symbols to form a single idea,* "whose meanings are deducible either from their position or supposed relative influence upon each other. Thus, the union of sun and moon expresses brightness, two trees stand for a forest, woman and broom denote a wife," in reference to her household duties. It is interesting to note the origin of ideas in the building up of the characters of the Chinese language. Prof. Douglas says: "For instance, if we analyse the

---

* "Middle Kingdom," Dr. W. Williams.

character sin 信, 'sincere,' we find that it is formed by the combination of the characters 人 jin, 'a man,' and 言 yen, 'words,' a collocation of ideas which speaks well for the ancient truthfulness of the Chinese, and which, when the unfortunate failing of their descendants is borne in mind, is decidedly opposed to the Darwinian theory as applied to language." In an ingenious analysis of characters containing the word "west," a writer in the *Chinese Recorder* has endeavoured to trace the western origin of the Chinese race. 要 consists of 西 west, and 之 che, going to, or to return to the west.

耍, from 西 west, and 女 neu, woman, the Chinese version of "The girl I left behind me."

粟, from 西 west, and 米 mu, rice. Suh, a general name for all cereals, apparently to acknowledge that all cereals were imported from the west, doubtless brought by the Chinese themselves when they first emigrated into this country.

The elephant is the Chinese ideal of form, hence the character by which it is expressed also means form or figure.

The beautiful and good are denoted by the character for sheep combined with another; a fine large sheep is beauty; a sheep's mouth is goodness, and my sheep is righteousness.

The fourth class, or "chuen chu," inverted meanings, numbers 372 characters, and is formed by uniting or reversing characters or sounds. Thus, ⼂ show the hand turned to the right, means right, and ⼂, reversed, left.

The fifth class, "kiai shing," contains 21,810

characters, each one made up of the union of phonetic with determinative symbols.

This class includes about two-thirds of the characters in the language. The first symbol affords a clue to the meaning of the entire character, while its companion supplies the sound. "In this respect," says Dr. Williams, "Chinese characters differ from and are superior to the Arabic numerals, to which they have often been likened; for combinations like 25, 100, &c., although conveying an identical meaning to all nations, none of them can indicate sounds."

This system of combining determinative and phonetic symbols was perhaps the most important advance which the Chinese made in the art of writing, as it enabled them to increase the number of their characters to an indefinite extent.

The sixth class, called "kia tsie"—lit., borrowed meanings—numbers 598, and consists of characters having a metaphorical meaning. For example, the symbol for a written character is composed of "a child" under shelter, characters being esteemed as the well-nurtured offspring of hieroglyphics.

The foregoing classification is modern, and was adopted as a convenient mode of arranging the already existing words of which the Chinese language is composed.

The actual number of characters in the language has been variously estimated. Magalahaens sets it down as 54,409, Sir George Stanton at 80,000; Dr. Williams puts down 25,000 as about the number of characters in actual use. One would imagine that to commit this number of words to memory is a task beyond the power of the most gifted native scholar. Nevertheless, there are men in China who have learned some of the classical books off by heart, and can repeat them line for line. Students of native literature have greatly reduced this number of characters, and increased the meanings of those in use. A knowledge of ten or twelve thousand words is deemed sufficient for all purposes, and implies a fair acquaintance with the language.

There are six recognised styles of writing, and the fancy is left free to form an indefinite number of others. The handwriting of an individual Chinaman can seldom be identified as peculiarly his own. The lines, or strokes, are too rigid to admit of the differences we recognise in English caligraphy.

The recognised styles are the Chuen shoo, seal character; the Li shoo, official character; the Kiai shoo, or model character; the Hing shoo, or running character; the Tsau shoo, or grass character, and the Sung shoo, or Sung dynasty character. "An extraordinary specimen of the quaint style of caligraphy sometimes employed is to be seen in the Chinese library of the British Museum, where there is a copy of the Emperor Kienlung's poem on Moukden, printed both in Chinese and Manchu, in thirty-two kinds of strangely fanciful characters."*

There is always a marked difference between the language as it is spoken and the language as it is written. In the latter, there are many words having the same sound, their true meaning being indicated by the mode of writing them. It is impossible to understand these words when spoken unless they are united with some other word of

* "The Language of China," Prof. Douglas.

like meaning, just as if in English one required to say sky—sun, child—son, or look—see.

An indication of the meanings of Chinese characters is found in a series of 214 determinatives, under which, as headings, the characters of the language have been arranged. It is thus that some native lexicographers have planned their works.

Dr. Williams observes that the determinatives are placed in different parts of the compound character, showing that no fixed rules had been followed in their original construction. They must all of them be committed to memory before the student can hope to make way in the language.

Many characters formed under different determinatives have the same meaning—this repetition of differently formed synonyms adds to the difficulty of acquiring the language. Thus the word "tsien"*—a small cup—is written under three determinatives—gem, porcelain, and horn, the substances originally used in making it.

Purely phonetic words have been introduced in modern times, composed of certain determinatives and primitives. They are simply the phonetic equivalents of common names, titles, and scientific terms borrowed from other languages. Thus Mr. would be written, as the nearest approach to its sound, Mi-sz, meaning, in reality, "beautiful scholar."

The materials used in writing are, as with us, paper, pens, and ink; but the paper is made from bamboo, the ink from soot, and the pens resemble the brushes used in water-colour painting. The brush, when full of ink, is finely pointed, and held

* "Middle Kingdom," Dr. W. Williams.

between the thumb and two fore-fingers vertically, so that the flow of ink may be continuous and regular. In this position it is used with great skill in forming the strokes of the characters.

There are eight elementary strokes employed in forming the whole of the characters in the language. When all combined they produce the word 永, yung, eternal.

The sounds of the Chinese tongue, court dialect, are about 500. In the spoken language of the South of China they are, according to Medhurst and others, more numerous. They bear, nevertheless, a very small proportion to the number in the written vocabulary of monosyllabic words. When treating on the subject of the limited scope of Chinese syllabic sounds, Douglas observes that the difficulty of pronouncing 30,000 odd words, with 500 available sounds, has been ingeniously overcome by this curious people. To use his own words, "Three methods have been adopted to prevent the confusion which at first sight would appear inevitable." First, the word spoken must be allied to another of like meaning, as has been already pointed out, just as if in English we were to say sky—sun, child—son, &c. Second, in the case of noun substantives, "by placing certain classifying words between them and the numerals which precede them. These classifiers have some resemblance to our expressions herd, head, fleet, troop, &c. For example, the word pa, to grasp with the hand, is used to precede anything which is held in the hand, such as knife, spoon, &c." Thirdly, "by dividing the words of the language among eight tones." These are divided into an upper and lower series of four each, rendering the spoken language more or less musical, in so far as each word has its recognised tone which carries its meaning to the ear. They, however, bear a closer resemblance to the accents of our own language. In English a false accent will completely destroy the drift of a sentence. In Chinese it is not the accent on a dissyllabic word, but the false rendering of the tone of a monosyllable which changes its meaning.

The grammar of the language may be described in the words of Remusat:—

"In every Chinese sentence the elements which enter into its composition are arranged thus: the subject, the verb, the complement direct, and the complement indirect.

"Modifying expressions precede those to which they belong; thus, the adjective is placed before the substantive, subject, or complement; the substantive governed before the verb which it governs; the adverb before the verb; the preposition, incidental, circumstantial, or hypothetical, before the principal proposition to which it attaches itself by a conjunction expressed or understood.

"The relative position of words and phrases thus determined supplies not unfrequently the place of every other mark meant to denote their mutual dependence, whether adjective or adverbial, positive, conditional, or circumstantial.

"If the subject be understood, it is because it is a personal pronoun, or that it is expressed above, and that the omitted substantive is found in the preceding sentence, in the same quality of subject.

"If the verb be wanting, it is because it is the substantive verb, or some other easily supplied, or one included in the preceding sentences with a different subject or complement.

"If a number of substantives succeed each other, they are either linked by construction or they explain and determine each other.

"If several verbs follow in succession which are neither synonymous nor employed as auxiliaries, the first should be taken as adverbs or verbal nouns, the subjects of those which follow, or, as verbal nouns, the complements of those which precede them."

Sinologues agree in expressing regret that a language so copious as the Chinese should have yielded no higher results than are found in its literature. It would appear, indeed, that the polite and classic mode of expressing thought, prevalent for so many ages, has blighted the genius of the people.

The language presents a strange union of the living with the dead. Its rigid characters are the relics of the old world, invented to express old world notions, dead to all that is vital and progressive. As well might the student expect to find, in the fossil skeleton of some pre-historic animal, the grace and beauty of its living form as the fire of genius in the literature of China.

The ancient classical writings are comprehended under the "Wu King, or Five Classics," and the "Sze Shoo, or Four Books."

The first in order is the "Yeh King—Book of Changes," the oldest work in the language, and much venerated by scholars. It was penned in prison by "Wan Wang, the Literary Prince," about 3,000 years ago, and is made up of a system of mystic philosophy which perplexed Confucius and his disciples, and is to this day only partially understood.

It contains "the eight diagrams," and crude imaginings about the creation of the world, the production of all things, animate and inanimate, from the Yin and Yang—the male and female—first causes.

This work, in common with others treating on mystical, astrological subjects, medicine, &c., was excluded from the general destruction meted out by Che Hwangti, of the Tsin dynasty, to the works of the ancients.

The "Shoo King, or Classic of Ancient History," contains a chronicle of Chinese History, commencing about the time of Noah, and continued to nearly the end of the eighth century B.C. "It includes," says Dr. Williams, "some documents upon which the early sovereigns conducted the affairs of state."

This is followed by the "Shi King—Book of Odes," the "Li Ki—Book of Rites," and the "Chun Tseu—Spring and Autumn Annals."

The latter is an historical work written by Confucius, embracing the interval between the time when the records of the Shoo King were brought to a close up to B.C. 560. The older classics were all of them edited by the sage, who displays in his writings a falling off from the older philosophers. "I will mention," says Dr. Legge, "two subjects in regard to which there is a growing conviction in my mind. . . . . The first is the doctrine of God.

This name is common in the 'Shi King' and 'Shoo King.' Te, or Shang-Te, appears there as a personal being, ruling in heaven and on earth, the author of man's moral nature, by whom kings reign and princes decree justice. . . . . . . Confucius preferred to speak of heaven. Not once throughout the Analists does he use the personal name. . . . . **Thus he** prepared the way for the speculations of the *literati* of mediæval and modern **times** which have exposed them to the charge of atheism."

While Confucius failed to recognise the personality of God, he adhered to all the ancient superstitions regarding spirits. " He sacrificed to the dead as if they were present; he sacrificed to spirits as if they were present." He was silent as to the exact nature of his own belief, and most ingeniously evaded the direct questions of his disciples. Tsze-Kung, his grandson, asked him, "Do the dead have knowledge (of our services, that is), or are they without knowledge?" The master replied, "If I were to say that the dead have knowledge, **I am** afraid that filial sons and dutiful grandsons would injure their substance in paying the last offices to the departed; and if I were to say that the dead have not such knowledge, I am afraid unfilial sons should leave their parents unburied." Dr. Legge thinks that Confucius doubted more than he believed, and was affected by a lack of sincerity and truthfulness which has left its traces on the people and government to the present day.

The "Shi King" is a collection of the most ancient, national, eulogistic, and sacrificial poems, whose chief merit is their great antiquity.

The "Li Ki—Book of Rites," is a work dating from the twelfth century B.C., which had more influence than all the others put together in moulding Chinese character and institutions. It contains the time-honoured rules for the guidance of prince and people in all their political and social relations. Its laws of ceremony are so faithfully followed as to root up nature, and make men slaves of custom. Old established rites are the rule among the people, while their rulers are the slaves of rites and ceremonies. The yielding grace of nature is politely hustled out of the land. The people are introduced to life—eat, sleep, marry, and die by rule. A babe is ushered into the Flowery Land with ceremony, grows to maturity, breathes his last, and is buried after the old, old fashion. Even then he has not done with ceremony; his spirit must wake up at set seasons to receive its dole, and breathe the incense offered at the grave by pious relatives.

The seasons may not come unbidden; they must follow the order of the imperial Chinaman, and spring-time is only recognised when the Emperor has gone out to welcome her budding leaves, and drive the plough into the sod. The very sun itself shines for China, and eclipses are heavenly rites which mark the progress of events in this favoured land. Trees and shrubs must bend before custom, and be tortured into forms to deceive the eye. But this is not all; there is too frequently no more sincerity in the obsequious gestures and prostrations of Chinamen than there is in their ceremonious lying.

The sacred books have brought about this sad end. The cold Confucian philosophy may be likened to a broad stream, and the literature to pebbles thrown up upon its banks, all of them uniformly rounded and polished, and none of great intrinsic value to the world. They have all yielded to the silent wearing of the stream. No rough sparkling gem shines on the shore. Pick a pebble at random; let it be a page of ancient history, a record of human events that might have kindled the enthusiasm of the dullest writer. What do we find? The majority of the kings and statesmen are represented as virtuous and wise. Their commonest sayings are carefully recorded, while events affecting the national destiny are summarily disposed of. For example, in the "Shoo King," the canon of Yaou begins thus:—"Examining into antiquity, we find that the Emperor Yaou was called Fang-heun. He was reverential, intelligent, accomplished, and thoughtful, naturally and without effort. He was sincerely courteous, and capable of all complaisance,"* &c.

Whereas in the preface to the "Shoo King," great events are dealt with thus:—"T'ae-K'ang lost his kingdom, and his five brothers waited for him on the north of the Lo." The reader is left in much doubt as to who T'ae-K'ang was, and how he came to lose his kingdom; where his kingdom was, whether it had any inhabitants other than the king and his five brothers; what became of the king, his brothers, and the kingdom.

The writings of Mencius, the last of the Four Books, are remarkable for their bold and independent utterance, and for the recognition which he bestowed upon the people. Unlike his predecessor

* Legge's Classics, "The Book of Tang," Part I.

Confucius, he was no courtier, and his estimate of a sovereign was based on the condition of the subjects under his rule.

As an example of the ancient poetry of China, the following, eulogistic of the virtues of Yu, is given among others contained in the "Book of Poetry":—

>*" Yu travelled wide and long about
> When the nine regions he laid out,
> And through them led the nine-fold route.
> Men then their temples safe possessed,
> Beasts ranged the grassy plains with zest,
> For man and beast sweet rest was found,
> And virtue reigned the kingdom round."

Then follows a brief account of the unprofitable pursuits of Yu's successor, which displays the art of the writer in placing the outlines of Yu's brilliant achievements against a dark background:—

> "Then took E. E. the Emperor's place,
> His sole pursuit the wild beast's chase.
> The people's care he quite forgot,
> Of does and stags alone he thought."

Then follows the moral seldom wanting in these early compositions:—

> "War and such pastimes we should flee,
> The rule of Hea soon passed from E,
> A forester, these lines I pen,
> And offer to my king's good men."

This historical scrap is not without its value, as it embodies certain facts, and breathes the spirit of the patriarchal system so characteristic of the government of China in ancient and modern times.

* Legge's "Chinese Classics," vol. iv., Part I.

The people, according to these lines, owed all their prosperity to their ruler, just as children do to a father.

The devotion of the people to their prince's memory is given in the following lines from the "Shi King," showing that they worshipped the trees beneath which he rested:—

> "[This]* Umbrageous sweet pear-tree,
> Chip it not, hew it not down,
> Under it the chief of Shaou lodged."

> "[This] Umbrageous sweet pear-tree,
> Chip it not, break not a twig of it,
> Under it the chief of Shaou rested."

> "[This] Umbrageous sweet pear-tree,
> Chip it not, bend not a twig of it,
> Under it the chief of Shaou halted."

Considering the position of woman in China, and the humble place she fills in society, the following may be taken as an early and exalted tribute to her worth:—

> "Lovingly confiding was the lady Chang,
> Truly deep was her feeling,
> Both gentle was she and docile;
> Virtuously careful of her person,
> In thinking of our deceased lord,
> She stimulated worthless me." †

The poet, not without effort, rises with his theme, and proves that even in these ancient times there were women so true as to scorn false hair:—

---

* Legge's "Chinese Classics," vol. iv., Part I., p. 26.
† Ibid., p. 44.

"Her black hair, in masses like clouds;
No false locks does she descend to.
There are her ear-plugs of jade,
Her comb-pin of ivory,
And her forehead so white,
She appears like a visitant from heaven!
She appears like a goddess!"*

We have yet to learn that celestial visitants dress well, wear ear-plugs and ivory hair-pins.

"How rich and splendid
Is her robe of state!
It is worn over the finest muslin of dolichos,
The more cumbrous and warm garment being removed."

In this style of poem one would almost expect to find the name of the court-milliner of the period and the estimated value of the robes; and one cannot fail to be impressed with the presence of vulgar fact and the absence of the ideal, the true attribute of poetic genius.

Who, for example, could take these lines for a piece of poetic imagery?—

"By the shores of that marsh
There are the rushes and lotus flowers;
There is that beautiful lady,
Tall and large and majestic."

A large woman on the shores of a marsh is a picture to perplex rather than to captivate the reader. It is suggestive of damp feet, colds, and probably an untimely end to all that is large and lovely in the wayward maiden.

On the subject of modern poetry, a recent authority† says, "A Chinaman and a poet. The

---

* Legge's "Chinese Classics," vol. iv., p. 77.
† Mr. W. H. Medhurst, "China Review," vol. iv.

two terms seem scarcely compatible. . . . That so cold-blooded, phlegmatic, and sensual a being as a Chinese should possess sufficient taste and sentiment in his composition to generate or keep alive the spirit of poetry, would appear at first sight to be simply impossible."

Nevertheless, Chinamen prefer verse to prose. Mr. Medhurst holds that Chinese poetry cannot be compared with that of other lands, as much of its beauty is sacrificed to obtain rhythmical effect, and to the inflexibility of the language.

The rules of Chinese metrical construction are so rigid as to prevent the poet "soaring into the higher regions of imagery."

"Popular songs and ballads are common, but they hold a low rank in native literature, although they are far above our contempt on this account," as they supply a clue to the folk-lore of the country.

The Chinese drama may be described as picturesque; it is held in little esteem among men of letters. The plays, consisting of a combination of tragedy and comedy, are most of them written in prose.

There is no style of verse to which the name of epic can properly be applied. "In the eyes of educated Chinese the essentials of poetic composition consist, as indeed they do in the estimation of most other peoples, in the justness of the sentiment and metaphor, the beauty of the imagery, and the harmony of the structure." Owing to the structure of the language, the latter feature gains undue prominence.

The following specimens have probably lost something of their force in translation if they have gained in other respects. The following stanzas, which are nearly rendered literally, form part of a poem on London, written by a native in 1813*:—

IV.

" Their fertile hills, adorned with the richest luxuriance,
  Resemble in the outline of their summits the arched eyebrows (of a fair woman).
  The inhabitants are inspired with a respect for the female sex.
  Their young maidens have cheeks resembling red blossoms,
  And the complexion of their beauties is like the white gem.
  Of old has connubial affection been highly esteemed among them,
  Husband and wife delighting in mutual harmony.

V.

" The two banks of the river lie to the north and south.
  Their bridges interrupt the stream, and form a communication.
  Vessels of every kind pass between the arches,
  While men and horses pace among the clouds " (fogs?).

Another descriptive piece, on a bed of autumn flowers, is by the pen of some loving observer of Nature, and begins thus:—

" See their slender shadows pictured on the fence, whilst their feeble perfume scents the garden walk.
  Their tints turn dark, there lights flash one against the other.
  The dew falling strengthens their frames.
  Hungry, they feed on air.
  What can with their bright colours compete?
  Chatting of them, one might pity their languor as that of an invalid.
  Delicate, they open with constitutions at best autumnal.
  Yet say not they live to no purpose,
  For did they not by their charms inspire Tao to poetry and conviviality?"

* Sir J. F. Davis, "The Chinese," p. 267.

The following example of a simple Chinese lyric is translated by Mr. Stent:—

From Tiny Rill.

"Over green fields and meadows 'Tiny Rill' ran,
    (The little precocious coquette);
She was pretty she knew, and thus early began
    Gaily flirting with all that she met.

Her favours on both sides she'd gracefully shower;
    One moment she'd kiss the sweet lips of a flower,
The next lave the root of a tree.

She'd leap from one rock to another in play,
    Tumble down on her pebbly bed;
Like a Naiad, let the dazzling sun-smitten spray
    Fall, in prismatic gems, round her head.

Sometimes she would lash herself into a rage,
    And rush roaring and seething along,
Till a bit of smooth ground would her anger assuage,
    Then she'd liquidly murmur a song."

Mr. Medhurst remarks that he cannot persuade himself that the original possesses all the prettiness of imagery and expression which appears in their metrical versions.

The Chinese are great prose writers, and express facts connected with all their civilisation and quasi-art and science with much accuracy. Their libraries are stored with works on medicine, astrology, astronomy, geography, hydrography, and religion. Many of their works are mines of native lore, and display an ability and knowledge which might have been turned to better account had the authors enjoyed free intercourse with the men of science of the West.

The Chinese possess a power of observation the most minute, supplemented by a patient and persevering spirit, which, even in the absence of higher qualities, will serve them in good stead when they take to the serious studies of western art and science.

In concluding this chapter, let us express the hope that the time is approaching when free intercourse with the great Christian nations of the world will open the eyes of this pagan people to the defects of their political, social, and religious institutions.

The dawn of a higher civilisation seems to be breaking over the land. Her students are being sent abroad to foreign universities; her merchants are employing steam to transport their wares across the seas, and the telegraph to transmit their messages from port to port; her statesmen are rising from the study of the past to view with alarm the progress of nations that a few centuries ago had hardly found a place in the history of the world.

THE END.

INDEX.

ARCHITECTURE, origin, 159.
—————, art, and industry, 159—188.
—————, city, 95.
Art, 169—174.
Agriculture, 216—239.
—————, implements, 220.
Aristocracy, 122.
Army and Navy, 256.
Altar of heaven, Peking, 189.

Births, 126.
Beggars, 134.
Banking, 156.
Bamboo and its uses, 182.
Bronzes, ancient, 185.
Buddhism, 199—206.

Canal, Grand, 10, 11.
Carpentry, 178.
Census, 83—85.
Chekiang, 30—32.
Chan-tang, 57.
Chinese labour in America, 93, 94.
Cities and villages, 95—116.
Confucius, 192—195.
Catholics, Roman, 206—208.
Christian missions, 208.
Customs, imperial, 259.
Characters, written, 267.
Classical writings, 276.

Death and burial, 131—134.
Dining, 153.
Dress of the people, 135—140.
Dwelling, gentleman's, 164—168.

Dynasties, ancient, 55—66.
—————, modern, 66—77.

Emperor Kwang-su, 76.
Emigration, 88.
Enamelling, 174.
Education, 125.

Fukien, 38—40.
Formosa, 47—50.
Fu-hi, 54.
First settlers, 78—80.
Foochow, 98—100.
Funerals, 134.
Food, 150.
Feng-Shui, 209—215.
Fires and fire-walls, 96.

Geographical position of China, 1—4.
Gambling, 140.
Grammar of language, 274.
Guilds, 155.
Government, ancient, 240—242.
—————, modern, 243.

Hwang-ho, or Yellow River, 4—6.
Honan, 24.
Hupeh, 26, 27.
Hunan, 34—36.
Hainan, 50—52.
History, 53—77.
Heaites, 55.
Hein-fung, 75.
Houses, 104.
Hong Kong, 260.

Imperial customs, 259.

Kangsu, 19, 20.
Kiangsi, 33, 34.
Kiangsu, 23, 24.
Kweichow, 37.
Kwangtung, 41—43.
Kwangsi, 43, 44.
Kienlung, 37.
Kwang-su, Emperor, 76.

Lakes, 9, 10.
Laoutze, 195—197.
Language and literature, 263—286.
————, ancient, 263.

Ming dynasty, 67.
Manchu dynasty, 68, 69.
Marriage, 127—130.
Music, 142—144.
Missionaries, Christian, 148, 208.
Metals, 184.
Mulberry, 232.

Ngan-whuy, 25, 26.

Opium, 144.
———— smoking, 145—150.

Provinces of China, 13—52.
Peichihli, 15—17.
Peking, 15.
Prince Kung, 75.
Population, 78—94.
Porcelain, 175—177.
Punishments, 249.
Painting, 169.
Paper, 183.
Progress, 260.
Poetry, 280.
Policy, recent Chinese, 254.

Rivers, chief, 8, 9.
Races, 118—120.
Religion, 189—215.

Religion, State, 190.
Rice, 216—219.
Rites, marriage, 127—130.
————, burial, 131—133.

Shanse, 17, 18.
Shense, 18, 19.
Shantung, 20—22.
Szechuan, 29, 30.
Shops, 101.
Social condition of the people, 117—158.
Society, 121.
Superstition, 209—215.
Sugar, 228.
Silk, 229.
Silk embroidery, 238.
Salaries of mandarins, 251.

Tsing dynasty, 69.
Tartars, 69.
Tsingle Yamen, 76.
Taipings, 85.
Theatricals, 141.
Taouism, 195—198.
Taxes, collecting, 248.
Taxation, irregular, 252.
Tea culture, 221—228.

Villages, 106—110.
Village strife, 111—115.

Women, 124—126.
Walls of cities and dwellings, 162.
Wall, fire, 96.

Yangtsze River, 6—8.
Yunnan, 44—47.
Yu, 57.
Yeh, of Canton, 74.

Zenfi, Queen Yamen, Tsingle, 76.

www.ingramcontent.com/pod-product-compliance
Lightning Source LLC
Chambersburg PA
CBHW030811230426
43667CB00008B/1160